The Spirit of Texas

DAILY READING BOOK

A Unique Approach to Learning TEXAS HISTORY

WRITTEN BY LAURIE COCKERELL AND YVONNE CUMBERLAND

Kinderfable Press
Fort Worth, Texas

Dedications

*To Charlie . . . who already loves books and I'm sure will patiently endure
many a Texas history story cuddled up on my lap.*
-Laurie Cockerell

*I would like to dedicate this book to the "men" in my life:
My grandpa, Cletus Batto, who first instilled in me a love for writing
with simple poems on a chalkboard behind the back door and who always, no matter what,
stopped and read every historical marker—even if we had read them the week before.
My daddy, Matthew Hutzler, who always made me feel special and find the positive in everything.
And to my three sons—Ben, Jeff and Luke, who accept me for who I am, encourage me and my crazy
ideas, don't roll their eyes when I run into someone I know every single time we go somewhere and
now, just laugh because if I don't run into someone I know, I've instead become friends with the
waiter or sales clerk. Love to you all, in heaven and on earth.   - Yvonne Cumberland*

Kinderfable Press
P.O. Box 10193
Fort Worth, Texas 76114
www.kinderfablepress.com

ISBN: 978-0-9845609-3-6

Printed in the United States of America

A GUIDE TO
The Spirit of Texas History Curriculum

Texas history.

Those two words evoke either cheers and smiles of pride, or eyes rolled with boredom. Families and teachers with strong Texas roots often instill an unbreakable bond and love of the Lone Star State in their children. They know the remarkable stories of Texas. Stories of fascinating Native Americans, eighteen-minute battles that changed the world, and fallen heroes trapped inside the walls of an old mission, fighting for liberty or death.

Unfortunately, history is also sometimes viewed as dry mountains of memorization. Names and dates. Rules and laws.

The authors of this curriculum view Texas history as a portal to adventure. Both have spent many years teaching, speaking, and writing about this fascinating topic, encouraging children to not only accumulate knowledge, but to see Texas as they see it: an incredible source of ongoing fascination and excitement.

The Spirit of Texas curriculum offers a unique perspective on teaching Texas history. The *Daily Reading Book*, used in tandem with the companion *Activity Guide* and *Reproducible Book*, provides a total, cross-curricular experience for your family or classroom. History doesn't stop with just the presentation of facts; a multitude of additional exercises and games offered within the activity and reproducible books will help build a foundation of knowledge and understanding beyond a simple reading of history. Extend your students' understanding of Texas facts and lore through math, writing, science, art, music, and other extension exercises. The curriculum is geared toward students between 4th and 7th grade, but can easily be adjusted for younger or older children.

Please note that there are three books included in this curriculum:
1. *Daily Reading Book:* This is the foundation of the curriculum: the history textbook.
2. *Activity Guide:* This book will lead your students through activities related to their reading of the day. Some activities are fully explained in the guide, while other directions will be found on the worksheets in the *Reproducible Book*. Copy work, recipes, and the answer key in the *Activity Guide* will be noted with the letters "AG" and page number location.
3. *Reproducible Book:* Reproducible activities and unit tests assigned in the *Activity Guide* are noted by the letters"RB" and the page number location.

We suggest your student begin each unit by reading from the *Daily Reading Book* (as your schedule allows), followed by the activities suggested in the *Activity Guide* (choose according to time available and suitability to your students). You will find a suggested nine-month schedule on page 6 of the *Activity Guide,* but this curriculum is designed to be flexible and meet your programming needs. Complete as much or as little as you prefer each day.

Texas history education doesn't end with the close of the book. Continue this fascinating journey of knowledge through visits to the many suggested museums and other landmarks listed at the end of each unit in the activity book. Select books from the *Suggested Reading* and make history come to life. Help your students understand that Texas is not just a place on a map or a list of facts and dates.

Teach them that THEY are Texas!

CONTENTS

(Please see this section for a comprehensive list of links and sources)

Unit One:
TEXAS STATE SYMBOLS

INTRODUCTION

Texas is a big state, and a big state means many things to many people. If someone asks you to describe Texas, you might talk about the land, the animals, the food, the plants, the flag … all of these *aspects* can be described in words, but they can also be reflected as a *symbol*. A symbol is a picture or design that represents a thing, an idea, or an action. States often *designate* popular or *native* objects or characteristics as *emblems* to reflect what is commonly seen and *valued* by its citizens.

As you will learn, Texas is very large and contains many different regions. That means there are also quite a few symbols selected to reflect

the *diverse* characteristics of our state (see page 10 for examples of official Texas state symbols). Although it might sound like a simple process, these selections are, in fact, not official until they are formally designated by the Texas Legislature.

First, someone must submit their symbol idea. Then it has to be approved by the Texas House of Representatives, the Senate, and the Governor. You can find a list of these *resolutions* and the date these symbols were officially designated at:

https://www.tsl.texas.gov/ref/abouttx/symbols. html

THE TEXAS FLAG

Six flags have flown over Texas since 1519: the Spanish, French, Mexican, Republic of Texas, Confederate, and United States of America flags.

The current Lone Star state flag originally served as the Republic of Texas flag from 1839-1845. When Texas joined the Union, this same flag continued to fly over Texas, but as a state, rather than the flag of the Republic. At that time, another star was added to the United States flag, giving our country's banner a total of twenty-eight stars.

The Texas flag uses the same colors and meanings as the United States flag: the blue of the *perpendicular* stripe along the left side of the flag stands for *loyalty*, the white of the star and upper *horizontal* stripe stands for *purity* and liberty, and the red lower horizontal stripe stands for courage.

SIX FLAGS
Flown Over Texas

SPAIN
1519-1821

FRANCE
1685 -1690

MEXICO
1821-1836

REPUBLIC OF TEXAS
1836-1845;
State:1845-present

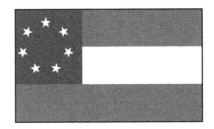

CONFEDERATE STATES
OF AMERICA
1861-1865

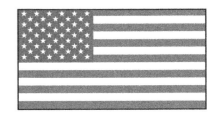

UNITED STATES
OF AMERICA
1845-1861, 1865-present

As you learn more about the history of Texas in the upcoming units, you will find this desirable land has been claimed by six different countries. From theme parks to historical museums, these six flags are often lined up on display, in order of their claim on the territory.

THE TEXAS PLEDGE

Most people know the American *Pledge* of *Allegiance*, but do you know the Texas Pledge? The Texas Legislature *instituted* this pledge in 1933. Many students in Texas classrooms and homeschools now start their day with both the American and Texas Pledges.

Before you recite the pledge, be sure to face the flag, remove your hat if wearing one, and place your right hand over your heart.

"Honor the Texas flag;
I pledge allegiance to thee,
Texas,
one state under God,
one and indivisible."

Did You Know?

Texas even has a State Hashtag!

No surprise here:

#Texas

Designated by the 84th Legislature in 2015

THE STATE SONG

The state song, "Texas, Our Texas," was written by William J. Marsh and Gladys Yoakum Wright. It was selected as the official state song after a contest sponsored by the state legislature in 1929. You can find complete lyrics to the song here:

https://www.tsl.texas.gov/ref/ abouttx/statesong.html

THE STATE SEAL

The Texas State Seal, *affixed* to official state documents and seen on the floor of the Texas State Capitol, has undergone several changes over time, but is still very similar to the original design *adopted* in 1836.

The Texas Constitution describes the Great Seal of Texas and notes the front side must consist of:

". . . a star of five points,
encircled by olive and live oak branches, and the words,
The State of Texas."

The *reverse* side of the Great Seal is quite interesting and colorful. In 1991, the Legislature decided the reverse side of the seal would have a shield, with the lower half divided into two parts: the Gonzales "Come and Take It" cannon is depicted on the bottom left section and Vince's Bridge is shown on the lower right.

On the upper half of the shield is an image of the Alamo. Live oak and olive branches circle the shield, and the six flags which have flown over Texas encircle the shield and branches. "Remember the Alamo" and "Texas One and Indivisible" are found above and below the shield. A five-pointed lone star sits at the top, centered between the flags.

You can find a color example of the seal's reverse side here:

www.sos.state.tx.us/statdoc/ seal-additional.shtml

TEXAS STATE SYMBOLS

There are numerous official state symbols. Here are a few examples:

State Motto: Friendship
Tejas, or *Texas*, was the Spanish pronunciation of a
Caddo Indian word meaning "friends"

State Bird: Mockingbird

Large Mammal: Longhorn

Small Mammal: Nine-Banded Armadillo

State Flower: Bluebonnet

State Tree: Pecan

State Fish: Guadalupe Bass

State Gem: Texas Blue Topaz

State Insect: Monarch Butterfly

State Pie: Pecan Pie

State Plant: Prickly Pear Cactus

State Reptile: Texas Horned Lizard

State Sport: Rodeo

State Dish: Chili

Unit Two:
REGIONS OF TEXAS

Texas history is filled with wonderful stories of adventure and excitement! Before you learn about the Native American tribes and the battles and the cowboys, take a look at the land of Texas from the ground up. Find out where Texas is located in relation to the rest of the United States and the world. Learn about its landforms, climates, and different regions. Study the native plants and animals, and discover why Texas is considered one of the most beautiful and most valuable spots in the world.

After completing this unit, consider taking a trip to some of the sites on our "Places to Visit" list. Someday, you might want to take a trip all around Texas. You'll be able to experience everything from canyons to beaches, from forests to deserts, from tall mountains to hills to flat plains. Once the itinerary is set, you will be the expert tour guide!

OUR PLACE IN THE WORLD

Look outside your window. What do you see?

Do you see mountains and prickly pear cactus? Do you see palm trees and gently rolling waves? Or do you see tall pine trees? Maybe even flat, flat land with nothing in sight except for a mesquite tree here and there?

Texas covers a very large amount of land, and that land is so big, it can be divided up into many *regions* based on *climate* and *landforms*. It is the second largest of all the United States, giving Texans good reason to often claim we are the biggest and the best! Texas land covers a total of 268,956 square miles. If you draw a straight line from the northwest corner of the Panhandle to the most southern tip of the state at Brownsville, the total distance is 801 miles. If you draw another line traveling east and west, from Orange to El Paso, you would have to travel 762 miles. Many people are surprised to find that El Paso is closer to San Diego, California, than it is to Houston!

Texas borders four states: New Mexico, Oklahoma, Louisiana, and Arkansas. Its longest boundary is formed by the Rio Grande River; the Red River and the Sabine River also separate Texas from its neighbors.

Since it might be hard to describe or locate a very specific spot on the earth, people invented imaginary lines you can see on maps and globes called lines of *latitude* and *longitude*. Look at a map and find the *equator* (the line that circles the middle of the earth, like a belt). Now notice the horizontal lines that *parallel* the equator, circling the earth as they continue towards both the North and South Poles. These are called lines of latitude. Now notice the vertical lines that connect the North and South Poles, also circling the globe. These are called lines of longitude. Each of these lines is given a number. If you are given the number for both the latitude and longitude lines, you can find where they *intersect* and locate any particular place on earth. Check your Texas map and you will see that the latitude at the very southern tip of Texas, near Brownsville, is located at 25° 50′ north and the latitude at the northern boundary of the Panhandle is 36° 30′ north. The far eastern boundary of Texas can be found at 93° 31′ west, and the western boundary near El Paso at 106° 38′ west.

Now imagine you could magically zoom out of that window and up high above your home. The higher you climb, the farther you can see in the distance. Now look down and pretend all of the borderlines we see on a map are visible. You see our state lies on the central and southernmost edge of the United States, and is considered the southernmost part of America's Great Plains. It is positioned above and sharing a border with the country of Mexico and is part of the North American continent. One-fourth of the border of Texas lies along the Gulf of Mexico, and fifteen major rivers flow through this large and *fertile* state, bringing much needed water to its many regions and providing access through the Gulf to the oceans of the world.

Now fly even higher.

Notice our North American continent can be found on the top half of the planet, north of the equator. Land and water located above the equator are considered part of the Northern *Hemisphere*. North America lies between the North Atlantic and North Pacific Oceans, with the Gulf of Mexico tucked between Florida and Mexico and bordering all the southern states in between. North America is also considered to be located in the Western Hemisphere, which includes all of the Americas, the western portion of Europe and Africa, the most eastern tip of Russia, and a portion of Antarctica.

Fly over the North Atlantic Ocean and compare the size of Texas to European countries. Texas is about the size of Ukraine, as well as the countries France and Switzerland combined. There are fifty states in the U.S.A., but Texas takes up about 7% of this country's space and is larger than the smallest fifteen states' areas combined.

Keep going up and up and up … Texas lies under 20,000 miles of air in the earth's *atmosphere*. It rests on top of 4,000 miles of rock, from the surface of the earth to its core. The top layer of that rock, called the *crust*, is formed from thirty miles of rock that continually rise and sink. This movement of the crust, along with the weathering and *eroding* of rock, helps to create the landforms of the regions of Texas. You'll find escarpments, buttes, sand dunes, canyons, caves, caverns, and offshore islands.

Falling rain sometimes sinks into spaces between these rocks, providing Texans with a treasured source of water. This water can be brought out of the ground by the use of pumps, especially vital to areas which do not receive enough rain to meet their needs.

When our state's hero Sam Houston first came to Texas, he wrote, *"Texas is the finest portion of the globe that has ever blessed my vision."* As you read about the land and history of Texas and its people, we think you might agree with the great general.

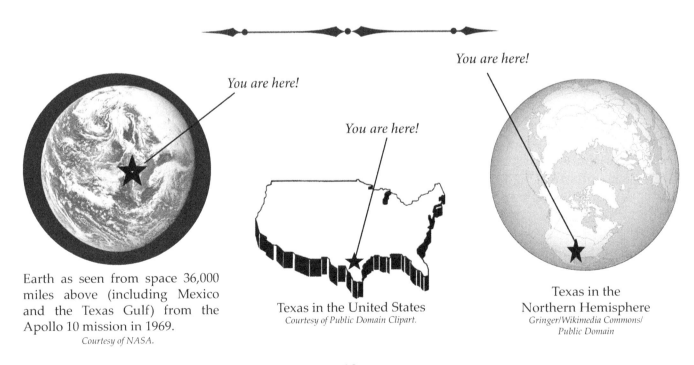

Earth as seen from space 36,000 miles above (including Mexico and the Texas Gulf) from the Apollo 10 mission in 1969.
Courtesy of NASA.

You are here!

Texas in the United States
Courtesy of Public Domain Clipart.

You are here!

Texas in the Northern Hemisphere
Gringer/Wikimedia Commons/ Public Domain

Texas Rivers

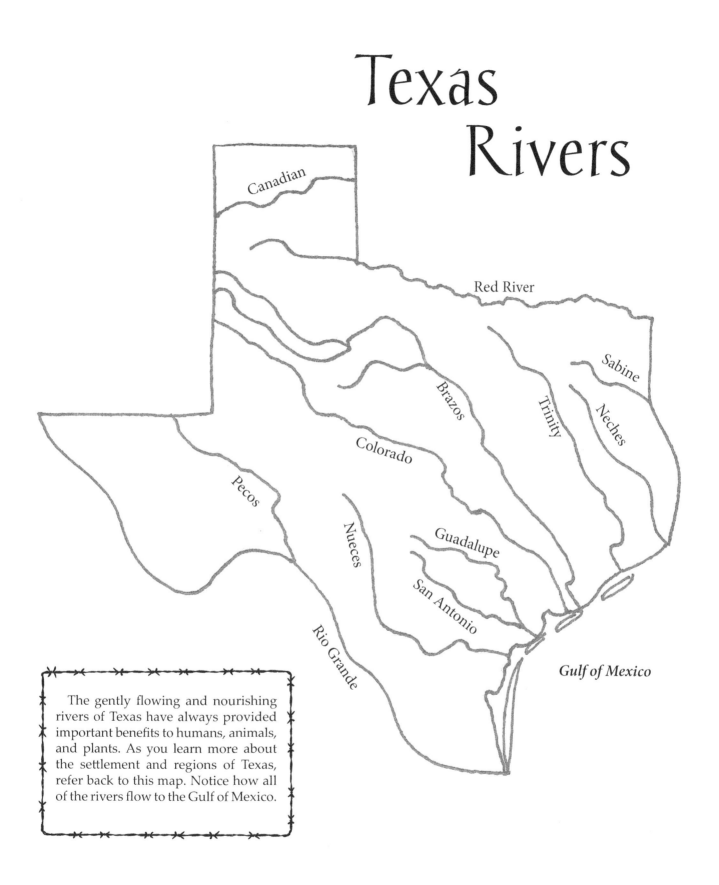

The gently flowing and nourishing rivers of Texas have always provided important benefits to humans, animals, and plants. As you learn more about the settlement and regions of Texas, refer back to this map. Notice how all of the rivers flow to the Gulf of Mexico.

INTRODUCTION TO REGIONS

Texas is unique. Unlike the majority of our country's states, you can drive for many miles and many hours as you travel from town to town across Texas. You might start your trip early on a bright summer morning in a forest with tall green trees in East Texas. Perhaps you stop for lunch at the beach along the Gulf of Mexico, then drive until you are hungry for dinner somewhere in the hills of Central Texas. Then get ready for the long ride to far West Texas, where you might climb a mountain and observe the view from the tallest point in Texas. You might even drive north into the Panhandle region and watch a beautiful sunset over gaping canyons.

Texas is home to a large variety of landforms, water sources, and climates. We call these different areas with common features "regions." These regions can be broken down into a number of separate areas, but we have chosen to use the seven regions frequently referenced on maps and in other books: *South Texas Plains, Prairies and Lakes, Big Bend Country, Piney Woods, Hill Country, Gulf Coast,* and *Panhandle Plains*. This unit will help you better understand what each region looks like and how its resources and people contribute to all Texas has to offer.

Be sure to check out the list in your *Activity Guide* of the many interesting sites you can visit within each region. Texas is a big state, so sit back and relax as we take you on a tour of the seven regions of Texas!

Region #1:
SOUTH TEXAS PLAINS

When you look at the Texas map, you will notice the South Texas Plains region lies just west of the Gulf Coast region and is bordered by the Rio Grande River. Most of the land is fairly flat, covered with grass and thorny brush. The Rio Grande Valley lies near the southern tip of the state, and it possesses a more *subtropical* climate. This means shorter and *milder* winters, and the ability of *citrus* trees to grow fruit in this fertile area along the river. *Annual* rainfall averages 20-32 inches each year.

Major rivers in this region include the Guadalupe, San Antonio, Nueces, Lavaca, and the Rio Grande. A few lakes are found in the South Texas Plains region, along with *marshes* and ponds which began as *resacas*. Resacas are similar to *ox-bow lakes*; these resacas were created many years ago when the Rio Grande flooded during the spring. The overflow of the water created new river channels, separate from the main flow. When the flooding ended and the water eventually receded, the *channel* ultimately dried up. At times these areas refilled with water and *silt*, bringing transferred plant and animal life to a new marsh or pond.

Native plants in the region include oaks, yaupons, wax myrtle, other thorny shrubs, and palms. Common wildlife found in the South Texas Plains region are roadrunners, white-tail deer, quail, tortoises, snakes, catfish, and the *caracara*. *Tropical* birds from South America even frequent this region! Of course, this means visitors can enjoy many available birding opportunities. The World Birding Center, a favorite destination for "birders," has nine nature sites set up for birds and their *habitats' conservation*.

The region is also a popular spot for hunting, camping, and water sports. Goliad State Historical Park and the Fannin Battleground provide lessons in the mission system and the Texas Revolution. Other important cities in this area include McAllen, Eagle Pass, Brownsville, Goliad, and Laredo. Although San Antonio is sometimes listed in the South Texas Plains region, it has been included within the Hill Country section in this book, as it sits along the border of these two regions.

Industries important to the economy are oil, gas, farming, tourism, cattle, and citrus crops.

Bentsen-Rio Grande Valley State Park, Tx: Vince Smith/Flickr/CC BY 2.0

Region #2:
PRAIRIES AND LAKES

The *Prairies and Lakes* region covers a big stretch of land in the central and north central areas of Texas. The land is gently rolling to hilly prairie, with patches of woodlands, grasslands, and fertile black soil. As its name implies, many lakes (almost all Texas lakes are man-made *reservoirs*), rivers, and streams run through the valleys of this region. In fact, Prairies and Lakes is home to the most reservoirs in the state.

Three separate *ecoregions* make up the Prairies and Lakes area: *Cross Timbers, Blackland Prairies,* and *Post Oak Savannah*. The Cross Timbers section is found on the west side of the region; this is a land of hilly, steep slopes and long cliffs where patches of trees cross **prairie** grasslands. The Blackland Prairies, in the center of the region, was originally a land of tall grass prairies. This rich, deep black soil is very fertile, and much of this area has been plowed for crop production. Finally, the Post Oak Savannah (found north of the Brazos River) was once a land of grass, wildflowers, and post oak trees. Pastures of Bermuda and Bahia grasses now cover most of this area.

Major rivers of the area include the Trinity, Brazos, and Red Rivers. The Brazos, one of the longest rivers in Texas, measures 840 miles. The river begins in the Panhandle Plains, flows down through the state, and empties into the Gulf of Mexico near Freeport, Texas. The Paluxy River is home to the site of actual **fossilized** dinosaur tracks! You can see these tracks and learn all about the dinosaurs who lived in the area (including Tyrannosaurus Rex and Pleurocoelus) at Dinosaur State Park in Glen Rose. Seventeen different dinosaur fossils have been identified in this area. Maybe someday YOU will find an undiscovered fossil.

Annual rainfall in the Prairies and Lakes region is 26-40 inches. Native plants include cottonwood, pecan, and oak trees, as well as sumacs and bald cypress. Common wildlife are beaver, raccoons, quail, mockingbirds, hawks, and porcupines. Major cities in this area include Dallas/Fort Worth, Denton, Arlington, Temple, College Station, Gonzales, Glen Rose, and Mineral Wells. Important industries include crop production, cattle ranching, oil and gas production, and aircraft building and design.

Region #3:
BIG BEND COUNTRY

It's hard to imagine a state that is home to both beaches and mountains … but mountains are just what you'll find if you make the drive to the *remote* *Big Bend* region of Texas. This rugged and beautiful land sits in the far west portion of the state. Look on your Texas map for the Pecos River; it is the eastern border of this region. Move to the west and notice the rest of the region is bordered by New Mexico and the Rio Grande River.

Big Bend is also known as the *Trans-Pecos* (because the area lies west of the Pecos River) or the *Basin and Range* region. You'll find the only mountains in Texas here; some of the higher ranges include the Guadalupe, Davis, and Chisos. The highest mountain, Guadalupe Mountain, is 8,749 feet tall. That's as tall as 580 one-story houses stacked on top of each other! Although warm in the summer, these mountains are cold in the winter and even receive snow on their forested slopes at times. Hikers who make it to the top of these mountains enjoy spectacular views of the surrounding desert and mountains.

These mountains and rugged *plateaus* are surrounded by large desert valleys considered part of the Chihuahuan Desert of Mexico. Just as you would imagine, the desert area can be very hot during the day, but cools down quite a bit at night. As this is the driest part of the state, the annual rainfall average is only 8-20 inches per year. Compare that to the Piney Woods region on the east and opposite side of the state, which receives 40-50 inches of rainfall every year.

Evidence of life from ancient times appears in the *abundant* fossils found in the area. Additionally, the Salt Flats is a white *basin* area where ancient lakes dried up and left salt deposits on the surface. This salt has been mined and sold over time; a war was even fought over these salt deposits in 1877.

Look at the Texas map again, and you'll notice the Rio Grande River (one of the largest rivers in America) creates the border between Texas and Mexico, running along the southern edge of the Big Bend region. Can you guess where Big Bend got its name? See the big turn in the direction of the river? There's the "Big Bend!" Kayakers and rafters can be found floating and enjoying the beautiful *canyons* and other sights as they follow this natural border between two countries. If the boaters floating downriver look to the right, they'll see Mexico; if they look to the left, they'll see Texas.

The Davis Mountains

17

The Ernst Tinaja
Courtesy of photographer Deanna Ford.

There are not many cities or people in this region, so wildlife and plants abound. Native animals include pronghorn antelope, squirrels, mountain lions, skunks, roadrunners, coyotes, and jackrabbits. In the desert, you will find prickly pear cactus, yucca, and agave plants, just to name a few. Plateaus are home to short grasses and brush. In the mountains, several types of pine, juniper, and oak trees line the slopes. Of course, the river *wetland* is home to completely different plants and animals, including cottonwood, willow trees, and catfish.

If you are hungry or need gas, be sure to plot your path carefully. Look at the map and notice how few cities can be found in the Big Bend region. The biggest city you'll find here is El Paso, but there are many interesting sights and things to do in Balmorhea, Fort Davis, Marfa, Pecos, Presidio, and Fort Stockton. Of course, the most well-known attraction in the region is Big Bend National Park, found in the Chisos Mountains. Believe it or not, this park is about the same size of Rhode Island.

Although far away from the majority of the state's population, the Big Bend region was an important home to early American Indian and Spanish settlers. Paintings made by Native Americans have been found and can still be seen on cave walls, rock overhangs, and canyon walls. Examples can be observed at Hueco Tanks and Seminole Canyon State Historic Sites. These and other valuable *artifacts* teach us about the life and *culture* of some of the first *inhabitants* of Texas.

Most of the Big Bend region is covered with *grazing* ranches and parks, although oil and gas fields lie on the eastern edge of the area. Other industries include tourism, agriculture, and health and education services.

Region #4:
THE PINEY WOODS

The *Piney Woods* region is found in far East Texas, between the border of Louisiana and the Prairies and Lakes region. The southern part of this area is very flat and home to the Big Thicket, a low-lying area of mostly **swamps** and wetlands, although grassy prairies and forests are also found in this *ecological* region. As you move farther north past the Big Thicket, the land begins rolling with gentle hills. There you will find deep woods, farms, and cities. Underneath the tall hardwood trees of the forests, beautiful blossoming trees such as redbud and dogwood bloom in the spring. The forest system of this region extends into other states: Louisiana, Arkansas, and Oklahoma.

With between 40 and 52 inches of rain every year (the greatest rainfall in the state), the Piney Woods is **humid** and home to many trees and lakes. One of these, Caddo Lake, is said to be the only naturally formed lake in Texas. Major rivers in the region include the Sabine, Cypress, Sulphur, and Red Rivers. The cloudy water found in these slow-moving rivers and streams is a result of leaf litter and muddy river bottoms.

Native plants include pine, oak, redbud, cypress, and magnolia trees. Common wildlife are opossums, bullfrogs, river otters, foxes, skunks, and bobcats.

Major cities in the Piney Woods include Texarkana, Tyler, Longview, Nacogdoches, Huntsville, Canton, Alto, and Jacksonville.

Natural resources contribute a great deal to the area's economy. Thanks to the heavily wooded land, the Piney Woods is the source of most commercial **timber** products, so **lumber** production is a major industry. The soil and climate are excellent for growing a variety of fruit and vegetable crops, and cattle ranching is widespread. Oil discovered in the region in 1931 has also contributed to the area's economic growth.

Region #5:
THE HILL COUNTRY

The *Hill Country* region is one of our state's most scenic and popular spots. You will notice it is located below the Panhandle Plains, right in the center of Texas. This rolling to hilly grassland sits on Edwards Plateau, which has eroded over time to become the Hill Country. Steep slopes and rugged hills dot the landscape where *granite* and *limestone bedrock* lie under thin soil.

This region sits atop the Edwards Aquifer, a huge underground water source created when water seeped through cracks in the limestone found just below the soil. Water can bubble up from the *aquifer* in the form of *springs*, and the Hill Country claims more springs than any other region in Texas. Perhaps you have gone for a dip at Barton Springs near Austin. If you have, you know that the water is cold! Water from this aquifer is a very important source for drinking, *irrigation*, and recreation. *Caverns* are also a result of this system, and are popular tourist attractions for *spelunkers* ready to explore these cool and eerie attractions.

Large granite *domes* or *uplifts*, such as Enchanted Rock, are located in the Hill Country. They are pretty to look at and fun to climb. Major rivers in this region include the Colorado, Guadalupe, and Nueces. Many Texans canoe and tube down these rivers: a popular Texas tradition and vacation choice. Rainfall in this region averages between 15 and 34 inches every year.

Common plants include oaks, pecans, junipers, bald cypress, mesquites, and grasses; you will also find open *grasslands* along with thick *woodlands*. White-tail deer, raccoons, armadillos, tarantula, mockingbirds, Rio Grande turkey, and herons are only a few of the many native animals found in the Hill Country. If you visit Austin during the summer, be sure to check out the world's largest *urban* bat colony (1.5 million bats!) living under the Congress Avenue Bridge. Every evening during the summer, these Mexican free-tailed bats *emerge* from beneath the bridge to hunt for insects. It's quite a sight to see!

Our state's capital, Austin, is located in this region. Other important cities include San Antonio, Boerne, Del Rio, Fredericksburg, Sonora, San Marcos, New Braunfels, and Camp Wood. The influence of early German settlers and their heritage can be seen throughout the area.

Granite *quarries* provide stone for building projects. Ranching, farming, and tourism are also important to the Hill Country's economy. Popular destination sites include Garner, Pedernales Falls, Lost Maples, and Lyndon B. Johnson State Parks as well as Longhorn and Kickapoo Caverns. Visit the Alamo, explore the Texas Capitol, find fields of bluebonnets, or check out a ghost town. The Hill Country has something for everyone!

Enchanted Rock

Region #6:
THE GULF COAST

Wish you could relax on a sandy beach, listen to the waves as they lap the shore, build a sand castle, or wet a hook and catch a shark? If you live in Texas, just head on down to the *Gulf Coast Region*: one of our state's favorite vacation spots.

This region stretches from the Sabine River mouth on the Louisiana border, and traces its way over 300 miles to the Rio Grande delta on the Mexican border. Many streams and rivers make their final exit into the Gulf of Mexico, emptying massive amounts of thick *sediment* eroded upstream and carried to the mouth of the river and into the gulf. It is believed that over time, changes after the last Ice Age, along with wind and waves, pushed and deposited that sand into what are now *barrier islands*. Look at your Texas map and notice this thin chain of islands that run along the coast. You'll find Galveston, Padre, Matagorda, Mustang, and many other islands along the shoreline. These islands are not just for swimming and fishing. They also offer protection for the coast and shallow *bays* (the water between the islands and the mainland coast) from storms which frequent this area.

Along with the coast and barrier islands, this region is also home to salt grass marshes, *estuaries* (where salty sea water meets fresh river water), and bays. Important rivers located and meeting the Gulf here include the Trinity, San Jacinto, Brazos, Nueces, and San Antonio rivers. Tall woodlands can be found on river bottom land, with areas of oak, tall grass prairies, and flat plain making up other portions of the region.

Galveston Beach

Galveston Fishing Boat

Did You Know?

The gulf was also a home to German submarines during World War II. Enemy U-Boats were stationed all along the Gulf of Mexico to target and sink oil tankers coming out of these ports, as oil was a necessary fuel in fighting a war. Galveston was on high alert during this time, protecting oil tankers by enforcing nightly blackouts, so the U-boats could not see the ships' *profiles* against the city lights.

The Gulf Coast sees quite a bit of precipitation; it averages 40-60 inches of rainfall every year. You'll notice this region *encompasses* some *inland* area, too. Cities in this area include Houston (home of the state's largest population—over two million residents!), Galveston, Victoria, Beaumont, Corpus Christi, and Baytown. *Seaports* have been very important to the economy in this region (look at the map and see why many ships transport materials in and out of the region), and *petrochemicals* and *aerospace* industries employ many of its citizens. Tourism is of course an important business along the coast, but cattle ranching (as found at the King Ranch) and agriculture (including cotton, rice, and other grains, vegetables, and citrus fruits grown in the Rio Grande Valley) are also significant to the economy.

Native plants of the Gulf Coast region include grasses, oaks, elms, hollies, and occasionally *copious* amounts of *migrating* sargassum seaweed (not native to the area, but often an annoyance to beachgoers). Numerous interesting animals live in the wild, including coyotes, river otters, bottlenose dolphins, alligators, pelicans, shrimp, crabs, and of course … sharks! State parks and wildlife refuges are great places to observe and learn more about these interesting plants and animals.

Multiple important historical events occurred in the Gulf Coast region, and you can learn more about the state's history by visiting monuments and historic sites in the area. The San Jacinto Monument in La Porte marks the final battle site of the Texas Revolution, where Texas won its independence from Mexico and became a Republic. It's also home to the Battleship Texas, located within walking distance of the monument. Other important battlefields, lighthouses, early capitals of the Republic of Texas, and Galveston—the city that actually built up its *elevation* and a *seawall* after the devastating 1900 hurricane—are located in the region. NASA's Johnson Space Center has provided training for astronauts, served as Mission Control, and contributed numerous other areas of support for our national space program.

Region #7:

PANHANDLE PLAINS

The *Panhandle Plains* region of Texas is perfectly named. Notice the shape of this region. The northern section looks like a handle, and the broader area below looks like the base of a pan. You can't cook in this pan, but you CAN enjoy beautiful scenery and historic sites.

Most of this region is a flat, grassy, treeless *plain* sitting on a high plateau known as the High Plains, or the Llano Estacado "Staked Plains." The High Plains are the southern part of the Great Plains which extend north through the United States, all the way to Canada. As you travel east within the region, an area known as the Rolling Plains becomes less flat and receives more precipitation. The High Plains and Rolling Plains are divided by a steep *escarpment* called the Caprock. Colorful walled canyons created by rivers and tributaries cut into this escarpment. You can see these spectacular views at Palo Duro Canyon (800 feet deep!) and Caprock Canyon State Park.

The Panhandle Plains region is bordered by two states: New Mexico on the west, and Oklahoma on the north and east. Major rivers of this region include the Canadian, Colorado, Brazos, Pecos, and Red Rivers. The average yearly rainfall is only 15-28 inches, but fortunately the Ogallala and other aquifers provide additional water for the region.

Another source of water for this area is furnished by the 19,000 *playa lakes*: water holes, averaging about fifteen acres in size, which fill with three to four feet of rain during spring and summer thunderstorms. The shallow lakes eventually *evaporate*, so depend on future rainfall to stay full. At one time these temporary lakes served as bison and Native American watering holes; today many migratory birds winter nearby.

Native plants in the region include mesquite, cottonwood trees, cactus, yucca, and sumac. Common wildlife found in the region are roadrunners, prairie dogs, mule deer, snakes, and pronghorn antelope . . . creatures adaptable to an area with less water and precipitation.

Much of the area's economy is based on ranching, farming, and oil and gas production. Strong winds are prevalent across the plains, so the area is also becoming one of the fastest growing *wind-power* producing regions in the United States. As you drive across the region, fields and fields of windmills can be seen, as well as many oil pumps, looking like horses bobbing up and down.

Midland, Abilene, San Angelo, Brownwood, Amarillo, and Lubbock are some of the larger cities of the Panhandle Plains. Universities, museums, and historic frontier sites such as Fort Griffin and Fort Richardson provide great reasons to visit and live in the region.

Llano Estacado near Amarillo

NATIVE PLANTS AND ANIMALS

You've learned all about the regions of Texas, along with examples of plants and animals you might find in the different areas across the state. Let's pause a moment to take a snapshot of the big picture: imagine you have a giant telescope out in space. We've been focusing on each region, but now zoom out and take a look at the entire state. Imagine all of the colors you might see from the different landforms and vegetation. Imagine all of the different animals making their homes in these habitats, perfectly fitting their needs.

In this section, you will have the opportunity to study native plants and animals of Texas. Perhaps you might then be able to identify and even help protect some of the lifeforms which make Texas so unique.

Native Animals

There are numerous types of animals in Texas. You know the general categories: mammals, reptiles, amphibians, birds, fish, and *invertebrates*. However, just because you can find a particular animal in Texas today, doesn't mean that particular animal and its *ancestors* have always lived in Texas.

Over the centuries, humans *intentionally* or accidentally brought new animals to Texas; these creatures had never lived in the area before that time. For instance, we always think of Texas Longhorn cattle as a symbol of the state, but actually these animals were introduced by the Spanish, who brought them to the Americas during the 1500s. Cattle have since become an important part of the Texas economy, but some non-native animals have caused many problems for the state. Nutria, red fire ants, and Zebra mussels are considered "*invasive* species," and can cause harm to the environment and/or people's health.

Some of the earliest native Texas animals are now *extinct*. Fossils and tracks of dinosaurs found in Texas include the Iguanodon, Alamosaurus, and of course Tyrannosaurus Rex! Other prehistoric animals, some being distantly related to modern animals, include giant armadillos, mammoths, mastodons, and large cats.

Today, more than 540 species of birds and 141 species of native land mammals can be found in Texas. This large variety is due to the many different environments and climates of Texas. You'll find everything from cave critters (like bats and salamanders), slithery reptiles (watch out for that rattlesnake) in the desert, sea turtles on the Gulf Coast, woodpeckers in the Piney Woods, and prairie dogs in the Panhandle. While most of these animals are fairly *docile*, Texas is also home to several types of poisonous snakes. Every Texan should be able to recognize and avoid copperheads, rattlesnakes, water moccasins, and coral snakes.

Endangered Animals

Some animals are *dwindling* in numbers, and the Texas Parks and Wildlife Department has named these species at risk. *Endangered species* are those animals at risk of statewide extinction. Examples of endangered species in Texas are gray and red wolves, whooping cranes, leatherback sea turtles, Kemp's ridley sea turtles, and the ocelot.

Threatened species are considered likely to be endangered in the future. Black bears, jaguars, bald eagles, Texas horned lizards, and paddlefish are just a few of the threatened animals in our state.

Organizations such as Texas Parks and Wildlife are working to research and protect these species and habitats which might be in danger of extinction. Many animals are protected from being hunted, and others require licenses and permits. Additionally, rules have been put in place to govern the trapping, killing, or selling of particular species. For instance, fishermen may only keep a certain number of some fish and crabs, and they must meet minimum lengths. Hunters may hunt some animals only at particular times of year. Of course, some animals are protected from any harm or capture.

http://tpwd.texas.gov/huntwild/ wild/rehab/protected/

Native Plants

Just as we have seen with animals, Texas has a wide variety of native plants. This is due to diverse soils and differing rainfall across the state. While you'll find many varieties of trees and grasses in East Texas, fewer trees inhabit the gulf area and instead, salt marshes take their place. Honey mesquite abounds in the Panhandle, while piñon pine and juniper are easily found in far West Texas.

Plants are usually classified as grasses, shrubs, and *forbs* (flowers), and Texas is home to various species of each. Most people love to travel Texas highways during the spring, stopping on the side of the road to take family pictures in a bluebonnet field. There are actually over 5,000 flowering plants in Texas, with most wildflowers blooming during the spring and summer. It's always a good idea to keep a pamphlet or book with a listing of Texas wild flowers in your car, so you can identify these beautiful treasures when you happily discover them.

http://www.texashighways.com/travel /item/7341-wildflowers-of-texas

Just as with animals, some plants found in Texas are not native to the state. These plants can often be troublesome, crowding out native plants. Examples of *invasive* plants are Japanese honeysuckle vine and *kudzu*.

Plants can also be considered at risk in Texas, and a list of endangered and threatened native plants is available so Texans can protect these plants from extinction. Threatened plant examples include the Pecos Sunflower and Earth Fruit. Several of the endangered species are Star Cactus and Texas Snowbells.

A joyful sign of spring each year throughout Texas . . . bluebonnets!
Photo courtesy of Lauren Tenery.

West Texas Cotton Fields

Unit Three:
NATIVE AMERICANS OF TEXAS

Long before Columbus discovered America— and long before the Spanish and French explorers set foot on this soil—Native Americans lived throughout the North American continent. Evidence exists that these people, also called "Indians" (we will use both of these terms), made their home in the land we now call Texas. There were no signs proclaiming "Welcome to Texas!" The border lines we see on maps today were non-existent. Just wide open spaces: home to the first humans to hunt, farm, trade, and raise families in this area.

Without formal transportation, Native Americans lived in fairly small groups, scattered in what you now know are very different regions and with varied natural resources. These small groups were abundant, resulting in the development of different tribes, customs, lifestyles, and languages but who were, through the years, forced to adjust and change to survive. Over time, and for many reasons, most of these tribes either ceased to exist or were driven away to other parts of the country.

We often see Native Americans portrayed in movies, or maybe you've played "Cowboys and Indians" with your friends ... but what were these tribes and individuals really like? How did they survive? Where did they live and how did they communicate?

Before we answer, let's begin by asking the question: *How did Native Americans get here in the first place?*

No one knows exactly how or where the first Indians set foot on American soil, but there are several theories. Most *archeologists* believe families migrated from Asia during the last Ice Age. At that time, northern Asia and North America were covered with thick sheets of ice. All of this ice held a large portion of the earth's water, which created shallower oceans and exposed what is now thought to be a land bridge between Siberia and Alaska. It is believed these families followed big mammals (like mastodons and mammoths) over the land bridge and the Bering Sea into what is now the North American continent.

Scientists think once people crossed the land bridge, a *corridor* between ice sheets created a path, and the first Americans then migrated down that path into what is now North, Central, and finally South America. As they spread out, some families stayed in different areas throughout the continent, giving rise to what would eventually become the different Indians tribes we know today.

When groups of these immigrants eventually arrived in what is now Texas, some chose to end their travels and settle their families to live out their lives as Texas's first citizens. Texas didn't look or feel exactly like it does today, though; this was still the Ice Age, so the climate was cooler and the first Texas Indians shared the land with very large animals!

How do archeologists develop theories about these first people and their lifestyle? The only clues are found in the discovery of artifacts and rock art left behind. These clues help scientists piece together a giant puzzle—the story of prehistoric Indians.

EARLY PREHISTORIC INDIANS

Prehistory covers a very long time: all the time the earth and man existed before man began recording the world around him using words. Some societies began using *decodable* written language very early, thus we know much more about Europe and the Middle East since we can refer to their writings, thousands of years old. These early records can be studied to help us better understand the environment and lifestyles of men during a particular period. Unfortunately, the *relics* left by Native Americans who lived in today's Texas (and over the American continents) are much more limited, and there are no written documents available until the Europeans arrived and recorded their observations in the 1500s.

Archeologists study the available relics and devise theories about the Prehistoric Indians' lives. They believe these early Americans lived in caves or shelters made of brush, rock, or animal skin; rock paintings still exist today in rock shelters and overhangs, especially in the Lower Pecos area. During the Ice Age, the main source of food was meat, so people were constantly on the move, hunting for mammoth, mastodons, giant armadillos and sloths, saber tooth tigers, native camels, or bison. While meat was their main source of protein, Prehistoric Indians consumed some types of plants as well.

Wheels did not exist in this part of the world, so individuals walked and carried supplies themselves or with the help of *domesticated* dogs. *Edible* plants were limited, therefore the people gathered what they could find. We call these nomads *"hunter-gatherers,"* because that is how they lived to survive. Spears and *atlatls* (spear-throwing sticks) were used to bring down large game. Stone tools were then used to chop and scrape the remains for food, shelter, clothing, and tools.

After the Ice Age, when the earth began to warm, many of the larger animals became extinct. The Indians living at this time hunted for smaller sized game, such as rabbits, deer, rodents, snakes, birds, and fish. They continued to use spears, with an assortment of points which varied by region. *Chert*, or *flint*, was chipped into fine points to use on both the end of the spear, and later on arrows.

The Indians also continued to gather what was likely a larger variety of edible plants to *supplement* their diet. They would often find and prepare prickly pear cactus, Texas persimmons, sotol and lechuguilla bulbs, and nuts. Stone *metates* and *manos* were used to grind some of this food into a fine flour-like powder, and meals were usually cooked on rock mounds.

Eventually, some groups found land suited for farming, and began to plant seeds and start an agricultural society. Early gardens frequently included *maize* (corn), pumpkins, beans, and squash. As time went on, some tribes began to trade their goods with other groups who perhaps lived nearby. One of these groups, the Late Prehistoric Caddos, were peaceful farmers who created woven baskets and clay bowls valuable for trading. Large, flat-topped mounds, built as a foundation for large wooden *temples*, have also given the Caddo a unique place in history. Interestingly, about every eighty years the temples were burned to the ground. More earth was carried to the mound in baskets and a new layer was added to support a new temple. You can visit and learn more about these fascinating people at Caddo Mounds State Historic Site in East Texas.

Finally, as we begin our study of Texas Indians, it is important to remember this: before the Europeans arrived, Native Americans were plentiful—perhaps millions of individuals living in North America by 1500 A.D. Their rich culture and contribution to this country were influential long before they met European colonists and incoming settlers. As we study the primary Texas tribes, remember also their impressive ability to adapt and change as the world changed around them.

Caddo Mound at Caddo Mounds State Historic Site
Photo courtesy of Cindy Freeman.

BUFFALO

As you will learn, many plants and animals were used by Native Americans for food, clothing, and shelter. The geographical area where each tribe lived determined the resources available to each group. Some survived on small animals and wild plants; others were able to cultivate their own gardens with plants which grew well in their homeland's particular climate and soil.

Alternately, the tribes who lived and roamed on the plains of Texas and the rest of the continent weren't the only living beings wandering in search of food across these wide spaces. Their four-legged neighbors were more than just an occasional triumph and dinner. They were the center of these tribes' lives, the source of food, clothing, shelter, tools, weapons, and other necessary items. They were the reason to get up in the morning, pick up their homes, and move across miles and miles of prairie lands.

The neighbor these particular Native Americans relied upon for the majority of their needs?

The BUFFALO!

THE ANIMAL

Although scientists usually refer to this particular animal as the American Bison, most of us—and most Native Americans—call this creature a buffalo. These mammals, which live and move in herds, are closely related to cattle. Buffalo are BIG! Some bulls can be as tall as six feet at their shoulders and weigh up to one ton (female cows usually weigh about half that of the bull). Both the male and female have a shoulder hump as well as horns and beards (although the males' horns are larger and beards are typically longer). Both have darker and lighter shades of brown hair over their body, and the bulls have thick hair on their forehead. During the winter, their coats grow heavier to keep the animals warm.

Buffalo are *herbivores* and mainly eat grass. During the warmer months of the year, they live and graze across the prairie. When winter sets in, they move to better protected areas near a water source, usually in the woods.

Buffalo roamed the North American continent long before the first Native Americans arrived. The earliest Indians hunted now-extinct giant buffalo, and when the first Europeans arrived, the animals could be found all over the continent east of the Rockies and north of Mexico; herds were especially numerous on the Great Plains. As Texas is located at the southern edge of the Great Plains, a large number of buffalo grazed throughout the Texas Panhandle High Plains area known as the Llano Estacado.

Even though buffalo appear bulky and not very intelligent, their speed and unpredictable temper make them quite dangerous to man. These animals are very fast and can actually run as quickly as a horse! Many humans have met their death by being trampled or *gored* by this huge beast.

An American Bison
Courtesy of National Archives.

The Hunt

Native Americans hunted buffalo long before the Spanish introduced the horse to North America. Buffalo hunts were best performed during the fall, when the animals' bodies had developed more fat and thicker fur. Often during this time, when a herd was spotted, hunters would close in on the buffalo from different directions. One hunter would wear a wolf *pelt*, and the other would cover himself in a robe made of a buffalo calf hide. The "calf " *imposter* would make bleating, distressed sounds. The real buffalo would hear the call and the cows would come to the aide of the "calf." The surrounding hunters would then attack and kill the buffalo with arrows and spears.

Other hunting techniques included driving the herd into a partially fenced area, chasing the buffalo into drifts of snow, or frightening the herd, causing them to stampede over a cliff. This technique was called a "buffalo jump" or a *pishkun*. Those buffalo who survived the fall were speared at the bottom of the cliff.

The Spanish brought horses to North America during the 1500s, offering another advantage to Native Americans for their buffalo hunts. The Indians first came to own horses through trade with the Europeans. Some Apaches even traded slaves for horses as early as the 1650s. By 1687, many tribes of Texas were hunting buffalo on horseback, and by 1770 all of the Plains tribes possessed horses.

This new mode of transportation made hunting the buffalo and carrying the remains faster and easier. Native Americans who used horses during the buffalo hunt could kill as many as four buffalo in one day. The Indian would ride bareback, and instead of a *bridle*, a rope was looped across the horse's lower jaw. As the trained horse chased the buffalo, the rider could aim his arrow directly between the animal's ribs and into its heart.

The Meat

Native Americans were careful to use every part of the buffalo's body. Of course, the meat was probably the most important part of all: it provided *protein* and *sustenance* to keep the tribe members alive. The tongue was usually the first part to be eaten. This was followed by other internal organs, including the kidneys, intestines, liver, and even the hump. The blood was made into a soup and the bones boiled for their grease.

The rest of the flesh was prepared in several ways. Some meat was dried in strips; this created a light, preserved, and long-lasting food for years to come. Another version of preserved buffalo was called *pemmican*. Once the meat was dried, the women would pound it into a floury powder. It was placed in a *rawhide* bag, sometimes along with dried berries, and covered with hot buffalo fat to help preserve the contents. The bag was sealed by removing all of the air.

"On the Trail" Buffalo Hunt
Courtesy of Library of Congress/Bain Collection.

Uses For the Rest of the Buffalo's Body

Once the meat was retrieved, it was time to harvest the rest of the animal's body for additional uses. Of course, the hides—that is, the skin—of the buffalo was turned into leather. This leather could be cut and sewn into everything from clothes to tepee covers, and from saddles to bags. When the hunt occurred during the fall or winter, the thicker fur was often used to create moccasins, gloves, and robes.

The tribal women would take the hide, stretch and stake it to the ground, and then use flint or bone to scrape off the outer flesh. If the skin was to be used for leather, the fur was removed as well. The resulting rawhide was very strong and fashioned for items such as boats, shields, and cradles.

With more processing, softer leather could be turned into tepees and clothing. A mixture of buffalo fat, brains, and liver was rubbed on the skin and then dried by the sun. The leather used for clothing would be smoked as it was prepared to be cut and sewed.

The buffalo's tail made an excellent fly swatter as well as a tool to flick water on hot rocks in the *sweat lodges*. Horns were utilized as *ladles*, spoons, cups, and headdresses and the animals' hooves were fashioned into rattles, doorbell-like chains for tepee entrances, and boiled for glue.

Sleds were created from the ribs of buffalo, and shoulder blades could become garden hoes. Other  bones were turned into war clubs, pipes, knife handles, and dogsled runners. The *tendons* were used as rope and thread; the stomach and bladder could be dried to become a water carrier. Even *dung* had a use! The dried buffalo "chips" provided an excellent fuel for the campfire.

Successful hunters were able to exchange their buffalo hides with fur traders for needed goods such as guns, cooking utensils, and clothing. The buffalo also served as food, clothing, and tools for fellow tribal members.

> ### Did You Know?
> The *phosphorous* found in buffalo bones was mined from the old pishkun buffalo jump sites during World War II, and was used to make explosives and fertilizer for the war effort.

Spiritual Aspects of the Buffalo

Native Americans held special views regarding all living things, honoring the animals who gave their lives so the people might survive. They viewed the buffalo and other animals as relatives and neighbors of the earth. Often the buffalo was seen as an intermediary to the Great Spirit: the people could speak to the Great Spirit and he could speak to them through the buffalo.

Apsaroke Bull Chief, c1908: Courtesy of Library of Congress.

After a buffalo hunt, ceremonies honoring the buffalo's spirit were performed. The animal's skull was often saved and used as a medium for prayer in sacred rituals. This great beast was considered a symbol of abundance and life.

Buffalo Today

Sadly, as more and more settlers moved west, the increase in hunting was sizable and the buffalo began to disappear. By the late 1800s, few wild buffalo remained. However, an effort to save the buffalo began in the early 1900s, and ranges were established where the buffalo were protected. Private ranchers began raising the animals as well.

Today the United States' buffalo population has fortunately increased to over 400,000 head. These beautiful beasts live protected on private ranches, Indian reservations, and in national and state parks.

Photographer: Carol M. Highsmith
Courtesy of Library of Congress.

HISTORIC INDIANS
Years: 1500 A.D. to Present Day

When Christopher Columbus discovered an island near the Americas, he named the inhabitants "Indians." Notice that the word India makes up the first five letters of the name. Columbus was confused and thought he had sailed to and found an island in the East Indies, so he incorrectly identified the people on the island as citizens of the Indian Islands—or "Indians." The people who were living at that time throughout North, Central, South America, and the Caribbean were, of course, not part of the Indies, but in fact were **descendants** of those brave families who courageously came to this new land thousands of years before the European explorers arrived.

Once Europeans began to explore and settle the land we now call Texas, they also began to meet and observe the Native Americans who had been living in the area since their great migration from Asia. These native groups were found living in the many different geographical regions of Texas, and were equally different in their lifestyles and languages. The European newcomers were fascinated with the citizens of the new land and wrote down observations to share with society back home. Fortunately, this gave us a much clearer picture and insight into the lives of early Native Americans. Prior to these writings, only tools, pottery, cave paintings, and other artifacts provided clues to their lifestyle. With these written records, the historic period began!

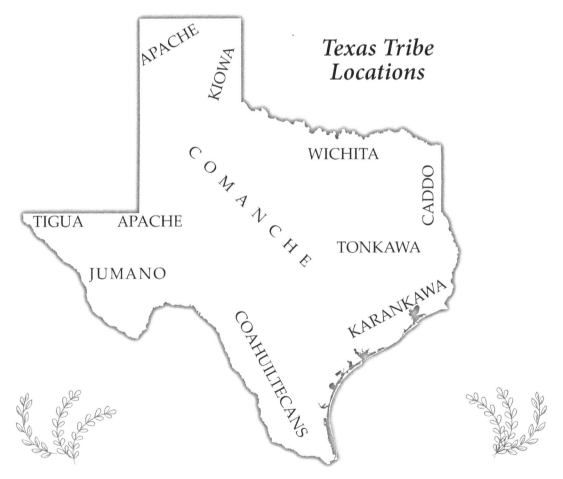

The Caddos

One of the Native American groups encountered by early European explorers were the Caddo (CAD-oh) Indians. As mentioned earlier in the unit, this particular tribe was present even during the prehistoric times, building ceremonial mounds and establishing early agricultural societies.

The Caddo were advanced in their tools and farming techniques, resulting in an excellent food supply. This *sophisticated* technology for that time meant the Caddo could live in more permanent communities and had no need to pick up their entire village to chase their next meal. It also meant more time to spend on building their culture and society, providing a fascinating story for us to study today.

Where Did They Live?

The Caddos lived in East Texas in the Piney Woods region. They first made contact with explorers as early as 1541, when some of Hernando De Soto's men came across these Native Americans. The French explorer La Salle also met with the Caddos during his time in Texas.

The Caddos were found to be a successful and advanced society. Three distinct Caddo groups lived in the area:
1) the Natchitoches (in the northwest corner of Louisiana),
2) the Kadohadachos (in northeast Texas), *and*
3) the Hasinai (who lived further south, near the original Caddo mounds).

It is said when early explorers met the Hasinai, the Indians greeted the Europeans with a word which sounded like "Tejas." The white men thought that the Native Americans were sharing the name of their people or their land when, in fact, "Tejas" meant friend, or friendship. The name stuck, and Tejas eventually evolved into the word "Texas."

What Did They Eat?

Living in a region with plenty of rain, trees, and natural resources, the Caddo were able to use their energies to create villages and an agricultural society, rather than merely survive. The fertile land and *ample* rainfall made the land perfect for farming. By 1250 A.D., corn was one, if not the most important crop; in fact, there were two varieties of corn planted at separate times within a year. The "little corn" was harvested in July, and the "flour corn" harvested in September. The corn could be prepared by roasting (cooked *unhusked* on hot ashes), boiled with other vegetables for a dish called *succotash*, or dried and ground with large wooden pestles and mortars into a flour to make bread, soups, and tortillas. Corn was also dried and used as seed for the upcoming season of planting.

Other important plants grown by the Caddo included many types of beans, squash, sunflowers, pumpkins, melons, and tobacco. In addition, the Caddo also foraged wild plants as a source of food, medicine, and dye.

A land with plenty of trees, plants, and water also meant a land full of wildlife for hunting. Once the tribe was introduced to horses, they were better able to hunt buffalo and bear. The buffalo provided plenty of meat for their people, and the bear was an excellent source of fat. Other important game included deer, wild hogs, and many types of birds. The Caddo were successful fishermen as well. They used *trotlines* (short baited hooks and lines attached to one big fishing line) to catch freshwater fish in the area.

What Did They Wear?

It's interesting to study the typical of particular Native American tribes, as the covering and accessories reflect the plants and animals available in the territory and within their environment.

Caddo men wore *breechcloths* made of animal hide, and the women wore deerskin blouses and skirts, fringed and decorated with colorful seeds along the bottom. The ladies were also known to wear breechcloths, but their "underwear" was made of straw and grass! Both wore soft *moccasins* for shoes. Hair was oiled and parted down the middle, and the women tied their hair with red-dyed skins from snakes and rabbits. The men either wore their hair short with a long section down the middle (which sometimes hung to their waist) with feathers attached or shaved, with all but a thin band of hair between their forehead and the back of the neck.

Men and women adorned their pierced noses and ears with shells, bones, teeth, and feathers and decorated their bodies and faces with elaborate tattoos.

How Did They Live?

Even during prehistoric times, the Caddo had an unusually complex social system. The people lived in villages or smaller *hamlets* with a common ceremonial center. The ceremonial center was home to the familiar earthen mounds used for fire mounds and burials.

Spiritual leaders helped tribal members communicate with the supreme god, Caddi Ayo, and assisted with important rites of the harvest and naming ceremonies.

The Caddo also worked together as a community to provide shelter for one another. In just one day, the village members would build a house, while the new homeowner's family prepared a feast to treat the rest of the village once the house raising was complete. The men would set up tall cedar poles in a circle (up to 40 feet high) and tie them at the top, leaving a hole for smoke from the inside fire to escape. These poles were then covered with bundles of dried grass, giving the home the appearance of a giant beehive. Most families owned one large home, with two smaller huts for work and food storage. Their beds were reed mats, raised off the floor by forked sticks and covered with deer or buffalo skins.

The Caddo were not only skilled farmers, they were also known for their ability to peacefully trade with both Europeans and other Indians. Even during prehistoric times, it is believed the Caddo participated in long distance trade. Common bartering items included *turquoise*, copper, bison hides, salt, *bois d'arc* bows, and of course their beautiful and well-made pottery.

What Tools Did They Use?

In addition to creating pottery, these skilled Caddo craftsmen and women wove reed mats, rugs, and baskets. They also created and used bows and arrows, made from the strong bois d'arc wood found nearby. Tools were normally constructed from wood found in the forest or bones from animals, such as buffalo shoulder blades for hoes. Instruments for ceremonies were made from *gourds* (for rattles), bird bones and hollow reeds (for flute-type instruments), and deer skin and hollow logs (for drums).

The Caddo's Place in History

Sadly, by the early 1800s, few Caddo remained in Texas. Many had died either from diseases brought to Texas by explorers and settlers, or by war. By 1859, the small number of Caddos left were moved by the U.S. government to the Indian Territory in Oklahoma.

This peaceful, friendly tribe likely provided a pleasant introduction to explorers and settlers entering Texas. A successful society of farmers and traders, the Caddos used their natural resources effectively and left behind artifacts and the amazing ceremonial mounds of their ancestors.

The Karankawa

Who Were They?

One of the first tribes to be encountered by Spanish explorers when they began journeying into what would become Texas was the Karankawa (kuh-RAHN-kuh-wah). Sometimes friendly, sometimes fierce (they were said to occasionally practice *cannibalism*), often smelly (they covered their bodies with alligator grease to keep away mosquitoes), and now extinct . . . this fascinating group acted as one of our state's first greeting committees and hosts.

Where Did They Live?

The Karankawa lived along the lower Gulf Coast and on the barrier islands from Galveston down to Corpus Christi. Their environment included flat prairies, marshlands, some wooded areas, and of course the coastlands and bays. The bands would rarely travel inland more than one hundred miles, although as *nomads* they moved frequently to find available food and better protection from bad weather.

Since this tribe lived near the gulf and wetlands, *dugout* canoes were *invaluable* forms of transportation. These canoes were made from tree trunks hollowed out through a technique of burning and scraping. Each boat was big enough for an entire family and their provisions. Instead of oars, long poles pushed the canoes through the shallow waters.

The life of a nomad requires homes easy to pick up and move quickly. A stay in one camp might only last a few weeks. The Karankawa huts were created with eighteen-foot-long willow poles, placed in a circle and connected at the top. These *wigwams* were then at least partially covered with animal skins to keep out the elements, but open enough to let out the smoke from fires built in the center of the home. Baskets and clay pottery, waterproofed with *tar* that had washed ashore, were used for gathering and cooking. Most meals were cooked in these clay pots and heated on glowing coals; oysters were merely thrown into the fire, as the heat caused the shell to pop open, ready to eat.

The Karankawa would often return to the same areas, and the discovery of shell *middens* give clues as to which were favorite campsites. These middens were *refuse* piles built up year after year by the Native Americans, who would return during their travels and pile their leftovers and rubbish in the same place during their occupation of that particular spot.

What Did They Eat?

The Karankawa were hunter-gatherer-fishers, so they hunted and ate meat, gathered edible plants (plant roots, nuts, and berries), and fished in the many available wetlands and shores of the Gulf Coastal region. They hunted deer, bear, birds, and *javelina* when closer to the shore; during their inland journeys, they would hunt bison as well.

Fish and shellfish were popular, and meals retrieved from the water included turtles, clams, oysters, scallops, porpoises, and even alligators. As mentioned earlier, these alligators were not only good to eat, but they also provided a natural, smelly mosquito repellent which was smeared all over the Karankawa's bodies.

Oysters served as a main source of food until spring. After that, blackberries provided the bulk of their diet. As the weather and available food sources changed with the seasons, the Karankawa would move between the mainland shore and the islands and sand bars.

During times when food was scarce, the tribe was also known to eat locusts and bear fat. They were just happy to have food! Even spoiled food and raw meat were part of their diet.

What Tools Did They Use?

The Karankawa were known for their long, red *cedar* bows which were almost as tall as the men themselves. Bowstrings were created by twisting fine deer sinew, and arrows were devised with three feathers attached. Amazingly, this tribe not only hunted with their bows and arrows, they also fished with them! Capturing seafood occurred through the use of traps and fish hooks made from shells as well. Other common tools used by the Karankawa included *lances*, clubs, and *tomahawks*.

Perhaps one of his ancestors kept mosquitoes away from the Karankawa! (Photo courtesy of Jeanne Diarte.)

What Did They Look Like?

The Karankawa were unusually tall compared to the other tribes found in Texas. The men stood at least six feet and were strong and muscular. They wore little clothing, other than moccasins and a breechcloth, sometimes accompanied with a long, fringed sash. The women wore skirts made from animal skins and *Spanish moss*, at times covering their shoulders with moss shawls. Ornaments included bracelets, necklaces, anklets, and feathers placed in their hair.

Both the men and women painted and tattooed their bodies, often piercing their lower lip with a piece of cane.

As scary as their appearance may have been, people who encountered the Karankawa said when food was plentiful and the Indians were not threatened, the people were generous and happy. They led a difficult lifestyle and had to be strong to withstand the hunger and cold of winter.

How Did They Live?

Although much of their time was spent hunting, gathering, and moving, the Karankawa found time for other activities as well. These strong men were physically competitive, and loved contests to test their strength in wrestling, swimming, knife throwing, arrow shooting, and running. While the men hunted and competed, the women erected and took down the huts, gathered wood, cooked, and picked edible plants.

These tribe members, while appearing quite *fearsome*, were very fond of their children. Babies were strapped and carried on *cradleboards* when they were young, but began to hunt or help their mothers at an early age. Children were given two names: one was a nickname only used by outsiders, and the other was considered a magical, secret name. When the time came for the child to *transition* into adulthood, a *shaman* performed a ceremony which included the application of tattoos.

Other religious ceremonies included *mitotes*, where circle dancing was performed with music provided by tortoise shell or gourd *tambourine* accompaniment.

Each band of Karankawa had a chief. One pioneer reported that the men painted their faces when on the warpath—half red and half black. Smoke signals were used to communicate in both times of war and also to send messages about social events.

The Karankawas' Place in History

Although the Karankawa lived a relatively quiet life, their influence and mark on Texas history is significant. When Spanish explorers were stranded during a shipwreck in the Galveston area, it is believed a tribe of Karankawa rescued Cabeza de Vaca and the other castaways, ensuring their survival but also "enslaving" the Spaniards. Finally, Cabeza de Vaca and his men escaped and made their way to Mexico. Their stories of life with the Karankawa resulted in an invaluable record of the world of these fascinating Native Americans.

The Karankawa next made contact with the Europeans through the introduction of French traders in the 1600s. When Spanish missions were established in the following century, the Karankawa refused to participate, but chose instead to continue their nomadic lifestyle, irritating many of their new neighbors. Trouble continued in the early 1800s with settlers and Mexican troops, and by the mid-1850s, the tribe had completely disappeared. These intriguing Indians either became ill and died from disease often brought to the Americas by explorers, or were victims of battles with other tribes and settlers.

The Coahuiltecans

Who Were They?

The name given to "Coahuiltecan" (ko-uh-WEEL-tee-kan) Native Americans really applies to people who belonged to hundreds of small, *autonomous* bands who roamed South Texas and Northeast Mexico. In fact, their name is more of a *geographical* term and is derived from the Mexican state of Coahuila, to which Texas once belonged, and where some of these Indians once lived.

These groups were diverse in many ways, including language and culture, but did possess some similar traits. They lived in small groups called bands, and each band was governed by a chief. As you read about the Coahuiltecans, notice how similar their lifestyles were to those of the Karankawa Indians. Both would be considered more primitive hunter-gatherers who spent their days taking care of their most basic needs, but the Coahuiltecan bands were normally found more inland than the Karankawa.

Where Did They Live?

The Coahuiltecans were nomads who lived down the coast from their Karankawa neighbors, and roamed from Corpus Christi south to the Rio Grande, and into northeast Mexico. Bands of this tribe also lived further inland, all the way to what is today's San Antonio area. Much of this dry land where they lived was, and still is, covered with thorny shrubs and small trees, so it was not a good place to grow crops.

Like the Karankawa, these families were hunter-gatherers and roamed the countryside in search of food. Their *foraging* area also included brushy South Texas, and since this tribe did not have horses, they roamed on foot.

The Coahuiltecans' homes were also similar to the Karankawas' movable shelters. They created a dome-shaped hut of *willow* branches, covered with reed mats or animal hides, and fires were built within each home. When a band would stop to camp, they usually selected an area within a *thicket*, and trenches were dug to encircle the camp. These trenches were used as a defensive position to protect the camp with bows and arrows.

When it was time to move to another area, families just picked up their belongings and carried them on their backs until they reached the next stop.

What Did They Eat?

The Coahuiltecans' diet was typical for the hunter-gatherers of the time. Deer, rabbit, antelope, and other small and medium-sized animals were hunted by the men. If they were very lucky, a few bison might roam into their area, but that was a rare occurrence. Sometimes they would trap javelina in pits covered with leaves and twigs, or work together to surround game, making for an easier kill. When an animal was taken down by hunters, the trail was marked and the women were then sent to retrieve the animal's body. Whichever hunter made the actual kill was allowed to keep the animal's skin, and the rest of the band shared the meat.

Bows were made from strong mesquite root with deer sinew for the string. The arrows were constructed with flint points and feathers were attached.

Another hunting tool called a "rabbit stick" was a curved wooden club thrown like a boomerang to kill game. Fish were killed with the bow and arrow, and nets (called *seines*) were used for fishing in shallower waters. Although fish were sometimes roasted and eaten right away, the favored treat was to wait until the dead fish sat a while and was covered by flies and other insects before devouring this delicious morsel!

While not nearly as exciting, edible plants were gathered and eaten as well. These included *sotol* and *lechuguilla* bulbs, pecans, the bulb of the *maguey* plant, mesquite beans, and the highly valued prickly pear cactus. The fruit of the cactus was considered a delicacy, and pouches were made from the cactus pads to carry water. Foraging, by using the rabbit stick, helped dig and pry plants from the ground. Food was stored in hollow gourds, and heavier loads were carried with a *tumpline*: a headband woven into a basket. Sometimes food was difficult to find in this harsh environment, so these families were happy to find and *consume* spiders, ant eggs, rodents, reptiles, and worms.

Everyday life was difficult. Although the Coahuiltecans could normally find sufficient food during the summer, winters were often a time of starvation and hardship.

What Did They Wear?

The Coahuiltecan men wore a knee-length breechcloth covering, decorated with animal teeth, shells, and seeds. The women wore deerskin or grass skirts and ornaments made from bone, shells, and feathers. Both usually went barefoot, although sandals were worn when walking through thorny areas. In winter, rabbit and coyote skins kept the people warm.

Men plucked the hair back from their foreheads and tattooed a line down the center of their faces and bodies. Tattoos weren't just for adults—even children were tattooed at a young age.

How Did They Live?

The Coahuiltecans led a hard and difficult life. Since this South Texas land had few natural resources, the people were constantly on the move, sometimes only halting for a few days or weeks at any given camp.

Cabeza de Vaca, in describing Coahuiltecans, mentioned that the people he encountered had a "fine *symmetry*" but were not as tall as the Karankawa he met earlier. He also noted the men had great *stamina* and were able to chase a deer for a full day, running without tiring.

The women stayed busy cooking, caring for the children, and hauling wood and water. Babies were carried on their mother's back when they were young, tied with animal skins to her body. When they were little, boys were even given small

bows and arrows for practice. As the youngsters aged, they were given more responsibilities, and young boys accompanied the men as helpers and lookouts on hunting trips. Once a boy proved to be a good hunter and a young girl a woman, special ceremonies were held in which the children were tattooed and became adults.

Little is known of their religion, but it is said ceremonies (mitotes) similar to the Karankawas' were held and overseen by the shaman, who was also considered a medicine man. These festivals of thanksgiving, or victory ceremonies, were usually held during summer or a time of ample food. Dancing with the accompaniment of drums and rattles took place around a fire, as relatives who had not been together were reunited and men and women met who would someday be married.

A running collared peccary or javelina (Pecari tajacu) in Big Bend National Park.
Wing-Chi Poon/Wikimedia Commons/ CC BY-SA 3.0

The Coahuiltecans' Place in History

The Coahuiltecans, like the Karankawa, also encountered Spanish explorers. The characteristics of their culture were recorded by Cabeza de Vaca, who spent time with bands of this tribe during the years after his shipwreck and before his escape to Mexico.

During the time of the Spanish missions in the 1600s, some bands lived within the protection of the missions, especially due to their fear of the Apaches.

Finally, during the late 1700s to early 1800s, the last Texas Coahuiltecans disappeared as they either migrated to Mexico to escape hostile tribes or died due to illness.

The Comanche

Who Were They?

The Comanche were nomadic buffalo hunters who migrated to Texas from the Rocky Mountains and Great Plains in the early 1700s. Excellent horsemen, they were sometimes known as the "Lords of the Southern Plains."

The Comanche were never unified as a group. Instead, they roamed in smaller groups in different territories. These groups had interesting names such as Honey Eaters, Liver Eaters, Buffalo Eaters, and Antelope. Feared by many, they were well-skilled at the art of *ambush*, and were known to attack their enemies and withdraw quickly.

As many as twelve of these different bands were present in Texas at any given time. The early Comanche *displaced* any current residents when they moved into their new Texas home, and continually fought off the Spaniards, Mexicans, other Native Americans, and Anglo settlers who might be considered a threat to their territory.

Horses were very important to the Comanche, and children often learned to ride before they could walk! Horses were first introduced to their tribe by the Spanish in the 1600s, and the Comanche soon realized how much faster they could hunt and battle with this new *mode* of transportation. Horses thereafter were either gained through *breeding*, trading, or theft and used for hunting, warring, raiding, and driving away other Native American tribes.

The Comanche believed the earth, sun, and moon were *supernatural* beings, but the supreme power belonged to The Great Spirit. Religion was mainly a personal matter, and a young man's vision quest ritual often marked his transition to adulthood. Comanches also believed in the healing power of the medicine man, who was thought to cure the sick. Peace chiefs provided advice and wisdom, and *councils* made important decisions regarding *alliances*, moves, and religious ceremonies.

Where Did They Live?

The Comanche's territory in the plains area was called *"comancheria."* It extended from the Cross Timbers region west to the Pecos River, and northward from the Edwards Plateau area into what are now Oklahoma and Kansas.

Since the Comanche moved frequently following buffalo herds, they chose homes that were easy to put up and take down, usually amongst trees and near a stream or other source of water. Like the Apache, they lived in tepees. Buffalo skin was used to cover sixteen to eighteen cedar or pine poles (about 12-14 feet high), often with doors sewn from bearskin. The hide-covered door flap always opened to the east, toward the rising sun. A hole was left at the top of the tepee so smoke from the inside *fire pit* could escape.

Pictographs were often painted on the outside of each home with scenes of daily life, battles, and deeds of bravery. Due to the many moves (and therefore, lots of practice), women were able to raise and take down the tepees in only 3-4 minutes. Once disassembled, the poles and skins were carried to the next camp on a *travois* (pronounced tra-VWAH) attached to a horse.

What Did They Look Like?

Since it was not unusual for Comanche to intermarry with captives, their dress and physical appearance were quite diverse. The Comanche men wore their hair parted (with the part painted) and braided, sometimes hanging to the ground. They decorated their scalp locks with yellow and black feathers, and plucked their eyebrows and beards. Shells and silver earrings ornamented their ten or more ear piercings. The men wore short, fringed aprons, breechcloths, *leggings*, and moccasins. The beautiful feather headdresses you often see in pictures and movies were worn in the later 1800s. Earlier warriors more likely wore a bison scalp and horn cap on their heads, perhaps with feathers and an ermine tail attached, and usually painted their faces red. They sometimes painted their horse's heads and tails red, where they might also tie a red ribbon.

Women wore *buckskin* or buffalo hide skirts (with uneven hems) and shirts. Their moccasins were decorated with fringe, beads, and *tinklers* (little iron bits attached to their shoes). The ladies wore their hair short, and painted yellow and red lines above and below their eyes. They even painted the inside of their ears red!

What Did They Eat?

To the Comanche, buffalo meat was the most important food, although they would also hunt and eat elk, black bear, antelope, longhorns, and even their own ponies. Most of the main hunts occurred during the summer, normally on horseback and with the use of three-foot bows and arrows. Each individual was given a particular assignment by the leader. Usually the hunters forced the bison into a circle, then shot an arrow into the animal's heart. The Comanche were also known to drive the bison to stampede off a cliff, then retrieve the animals' bodies at the bottom.

Once the animals were killed, the women skinned and cleaned the meat off the bones, saving every possible body part for another use. Some of the meat to be consumed later was made into pemmican, a mixture of dried meat, berries, and animal fat. The dried meat was then packed into colorfully decorated rectangular buffalo hide boxes called *parfleche*.

The Comanche did not plant crops. Instead, they foraged for wild edible plants, traded, or stole corn and other vegetables, fruits, and nuts. Favorites included grapes, persimmons, berries, acorns, pecans, roots, and plums.

Warring and Weapons

The Comanche were strong warriors and feared by many, so weapons were a very important key to battle, as well as hunting. Bows and arrows were essential tools and weapons to the men. The Comanche's three-foot long bows were usually made from Osage orange, hickory, or ash tree wood with buffalo or deer sinew strings. Carried on the hunter or warrior's back in a bag called a *quiver*, arrows were often carved from dogwood branches and fashioned with bone, steel, iron, or flint arrow tips. These men had excellent aim, and could shoot

up to twenty arrows per minute. In fact, it is said young boys could shoot a hummingbird out of the air!

Early Comanche used lances and feather-rimmed shields made of thick rawhide, decorated with bear teeth, *scalps*, and horse tails, but later bought, traded, or stole guns. *Battle axes* were also used in combat, as well as to cut firewood.

Close your eyes and imagine Comanche warriors in battle, leaning over the horse's side to protect themselves, riding at full speed as they hold and shoot arrows from under the horse's neck. That must have been quite an exciting sight!

The Comanche's Place in History

The Comanche were brilliant horsemen, fearsome warriors, excellent hunters, and a great threat to those who lived near their territory. As they saw their way of life endangered by a growing scarcity of buffalo, as well as incoming settlers and other tribes, their aggressive raiding, theft, and kidnapping increased. Eventually the Texas Rangers were sent to end their dangerous assault on other Texas citizens.

In 1867, the Treaty of Medicine Creek Lodge established a reservation in Indian Territory, but the Comanche continued their raids in Texas. The army eventually drove the remaining Comanche to reservations following the Red River War in the Panhandle region. After difficult years adjusting to reservation life, individual Comanche families were given 160-acre plots of land and the reservation broken up. Currently, many Comanche continue to maintain traditional ways while living in a modern, present-day world.

Four Comanches in front of a wigwam, Fort Sill, Indian Territory, 1873.
Photographer: John P. Soule. Courtesy of Library of Congress.

The Tonkawa

Who Were They?

The Tonkawa (TONG-keh-weh), whose name comes from a Waco Indian word meaning "they all stay together," were nomadic buffalo hunters. They began as small, loosely connected bands, but eventually united in the 1800s. The appearance of the aggressive and feared Comanche and Apache Indians changed both the lifestyle and the roaming region of the Tonkawa over time.

Where Did They Live?

The Tonkawa roamed throughout Central Texas and moved through an area from today's Hillsboro to San Antonio and Austin, throughout the Edwards Plateau. They were eventually pushed off the buffalo-rich plains and east of the Edwards Plateau by their Apache enemies.

Villages of scattered buffalo hide-covered tepees served as a home base for the hunters. When buffalo became *scarce*, low huts were crudely made from brush and grass and families foraged for food as best as they could.

What Did They Eat?

Although the Tonkawa were buffalo hunters, their hunting grounds became smaller when the Comanche and Apache moved into the area. The Tonkawa were forced to settle for smaller game such as deer, turkey, rabbits, fish, skunks, tortoise, shellfish, and even dogs and horses. Rattlesnake was considered a special treat! Meats were roasted over an open fire, and leftovers were preserved as *jerky* or pemmican.

When buffalo were available, more than the meat was put to use. Hooves were turned into glue for arrow making, the *sinew*, or tendons, became thread for bow strings and sewing purposes, horns became cups and spoons, and the buffalo tails were turned into rope.

Edible plants were also foraged. Favorites included nuts, herbs, acorns, and fruit from the prickly pear cactus. To remove spines from the prickly pear, the people used a pincer made from slivers of deer antler. Pecans were particularly important to the Tonkawa, as they traded these valuable nuts with Anglo settlers.

Farming was attempted during the late 1700s, but with little success.

What Did They Wear?

The Tonkawa men wore very long breechcloths, leggings, and moccasins; they also possessed *breastplates*, *chokers*, and ear *pendants*. Warriors painted themselves and their horses, and wore horned and feathered headdresses. The women wore deerskin skirts and painted their noses, mouths, and backs with stripes. Both wore buffalo robes during cold weather and tattooed and painted their bodies for both *adornment* and religious reasons.

How Did They Live?

Although known to be warlike with other tribes, the Tonkawa were friendly and traded with the white settlers. Tonkawa bands were led by tribal chiefs and the men were *notable* warriors, wearing protective leather jackets and colorful caps with ornaments of horn and feathers.

Lances, as well as bows and arrows, were their chosen weapons. Arrow tips were made of stone and later with metal after it was introduced by the Europeans. Believing mistletoe to be poisonous, they rubbed the plant on the end of their arrows and guns. *Firearms* were obtained from the Spanish through the trade of *tallow*, deerskins, and buffalo robes during the late 1700s. It is believed that the Tonkawa may have also participated in cannibalism in battle situations as a ritual, but not on a regular basis.

The Tonkawa believed in supernatural gods, with great emphasis on the spirits of the dead and rituals surrounding death. Friends and family,

Tonkawa babies were carried in a cradleboard until they were about eighteen months old.

(Although these are actually Apache babies, versions of these baby carriers were commonly used among different Native American tribes.)

Courtesy of National Archives.

chanting and swaying, would form rings around a member as he/she lay dying. Like many cultures, the dead were buried with their prized possessions. Sometimes even a horse was shot over an important warrior's grave.

The Tonkawa also believed that owls and wolves were *manifestations* of the spirits of the dead, and thus were careful not to hunt or eat these particular animals; they believed the wolf brought their people into the world. As with many other tribes, shamans served the bands as medicine men, helping treat illness.

Babies were carried in a cradleboard until they were about eighteen months old; at that time, they were given freedom to play within the camp area. Children also remained nameless until they were several years old and were rarely punished.

During the late 1500-1600s, the Tonkawa had contact with both the Spanish and French traders, beginning with their introduction to the De León expedition. Some members sought *refuge* in the Spanish missions during the 1700s to escape their enemies, the Comanche and Apache. Later, the Tonkawa signed a treaty with Stephen F. Austin during the early Anglo settlement days, and some tribal members agreed to serve as scouts for the Texas Rangers and the United States Army against the Comanche. Known to be curious of settlers' activities in their area, these Native Americans would often show up uninvited to church services and weddings, observing their neighbors with interest.

The Tonkawas' Place in History

These hunter-gatherer nomads saw their way of life change with the arrival of settlers, the Apache, and the Comanche. Somewhat receptive to the Spanish mission system, probably out of need for protection, the Tonkawa developed and usually maintained friendly relations with both Spanish and Anglo settlers.

Unfortunately, the Tonkawa population became greatly reduced over time. Today, their reservation is located near Tonkawa, Oklahoma.

The Apache

Who Were They?

Like the Comanche, the Apache were greatly feared by both settlers and other Native Americans. They lived in small family groups and called themselves "Tinde," or "Indé," which means "The People." There were primarily three groups of Apache that lived in Texas. The most well-known are the Lipan (lee-PAHN), who lived in the Hill Country and west to the Rio Grande. The Mescalero (mes-kuh-LAR-oh) lived in New Mexico, and from the Rio Grande to the Pecos River. Finally, the Kiowa (KYE-oh-wuh) Apaches lived along the Red River and, except for their language, were very much like the Kiowa Indians who lived in that same area.

How Did They Live?

The Apache were nomadic buffalo hunters who lived and traveled in small family groups, but would unite in bands during times of war. Since they had to move their homes to follow the buffalo, it was important that these *dwellings* be easy to put up and take down. The Apache lived in tepees, sometimes up to twenty-five feet high. Long poles, often made of sotol stalks, were used as the frame. Up to eighteen buffalo hides were sewn together, set upon the poles, and tied down with wooden pegs. The inner and outer walls were decorated with pictographs depicting scenes of hunting, war, and Apache life. The tepee materials were carried between camps on a travois, and the women were responsible for erecting the homes and breaking them down when time came to move on. Often, the tepees could be set up as quickly as only three minutes! Each tepee was usually accompanied by a large *arbor* made from brush, which provided a cool and shady place to rest and eat. *Wickiups*, small wooden frames covered with brush or hide, were also used as dwellings.

The Apache were quite frightened of the spirits of the dead, and in fact would not reuse the name of someone who had died. They also held the belief that every object and animal in the universe held either good or bad powers. Shamans held rites to heal, to encourage successful hunts, and to control the weather; they were also known to handle snakes and perform other similar tricks.

The Apache were excellent horsemen, and these animals were very valuable for both hunting and battle. While they preferred their four-foot *mulberry* bows and arrows for accuracy and efficiency, guns later became a weapon in the Apache *arsenal*. To protect themselves during battle, warriors carried three-by-two foot buffalo hide shields.

Apache women cared for the home and children, and created beautiful baskets with interesting shapes or animals woven into the design. They also made beads from bones, turquoise, amber, and other materials to decorate clothing and pouches, as well as for trade.

Children were important to the Apache. Contrary to the Tonkawa, they were given a name when they were four days old, but also spent their infancy attached to a cradleboard. Boys were encouraged to be brave and strong, training to build up their stamina and strength through contests beginning at a young age. The young men would usually become a warrior in their late teens.

What Did They Eat?

Since the Apache were hunters, meat was the most important part of their diet. Along with buffalo, the men would hunt deer, javelina, antelope, rabbits, and *rodents*. This meat might be baked, boiled, or dried into jerky; even the animal's blood was consumed in stews, soups, and puddings. Snakes, fish, and turkey were not eaten, as they were considered unclean.

Hunters would often smear themselves with animal fat before trailing game to cover the smell of their bodies. At times, they would also wear a deer mask over their heads, allowing them to sneak up on the animal for a closer shot. When he was successful, the hunter would immediately slice open the animal's carcass and eat the bloody liver, raw.

Women foraged the area for seeds, vegetables, fruits, nuts, and roots; favorites included the *agave* and sotol plants. The tender sotol leaves were roasted and the bulbs were cooked for days, pounded into sheets, then either eaten or ground into a flour. Pinon pine nuts were also dried, roasted, or made into flour. Honey provided a special treat, and the women were responsible for smoking the bees from their hives and collecting the sweet product from inside.

Before the Apache acquired horses, the women would sometimes plant squash, beans, maize, and pumpkin, but were not particularly successful gardeners.

What Did They Wear?

Men either went without clothes at all, or wore breechcloths, leggings, and moccasins. When the weather was cool, they covered themselves with blankets and buckskin shirts. Loose-fitting *tunics* were worn for ease of movement and were fringed with ornamental beadwork.

Ladies wore fringed and beaded dresses, fringed buckskin trousers, skirts, and tops, leggings, and moccasins. The Apache moccasins were quite long, reaching all the way to the knee.

Animal hides were naturally rough and stiff, so a process called *tanning* was used to soften the skin. Buffalo brain, fat, and liver were rubbed on the hide, which was then pulled, stretched, and rubbed to result in a smooth and soft material.

Women wore their hair in a long, thick braid down their back, often with bead and copper earrings and clamshell necklaces. Men did not like hair on the faces, so they plucked out the hair from their eyebrows and beards, and smeared colorful paint over their face and bodies. Warriors cut their hair on the left side of their head, but left the right side to grow long, sometimes to the ground. This hair was then looped, tied, and ornamented with feathers.

Up to eight holes pierced their left ears, with another single piercing in the right, adding ornamentation for special occasions. War bonnets were made with eagle feathers, each *plume* representing a brave deed.

The Apaches' Place in History

The Apaches, who once lived on the Northern Plains and in Canada, arrived on the Texas Plains as nomads. Their great enemy was the Comanche, with whom they spent much time at war, as the Comanche pushed the Apache from their hunting ground.

Although the Lipan were at times friendly with white settlers, they were slowly forced from their hunting grounds. As they moved south, they frequently raided along the Texas-Mexico border. The Lipan were eventually forced onto New Mexico reservations, while the Kiowa Apache were sent to live on a reservation in Oklahoma.

Throssel, Richard, c1910/Museum of Photographic Arts/Flickr Commons/
Accession Number: 2003.003.027

An example of a Native American using a travois, attached to a horse to carry provisions.

The Jumano

Who Were They?

It's difficult to find agreement on an exact description of the Jumanos (hoo-MAHN-oh). It is believed that the Jumanos were distinct groups that lived and roamed in several separate regions in Texas, New Mexico, and Mexico. However, their homes and the lands where they lived were quite different from the coastal and wooded regions of the previous tribes mentioned.

The Jumanos are probably best known as both buffalo hunters and traders; in fact, they served as middlemen in the trade between other Indian tribes and Spanish colonies. Like the Karankawa and Coahuiltecans, these mysterious Native Americans eventually vanished.

Where Did They Live?

Native Americans identified as Jumanos are thought to have lived in several different areas. One group lived and attempted to farm land along the Rio Grande River, south of what is now El Paso. Another more nomadic group ranged from an area south of the Rio Grande and into the South Plains and Central Texas region.

The settlements in far West Texas were located in a dry, mostly desert area. Although they would plant their gardens along the Rio Grande River, the *arid* climate meant farming was not always successful. Plants grown included corn, squash, and pumpkin. Members would also forage for wild plants such as *mesquite* beans, agave bulbs, and prickly pear cactus.

Homes in this area were *pueblo*-style, made from *adobe* brick. Adobe is created from a mixture of wet clay, ashes, and sometimes dry grass. This blend was allowed to dry in the sun and then used as bricks to build homes. They often painted the walls yellow, red, and black. Half of the house was located below ground level, keeping homes cool and dark in the ferocious summer heat.

Other Jumanos were thought to be nomadic, with only *semi-permanent* settlements. These groups would set up camp in an area, often following bison, and attempted to plant food to eat. After harvest or in search of buffalo, the group would pick up camp and move on to another area. Since these families moved frequently, homes had to be easy to load and carry quickly. Animal skin tents usually served as shelters.

Some Jumanos worked as traders with other tribes throughout the state, sometimes going all the way into Caddo territory near the Red River. They provided items such as mesquite beans, cloth, feathers, *pigment*, turquoise, shells, and salt. Another popular item for trade was *wampum*: beads made from the polished ends of shells.

Others worked as *middlemen* and assisted trade between the Spanish and other Texas Indians, including horses and various other goods (after 1650).

How Did They Live?

Of course, the lifestyles of these two groups were very different. Encounters with Spanish explorers left *vague* records of their customs. Cabeza de Vaca mentioned one group of Indians (possibly the Jumano) who were quite unlike the bands of coastal Indians with whom he lived before. The Jumanos did not come out of their homes when guests initially arrived, but they were not unfriendly. The tribe prepared special houses for their guests, offering gifts of skin blankets. Guests were entertained with celebrations and dances around the campfire, where members kept rhythm with their hands and made musical flute sounds with their mouths.

It is thought that either one or two chiefs oversaw each village, and the communities were friendly with each other and neighboring nations and tribes.

Those hunting buffalo were usually forced to walk on foot, especially before the arrival of horses. These hunters at times used a dog travois to bring back the buffalo, often dried into jerky to lighten the load. A travois was made by attaching a piece of hide to two long poles; these poles were then attached to a dog to pull the load.

Food was cooked in an interesting fashion called stone boiling. Stones were heated directly on a fire, then placed into a container filled with water. Once the water began to boil, food was added and cooked. If the water became too cool, more heated rocks were added to the container. Food and other items were stored in hollow gourds, pottery, or pressed *rawhide*, and set into a hole in the ground.

Not much is known about Jumano weapons, although it is said bows and arrows were used for hunting. Long, sharply pointed sticks were used to dig gardens, and buffalo hide shields were used for protection.

What Did They Wear?
The Jumanos were reported to have a neat, clean appearance. The women wore deerskin skirts and *ponchos*, and the men wore long tanned hide breechcloths—and sometimes nothing at all!

Men cut their hair about half way up their scalps, with a large curl on the top of their heads, often decorated with feathers. Other ornaments included necklaces and nose and ear decorations made from turquoise and coral bands. Faces were tattooed with horizontal lines or bars.

The Jumanos' Place in History
The Jumanos have left many mysteries regarding their lifestyle and customs, and we in fact know less about the Jumanos than any other Texas Indian. Native artifacts and pictographs provide a little information, and some records exist regarding their relationship with explorers, as well as the Spanish and mission authorities.

We do know that when the Apaches arrived from the north, they began to cut off the Jumano trade routes and invade their land. Tribal members appealed to the Spanish for help, and some became attached to the Spanish missions, desiring protection from their invading enemy and in the process gaining an interest in Christianity. Unfortunately once again, disease, warfare, and migration eliminated another Native American tribe.

Mesquite Beans

Pierce, C.C., c1900-1910,
California Historical Society Collection, 1860-1960.
Courtesy USC Digital Library.

Prickly Pear Cactus

Sullivan, Jon/Wikimedia Commons/Public Domain

The Tigua

Who Were They?

The Tigua (TEE-wah)) were Pueblo Indians who originally lived in New Mexico along the Rio Grande Valley. They made contact with the Coronado expedition in 1540 and again as the Spanish began to settle the area during the 1600s.

In 1680, these Indians began a *revolt* to drive out the Spanish. A group of escaping Spanish settlers, along with 317 Tigua refugees, followed the Rio Grande down to what is now the El Paso area of far West Texas. The town of Ysleta del Sur was then founded in 1682, and the Tigua built the Corpus Christi Mission of Ysleta del Sur—the oldest church and mission in Texas.

During the late 1800s, the Tigua lost all of their land to settlers, leaving tribal members in poverty. Their lives improved in 1968 when the Tigua were finally recognized as a nation and a North American Indian Tribe. The tribe is governed by the Tribal Council; currently, the tribe elects a governor, lieutenant governor, bailiff, and other officers. The Tigua chief is called the "Cacique," and the War Captain is called "Capitan de Guerra." These two men serve in these positions for life and offer spiritual and traditional guidance.

Where Did They Live?

The Tigua did, and still do live, just outside El Paso in far West Texas. These Pueblo Indians live in adobe pueblo homes. The thick walls help keep the homes in this hot, dry region cool inside. Early pueblos didn't have a door on the first floor. Instead, one would enter through an opening called a *hatchway* in the roof. This protection allowed families to keep out intruders, as a ladder could be used when needed, then pulled up and away to deter unwanted guests. Fire pits for cooking were located inside the home, and the hatchway also served as a chimney for the smoke.

Villages made of these adobe homes also included separate *kivas* for meetings and ceremonies. You can still visit and see these pueblos in the historic Mission District, about fifteen miles from downtown El Paso. Families continue to live and work there and maintain many of the traditional Tigua traditions and customs.

What Did They Eat?

The Tigua were primarily farmers, although they also hunted deer, antelope, buffalo, rabbits, squirrels, and fish. To irrigate their crops, they developed a sophisticated system many years ago, using canals to bring water to their garden from rivers and streams. Corn was their main crop, but they also planted tomatoes, squash, beans, grapes, and fruit. Red and green chili peppers were grown to spice up their dishes, and were dried and hung with strings within their homes.

The planting and harvest of corn, beans, and squash was common among many farming Native Americans tribes. This trio of vegetables was known as "The Three Sisters," and a clever way of planting the seeds helped the plants grow successfully. First, a few kernels of corn were planted under a small pile of dirt. After the corn sprouted, the bean and squash seeds were planted next to the corn. The corn grew tall and the beans climbed up the corn, which supported the bean vines. The squash vines spread over the mound, protecting the soil from weeds and erosion. This practice is now known as "companion planting."

The Tigua tribe actually owned the land used for farming, but families were given plots to plant and harvest their own food. Men cleared the fields, women were responsible for digging holes with a sharply pointed stick to plant the seeds, and children helped by weeding the gardens. Big ceremonies were held at the time of harvest. The

Tigua cooked their daily bread in a beehive-shaped outdoor oven called a *"horno,"* which was heated with mesquite roots.

How Did They Live?

The Tigua wore cotton clothes, trimmed with cowhide leather; men wore breechcloths and coats were decorated with turkey feathers.

In earlier times, long wooden sticks with sharp points were used to hunt rabbit and smaller game; these tools were later replaced with guns and rifles. War captains led tribal hunts, beginning each with a prayer and a blessing. Using the old traditions, these hunts still take place today.

The Tigua became Christians, and today you can visit the Ysleta Mission church, built over 200 years ago. Over time, they have blended Roman Catholicism with their own Native American traditions and feasts.

Tigua pottery is still designed and created in the ancient Pueblo fashion. Clay is rolled into snake-like strings and layered atop a clay foundation. Once it is smoothed, the pottery is dried in the sun, painted, and then fired to complete the process.

Very old pictographs created by the Tigua can be found at Hueco Tanks, east of El Paso. The pictographs in this desert area were created on cave walls and overhangs.

The Tiguas' Place in History

The Tigua may have originally come to Texas either as refugees or against their will, but they contributed a great deal to the advancement of farming and cultivation in West Texas.

They also built the earliest mission and church in what would become Texas, and brought the pueblo-style adobe home to the area as well. Tigua men served as scouts for both the United States Cavalry and the Texas Rangers until 1881, helping to protect Texans from aggressive Comanche and Apache. The Tigua are still living out their traditions and culture, providing a living history lesson for Texans and other visitors.

Ysleta Mission
La Misión de Corpus Christi de San Antonio de la Ysleta del Sur

McGee, Shannon/ *Ysleta Mission*/Flickr/ CC BY-SA 2.0

Other Texas Native American Tribes

We've named only a portion of the Native American tribes and bands who have lived in Texas throughout history. The Wichita, Concho, Cherokee, Choctaw, Shawnee, and Seminoles have also called Texas home at one time.

You might enjoy doing some further research on these interesting people and their cultures. Most of the Native Americans that lived in Texas either moved away on their own, were relocated to reservations in other states, or are no longer in existence.

Today, three tribes possess reservations in Texas: the Tigua (near El Paso), the Alabama-Coushatta (near Livingston in the Big Thicket area), and the Kickapoo (near Eagle Pass and the Mexico border).

The 1900 *census* in Texas listed only 470 Native Americans living in Texas, but today the population is closer to 125,000.

1. **Cherokee**: The Cherokee were originally from the area around Tennessee and North Carolina. The U.S. Government and settlers kept pushing the Cherokee west, to Arkansas and eventually Oklahoma and Texas. Sam Houston lived with the Cherokee twice during his lifetime!

2. **Concho**: The Conchos lived near where the Rio Grande and Rio Concho rivers meet, and they had a similar lifestyle and culture to the Jumano Indians. It is believed they encountered Spanish explorers, but eventually died off or were absorbed into other tribes.

3. **Wichita:** Four different associated groups made up the Wichita—the Waco, Wichita, Tawakoni, and Taovaya. Waco, Texas, is name for the Waco Indians who settled in the Central Texas area where the city is now located.

4. **Choctaw:** The Choctaws arrived in Texas during the 1830s and had a good relationship with their settler neighbors. However, most were forced out of Texas with many other Native Americans in 1839.

5. **Shawnee:** The Shawnee also maintained good relationships with the settlers and were allies with the Cherokee. They came to Texas in 1822, settled along the Red River, and were forced out as well in 1839.

6. **Seminole:** The Seminoles left Florida in the early 1800s and moved west. Slaveholders in the South were unhappy with the Seminoles because they allowed runaway slaves to live in a separate commmunity within their group. Although the runaways were considered slaves with Seminole masters, they could ranch and farm their own land, only being required to share a portion with their Indian masters.

7. **Alabama-Coushatta:** These two tribes originally came to Texas from Alabama and Louisiana in the 1780s. They lived in the Big Thicket area and, interestingly, were not forced out of Texas in 1839 with the other Native Americans. Instead, the tribes were granted a reservation in Polk County, Texas, and eventually combined as one tribe.

8. **Kickapoo:** The Kickapoo originally lived in the Great Lakes area and Kansas, came to Texas, but were then forced to leave in 1839. In the 1980s, the Kickapoo were granted land in El Indio, Texas, where many members work as *migrant* workers, frequently crossing the border into Mexico.

By now you have learned all about the land of Texas and the first Texans: the Native Americans. In this unit, we will begin by discussing early exploration of the world. Then we'll move on to how it impacted the first Spanish and French explorers in Texas. These brave men paved the way for the settlers, who would later join the Native Americans and share the land we now call Texas.

You'll also learn about the missions and presidios of Texas, and why they are important to the colonization of the region.

WORLD EXPLORATION

For many years—in fact, for most of the years man has lived on earth—people spent the majority of their days just trying to find food and shelter. Hungry or being chased by wild animals or unfriendly neighbors, one did not have time to worry about anything other than staying alive and protecting the family.

Eventually people began to settle in groups. They grew their own food and domesticated animals. They began to share in the responsibilities of their community, focusing on specific services or products (like grinding grain or making pottery) which they could either sell or trade to support their families. Once their lives were more stable and their basic needs fulfilled, they had time to think about other things ... like adventure!

People became curious about other lands. They looked at the possibility of moving families to new regions (colonizing), but they also searched for new sources of wealth. Men like Marco Polo (1254-1324 A.D.) traveled overland from Europe to Asia, discovering wonderful spices and silks which could be carried back home and sold for a great deal of money. People wondered if there might be a faster way to reach Asia and began to look for new trade routes, using the oceans and seas as their highway.

There was a great deal of glory in bringing back riches and the news of discoveries, claiming and planting their country's flag on the shores of a land full of wonderful resources.

We call this period of time the *Age of Exploration*, taking place in an exciting era known also as the *Renaissance*. Explorers of the 1400s through the 1600s were curious about undiscovered parts of the world, braving the dangerous seas as they traveled to unfamiliar lands. Better understanding of science led to better shipbuilding and navigation. Explorers began to draw maps as they discovered new lands, opening the door for investigation. Of course, kings and queens wanted their country to take credit for being the first to discover these new lands and reap the riches, so they would often *fund* the explorers' trips with enough money to purchase ships and supplies, as well as pay sailors to search for these new lands and routes.

Exploration was a dangerous business. Storms destroyed ships and dashed hopes. Unfriendly natives and aggressive explorers often meant war and loss of lives. As they entered unknown seas and lands, the explorers risked becoming lost, never to return home again.

And remember, when these explorers "discovered" these new lands, very often native people—whose ancestors had found and settled the land long ago—were already living on that land. Sometimes the explorers were respectful and the natives friendly, but as you can imagine, very often the natives were not thrilled with the appearance of newcomers who sometimes took their land, their riches, and even their people.

51

TIMELINE OF EXPLORATION

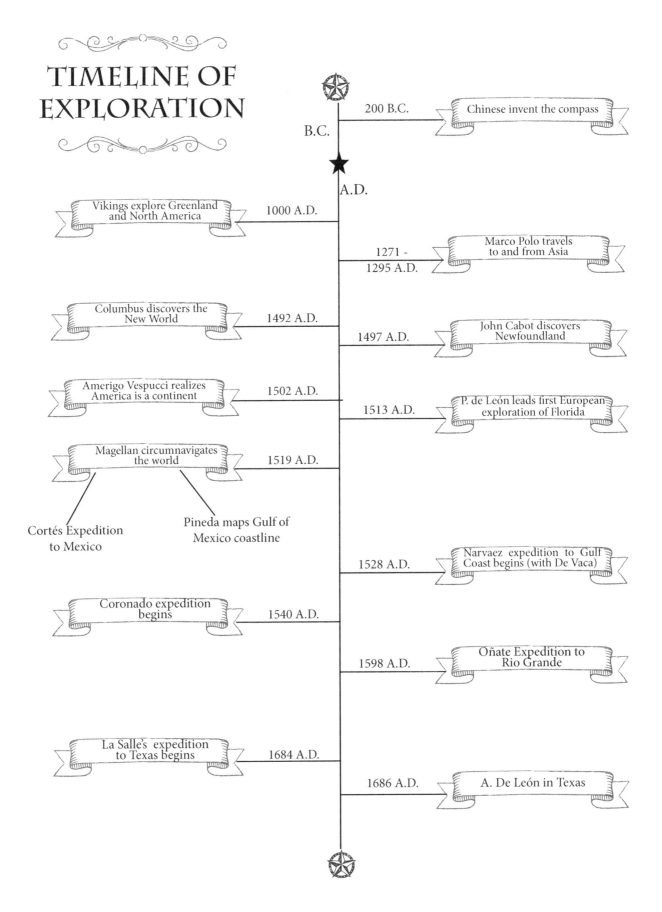

200 B.C. — Chinese invent the compass

B.C.

A.D.

Vikings explore Greenland and North America — 1000 A.D.

1271 - 1295 A.D. — Marco Polo travels to and from Asia

Columbus discovers the New World — 1492 A.D.

1497 A.D. — John Cabot discovers Newfoundland

Amerigo Vespucci realizes America is a continent — 1502 A.D.

1513 A.D. — P. de León leads first European exploration of Florida

Magellan circumnavigates the world — 1519 A.D.

Cortés Expedition to Mexico

Pineda maps Gulf of Mexico coastline

1528 A.D. — Narvaez expedition to Gulf Coast begins (with De Vaca)

Coronado expedition begins — 1540 A.D.

1598 A.D. — Oñate Expedition to Rio Grande

La Salle's expedition to Texas begins — 1684 A.D.

1686 A.D. — A. De León in Texas

Exploration and the Americas

Christopher Columbus
First European to Discover the Americas

Most people know the story of Christopher Columbus. He was the Italian who led three ships under the Spanish flag in 1492, searching for a new route to Asia. China was an area of many riches, but traveling the overland course was dangerous. Columbus convinced Queen Isabella and King Ferdinand of Spain to pay for his trip, since a voyage by ocean would surely be safer and maybe even faster. No one in Europe realized an entire continent lay between their homes and China, so Columbus set sail, heading west across the Atlantic Ocean. He was quite certain he would sail directly to the shores of Asia.

Instead, he stumbled upon San Salvador, an island in the Bahamas, south of today's Florida. He named the *inhabitants* "Indians" because he still believed he had landed on what was South or East Asia, known as "the Indies" during that time. This landing eventually led to the discovery of the continents of North and South America, which were then inhabited by Native Americans.

Over time, Spain claimed the land of today's Mexico, Central America, most of South America, many of the Caribbean Islands, and much of the southwest region of North America. Although

Columbus never actually set foot on the North American continent, his discovery set the stage for future European explorations and settlements, ultimately resulting in the *colonization* of a land which would, in time, take the name "Texas."

Engraving of Columbus by John Sartain. Courtesy of Library of Congress.

Hernán Cortés
Conqueror of Mexico

Cortés was a Spanish *conquistador* who is known for his conquest of Mexico. In 1519, Cortés sailed to the east coast of Mexico with 500 soldiers.

At that time, the native Aztec *empire* and its people controlled the land. Accompanied by a group of Native Americans who had earlier *rebelled* against the Aztec rulers, Cortés and his men marched to the capital, Tenochtitlán.

When the newcomers arrived, the Aztecs initially welcomed Cortés—they thought he was their god, Quetzalcóatl. Instead, Cortés took the Aztec emperor Montezuma captive, leading to Montezuma's death when he was killed by Aztec rebels.

Cortés and his men destroyed the city of Tenochtitlán, stealing Aztec treasures along the way. He then had a new city built on the ruins and called it Mexico, a name possibly based on an earlier name of one of the Aztec tribes, the Mexica. This city, Mexico City, then became the capital of Mexico.

Cortés was appointed governor of "New Spain"(which included Mexico and adjacent land to be claimed and conquered by Spain) by King Charles I of Spain in 1523. He was eventually removed from power and returned to Spain, where he died in 1547.

Hernando Cortés, engraving by W.Holl; published by Charles Knight. Courtesy of Library of Congress.

Alonso Álvarez de Pineda

Now that the New World had been discovered and the Spanish had conquered Mexico, the time had come to further explore the North American continent and attempt to make this new land easier to navigate through the creation of maps.

The governor of Jamaica chose the Spanish Captain Alonso Álvarez de Pineda (1494?-1519) for this mission. Pineda was expected to not only map the Gulf Coast from Florida to Veracruz, Mexico, but also keep an eye out for a possible *waterway* passage to India.

In 1519, Pineda set sail from Jamaica with four ships and 270 men. The sailors closely followed the coastline as they sailed along the shores of the Gulf of Mexico. Pineda kept careful notes and mapped islands, rivers, and bays encountered along the way. These maps were carefully drawn and preserved on *parchment* paper. He recorded plants he noticed growing near the shore, but saw no large villages or settlements along the route.

After several months spent mapping the shoreline, Pineda and his men reached Veracruz, Mexico. Upon his arrival, a suspicious Cortés took several of Pineda's men prisoner.

Pineda and the rest of his crew then retreated up the coast and eventually stopped to repair their boats at the mouth of a large river he named "Rio de las Palmas" (River of the Palms), thought now to be the Pánuco River near Tampico, Mexico.

As Pineda's men explored the area, the sailors came across forty small Indian villages. It is believed Pineda and his men decided to colonize the area. Although no one knows exactly what happened, Pineda and many others were later found to have been killed by natives, either on this trip or another voyage to the same settlement.

However, somehow Pineda's map eventually made its way to Jamaica. Although these explorers did not complete their mission of finding a passageway to India, they did something which would set the stage for many future explorers and settlers: they created an *accurate*, well-designed map used as a tool for further exploration. In fact, this map is the first known document in Texas history. Pineda and his men were the first Europeans to observe the gulf coastline of Florida, Mississippi, Alabama, Louisiana, and of course, the land that would eventually come to be known as Texas!

The map, as seen below, is the first to represent this coastline, as well as Texas. Notches in this sketch are thought to symbolize the mouth of the Sabine River and the Rio Grande, as well as Galveston, Matagorda, and Corpus Christi bays. It's interesting to note the barrier islands were not included on this map.

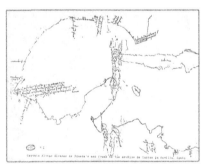

Section of Pineda's 1519 Map of the Gulf Coast

Courtesy of Texascounties.net/Public Domain

Pineda's Route

Gulf of Mexico

54

Álvar Núñez Cabeza de Vaca (1490? - 1555) was a Spanish explorer who served as treasurer on an expedition to North America led by Pánfilo de Narváez. In 1528, the king of Spain sent five ships to the newly discovered land we now know as Florida, hoping that men would colonize along the coast of the Gulf of Mexico and perhaps find gold and other precious metals. Landing on the west coast near today's city of Tampa, 300 of the explorers were ordered to leave the ships and march inland to explore land to the north. Four months later, the crew arrived at Apalachee Bay, having lost at least fifty men and encountering hostile Indians along the way. Now they were separated from their ships and had little food to eat.

Realizing their lives were in danger, the men built five rafts from timber, lashed together with *palmetto* husks and made waterproof with pine *resin*. Unable to bring their horses aboard, they slaughtered the animals for their meat, wove ropes made from the manes and tails, fashioned water bottles from horsehide and hollowed out horse legs, and created tools from their stirrups and horseshoe nails. They then sewed their capes and shirts together to create much-needed sails for their boats.

Sailing along the coastline for close to two months, nearly 250 men headed west on their newly crafted *barges*, hoping to eventually reach Pánuco, Mexico. Unfortunately, the sailors were greeted with a very violent storm near Galveston Island. Wind and rain tore apart their rafts' lashings and all of their supplies were washed away.

Only a few boats made it to shore; most of the men were lost at sea. Those who survived were weak and unable to care for themselves. Soon a group of about 100 Indians appeared with bows and arrows in their hands. The Spanish were probably quite frightened of these men who appeared very large and did not speak their language. In fact, Cabeza de Vaca would later recall the Spaniards' fear "made them appear as giants." It is believed that the coastal Native Americans encountered

were likely Karankawa and later Coahuiltecans.

As frightening as they appeared, these Indians were at first quite friendly, bringing the explorers food and clothing. Even so, most of the Spaniards eventually died from illness, exposure to the *elements*, and starvation. Six years later, only four of the Europeans would still be alive, including the journey's treasurer, Cabeza de Vaca, and a North African slave called Esteban the Moor (also known as Estevanico).

> *Did You Know?*
> We know Cabeza de Vaca and his companions landed on one of the Texas barrier islands, and it is believed to have likely been Galveston or nearby Follet's Island. However, at that time, the island had not been named.
> Cabeza de Vaca titled it accordingly:
> *Isla de Malhado*,
> which translates to
> *Island of Misfortune.*

Cabeza de Vaca spent the first four years traveling throughout the mainland as a trader, a healer, and a forced laborer as he moved among the local Native Americans. He observed and would later describe the Indians and their lifestyle, as well as the plants and animals of the region. The other remaining castaways also survived by serving as slaves to the natives, although Cabeza de Vaca recalled that his position as a trader allowed him more freedom. Separated from each other at times over these years, the Spaniards yearned to escape and return home.

Eventually Cabeza de Vaca reunited with the other three survivors. Finally, in 1534, the men escaped by night and traveled west, sometimes eating only dried grass along the way. They followed the Colorado and Concho Rivers and met and traded with many friendly Native American tribes.

These four Europeans began to be known among the Indians as the great healers: "Children of the Sun." The Spaniards were very popular and sometimes crowds of Indians would follow along as they traveled. Although the explorers were not trained physicians, they adopted the Indian custom of breathing on the patient, then would make the sign of the cross over him/her and offer prayers for their healing. Cabeza de Vaca was even known to perform operations, once removing an arrow from an Indian's chest. The Spaniards happily accepted their fans' gifts of food and clothing, and reported later that the patients appeared to always recover from their ailments.

The men were exposed to many different tribes' ways of life and cultures. They were fascinated by the Native American farmers who used irrigation as they *cultivated* beans and squash. They saw and ate buffalo. They wore little, if any clothing, walked barefoot, and slept on the ground. They lived the life of Indians.

Eventually the explorers crossed the Rio Grande River near today's El Paso. They continued to travel southwest with friendly Indian guides through New Mexico and Arizona, finally reaching a spot near the Pacific Coast and turning south into Mexico. After hearing other "Christians" were nearby, Cabeza de Vaca and Esteban had the good fortune to run into four Spaniards on horseback as they neared the city of Mocorito. Esteban ran back to find the others, and eventually the entire group made it to Culiacán, Mexico.

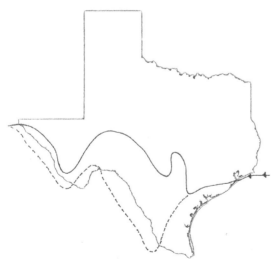

Historians have several theories about the route Cabeza de Vaca and the other men took across Texas. Two possible routes can be seen on this map.

Who Were the Conquistadors?

The word *conquistador* comes from the Spanish word "conquistadores," meaning "conquerors." These Spanish and Portuguese professional soldiers and explorers traveled to the Americas and other continents of the world, searching for gold, opening trade routes, claiming land for their country and colonizing the new territories, spreading their religion, and gaining glory as national heroes.

The warriors explored and conquered land throughout the Americas from the 15th through 17th centuries, sometimes bringing progress, and sadly, sometimes bringing death and disease to the native inhabitants. Famous conquistadors include Cortés, Pizarro, Balboa, Ponce de León, and Hernando De Soto.

The men were soon escorted to Mexico City, where Viceroy Mendoza honored the explorers with feasts and bullfights. The four men drew a map and retold the tale of their long and exciting eight-year adventure.

Cabeza de Vaca rested, then decided to return to Spain in 1537. He met with the king and then wrote the story of his travels—the first to tell of the land which would become Texas—in a book entitled *La Relación* in 1542. Although they were unable to complete their mission to find gold and other precious metals, these four explorers had an even greater claim to fame: they were the first non-natives to cross both Texas, and, in fact, the southern part of the North American continent.

While Pineda created the first written document regarding the land that would become Texas, Cabeza de Vaca wrote the first true description of the native people and their cultures. He became endeared to his new Native American friends, and expressed a compassion and concern about these families unusual for a man recognized as a conquistador.

The story of his travels became known throughout Europe, leading to an excitement and encouragement to further explore these lands across the ocean.

Fransisco Vázquez de Coronado

When the stories of Cabeza de Vaca and his adventures were told, Europeans began to be even more curious about this mysterious new land and its possibilities. Rumors began to spread about an area in the southwest portion of the North American continent, just above Mexico, called Cíbola. It was said that Cíbola possessed seven cities which were filled with gold, silver, and turquoise.

The highest Spanish official of Mexico, *Viceroy* Mendoza, put together a mission to find and claim these precious lands and treasures for Spain. To lead the expedition, he selected Fransisco Coronado (1510-1554), who had no trouble enlisting volunteers, excited about the prospect of participating in a venture leading to great wealth and rewards of rich land.

The great journey began in 1540 with a grand parade in Compostela, on the west coast of Mexico. The expedition consisted of 240 horsemen, 60 foot soldiers carrying *crossbows* and swords, 800 friendly Indians, hundreds of Black and Indian servants, 1,000 pack animals, and thousands of additional animals that would provide a source of food for the men along the way.

Only one member of this crew had previously visited the area north of Mexico: *Friar "Fray" Marcos de Niza*. He and a small scouting party had *trekked* through a portion of the area in 1539 to establish a trail for the upcoming expedition. The guide for this scouting mission was none other than Esteban, the slave who accompanied Cabeza de Vaca and the other remaining survivors of that journey before. Esteban forged his way forward in front of the rest of the *scouts* in order to talk to Indians up ahead. The party soon received word that Esteban had been killed by Indians. The death of Esteban frightened Fray Marcos, and so the small scouting crew returned to Mexico before completing their mission of establishing a trail for the impending venture.

Upon his return, Fray Marcos reported to Coronado that he had seen with his own eyes a large city in the distance, far across a green valley: Cíbola!

Encouraged, Captain Coronado and his huge *entourage* began their journey with high hopes. However, the movement was slow, weighed down with so many men and animals. One scout returned with a message from the Indians that they intended to kill white men who entered their territory. Coronado *persisted* and the crew continued in a northeastern direction, into land that is now near the border of New Mexico and Arizona. They crossed long, hot deserts and lost many animals to starvation and lack of water. It didn't take long for the men to become discouraged and frustrated.

By May of 1540, the men had traveled 1,000 miles and finally reached the area of Cíbola. They didn't see shining cities of gold. Instead, all they observed were adobe houses set upon steep cliffs in the distance. These were the pueblos of the Zuni tribe. The Zunis were unhappy to see these visitors from the south, and began throwing lances and shooting arrows at the crew. Realizing the Spaniard's guns were likely deadlier than bows and arrows, the Zunis quickly pulled up the ladders to their pueblos and huddled inside their homes. Coronado was wounded by an arrow and stones hurled during the brief battle, and at least twenty Zunis were killed.

Courtesy of Wikimedia Commons/Public Domain.

Coronado Sets Out
to the North
By
Frederic Remington

The tribe realized it was in grave danger and asked for a *truce*. Once allowed in the village, the expedition was friendly and offered many gifts to the Indians. The crew's *scribe* noted that the town was "a little, crumbled village" with no precious metals or stones.

Angry with Fray Marcos and his obvious lies about the Cities of Gold, Coronado ordered the friar back to Mexico. He also sent a message to the viceroy, notifying him that the Seven Cities of Gold were only seven little poor villages.

During this time, the captain also sent a scouting crew to investigate land to the west of Cíbola, led by a man named Cárdenas. This party, twenty days later, had the fortune to discover a monstrous chasm with a river twisting along the bottom. They were the first Europeans to see the marvel of the Grand Canyon!

Coronado also sent a scouting mission to central New Mexico. Located near what is now Albuquerque, the men came upon an area of twelve towns called Tiguex. The land was good for grazing and the Indians were friendly; they suggested the men winter in their towns and then proceed to the east, where rich land could be found. Coronado and the rest of the mission arrived at Tiguex but were demanding of the Indians, forcing them to provide housing and food. This angered the Indians and a violent battle began. The fighting lasted several weeks, with the Spaniards finally taking control.

The Native Americans, however, had the last laugh. They introduced the explorers to a Pawnee Indian who became known as "El Turco." He told the Spaniards all about his home that lay to the east. A land called Quivira was located near his home. He said THIS land was truly one of great riches and treasures. Intent upon fulfilling their mission and bringing great riches to their homeland, Coronado chose to believe El Turco and set out to find Quivira.

The expedition set off in April of 1541, heading east again. This time the men followed the Rio Grande to the north and crossed the Pecos River. Continuing east along the Canadian River, the crew reached a flat land, covered with buffalo. They named this area the Llano Estacado (Staked Plains). Although the land was flat, there were no landmarks and the grass sprang up after being trampled—making it impossible to create a trail and easy to become lost.

El Turco and the local nomadic Indians served as guides along this area of the Texas Panhandle. El Turco began to zigzag along the way, turning in a southward direction. Coronado became suspicious.

Did You Know?

The Llano Estacado, also referred to as the "Staked Plains," is actually a giant *mesa* that covers land in eastern New Mexico and northwest Texas. It begins at an elevation of 3,000 feet in the southeast and rises at about ten feet per mile to over 5,000 feet in the northwest area of the region. Its boundaries are the Canadian River (to the north), the Caprock Escarpment (a 300 foot cliff!) to the east, the Mescalero Escarpment (to the west), and a blending into the Edwards Plateau on the southern edge.

The men met friendly Tewa Indians who told Coronado that El Turco's claims about Quivira were false, and the town was certainly not in their path's direction. El Turco was placed in chains and a smaller expedition of thirty horsemen, six soldiers, a priest, and a new guide named Isopete were selected to continue the journey, as a smaller company could travel faster. The rest of the expedition was sent back to Tiguex to await the smaller group's return.

It is believed that Coronado and the smaller crew followed the Canadian River, meeting more friendly Indians along the way who gave them many buffalo robes as gifts. Suddenly the men came across a beautiful deep *gorge* with colorful rocky sides and a narrow stream at the bottom: the Palo Duro Canyon!

They then traveled up into what is believed to be Oklahoma and then Kansas, finally reaching the settlement at Quivira. Again, promises of riches and gold proved false. Quivira was only a town of grass huts and poor families. El Turco had lied.

The men spent twenty-five days exploring the area, and during that time discovered El Turco had advised the local Indians to kill the Spaniards. El Turco was tortured and finally confessed that his mission was to ensure the expedition become lost. Coronado's men executed El Turco on the spot.

This small group then turned around, returning to Tiguex (much faster this time, since they traveled in a straight line). They wintered there and finally returned to Mexico City in 1542. The explorers had journeyed 4,000 miles in two and a half years. Because they were unable to bring good news and return with riches and stories of streets lined with gold, the mission was considered a failure. Not one person was waiting to greet them on their return.

Looking back, we know this mission was *not* a failure. A great deal of information about this vast and fertile land, previously undiscovered by the Europeans, was obtained—although it was believed at the time that the land they observed was not suitable for settlement. Much information about the Indians and the land was now available to future explorers. Most important of all, Coronado had claimed all of the southwestern North American continent for Spain.

Like Cabeza de Vaca's travels, historians are unsure of Coronado's exact route. This path is believed by some to be Coronado's approximate course to Quivira and back to Mexico.

Robert de La Salle

As we have learned, the Spanish concentrated their exploration and settlements in Mexico and the southwestern portion of North America. After Coronado's expedition and his failure to find gold and precious metals, Spanish interest in Texas *waned* for about a hundred years.

Other Europeans were beginning to make their mark on the continent. English settlers crossed the Atlantic and settled along the east coast, and the French developed a system of trading furs with the Indians in Canada.

Robert de La Salle (1643-1687)—his full name was René-Robert Cavelier, Sieur de La Salle, so we'll just stick with La Salle—was a Frenchman who built trading posts and forts for French and Indian fur traders. The Indians brought animal furs to trade with the French, in return for items such as guns and cloth.

La Salle realized there was a great need for a *seaport* which could be used all year long to *export* these furs back to Europe. He decided to explore the possibility of following the Mississippi River to its mouth, hoping it would lead to a milder climate where the seaport could be located. La Salle followed the river and found that it indeed flowed into the Gulf of Mexico. He claimed the river, the Mississippi River Valley, and the land around it (including what would become Louisiana) for France.

La Salle then offered a *proposal* to King Louis of France: La Salle would build a fort and a colony where the Mississippi River met the Gulf of Mexico. This would become the year-long seaport he had

long desired. With plans to make *allies* of the local Indians, whom he hoped would help the French in any battles with the Spanish, La Salle convinced the king to pledge his support. La Salle also noted there was great potential for riches within the Mexican mines, not to mention priests could be included in the *venture* to help spread Christianity.

King Louis agreed, and four ships set out for the Gulf of Mexico in 1684. Aboard were 280 men, 100 soldiers, 30 volunteers, a handful of priests and friars, and a few women and children to begin the colony. While making a stop in the West Indies, one of the four ships was lost to pirates, along with many valuable supplies.

The remaining three ships continued along the coast, but somehow passed the Mississippi River *Delta*. Some believe La Salle just missed the area due to fog and poor maps; but others believe he intentionally passed the delta so he could continue closer to Mexico and its potential wealth.

Either way, the ships eventually spied Matagorda Bay and a large river we now know was the Lavaca River. La Salle, however, reported to the crew that they were nearing the Mississippi River. The waters of the bay were very shallow, and one ship ran aground. Unfortunately, a storm arose and the ship was destroyed, resulting in the loss of even more supplies.

La Salle and Captain Beaujeu, the mission's naval commander, never got along. Beaujeu and

René-Robert Cavelier, Sieur de La Salle
PS Burton/Wikimedia Commons/Public Domain

several other leaders decided to turn one of the ships around and leave La Salle and the others behind.

Now only one ship remained with the 200 colonists: the ship *La Belle*. Most of the remaining settlers were ill, many from a lack of fresh water. La Salle decided to seek another spot for the colonists to settle, where the water was clear and they felt safe from the local Indians whom they had already angered.

The remaining settlers moved about five miles inland, near a clear stream and closer to buffalo. They surrounded and protected their six mud-covered huts and larger meeting building with a tall *palisade*. Cannons and the French flag were mounted on the top of their new home, which they named Fort St. Louis.

La Salle made a journey with a group of sixty men to explore the bay area, meeting Indians and traveling as far as the Rio Grande. After the scouting group returned, La Salle decided to take twenty men with him to find the Mississippi River and make their way to Canada for help. During this trip, the explorers met Caddo Indians and stayed with them for a time in East Texas.

The men returned once again to Fort St. Louis, finding only forty-five settlers had survived illness and Indian attacks during their absence. To add to their troubles, *La Belle* had been torn apart by a *squall* and destroyed.

Deciding to make one more attempt to find the Mississippi River and assistance, La Salle left with about seventeen men and made their way east. His men were angry and blamed La Salle for the failure of the colony, and began to plot against their leader and his few remaining supporters. After killing La Salle's nephews and two friends, they murdered La Salle and left him near what we believe today is Navasota.

In 1689, some Spaniards came across the ruins of Fort St. Louis. The last remaining colonists had been killed by Native Americans, although four children were kidnapped by these Indians and eventually recovered by the Spanish and taken to Mexico.

While La Salle and King Louis' plans to colonize the Mississippi River Delta never came to pass, and it appeared the *venture* was a failure, the French presence in Texas had surprising results. When the Spanish discovered the French had attempted to settle in Texas and were apparently a threat to Spain's claim to the land, Spain became very concerned and realized perhaps they should begin to take a greater interest in the territory. This potential threat led to the Spanish decision to build forts, missions, and settlements.

The result? Villages would rise, more people would settle, and this new territory would begin to grow.

La Salle's Expedition to Louisiana in 1684
by Theodore Gudin (1844)

The ship on the left is *La Belle*, in the middle is *Le Joly*, and *L'Aimable*, which has run aground, is to the far right. The ships are at the entrance to Matagorda Bay.

AYER/Wikimedia Commons/Public Domain.

Six of La Salle's men continued on to Canada

Approximate site La Salle murdered (near Navasota)

Fort St. Louis

Matagorda Bay

Route to landing site and Fort St. Louis settlement, and La Salle's final exploration trek.

Hernando De Soto
and Luis de Moscoso Alvarado

Hernando De Soto (1495-1542) was a Spanish explorer who became wealthy after he helped conquer the Incas of South America in the 1530s. After hearing rumors about the riches to be found in North America, he sailed to Florida with a crew of 600 men, spending four years exploring the Southeast. De Soto became ill and died before he actually reached Texas, but prior to his death in 1542, made Moscoso (1505-1551) leader of the expedition.

Moscoso continued marching west, and it is believed he and his men likely traveled as far west as the lower Brazos River in Texas. Because they were low on supplies, Moscoso and his men marched back to the Mississippi River, sailed down to the gulf, then followed the coastline to Mexico.

Hernando De Soto

Juan de Oñate

Juan de Oñate (1550-1626) was another conquistador and explorer for Spain, born in Mexico. He led a large expedition in 1598; his excursion included 600 people, eighty-three wagons and carts, and 7,000 animals, establishing the first European settlement on the upper Rio Grande. Upon reaching the Rio Grande after a difficult journey, Oñate claimed the land for Spain and celebrated with a Mass and thanksgiving feast, almost twenty-five years before the *Puritans* held the more well-known Thanksgiving in Plymouth. Oñate crossed the river at "El Paso del Río del Norte," later called "El Paso." He finally reached the northern Rio Grande Valley, where he set up headquarters and formally founded the *province* of New Mexico.

Alonso De León

Alonso De León (1639-1691) was born in Mexico and educated in Spain. He was sent by the Spanish government to find and remove any French settlers. Making four trips into Texas from 1686 to 1689, he eventually found the abandoned Fort St. Louis settlement. He became governor of Coahuila (Spanish territory southwest of Texas) in 1687, and was the founder of the first East Texas mission, San Francisco de los Tejas, in 1690 with Father Damián Massanet. De León encouraged the building of more missions across the province.

Louis Juchereau de Saint-Denis

Louis Saint-Denis (1676-1744) was a French-Canadian explorer whose personality was apparently quite different from the other well-known (and apparently, less charming) explorers. During this time, the French continued to trade with the Native Americans, swapping guns and other supplies for the furs provided by the Indians. The French hoped to also begin trading with the Spanish in Mexico, but there were laws against trading with foreigners in New Spain.

Saint-Denis was sent in 1714 by the French governor in Louisiana to discuss the possibility with officials on the Rio Grande. His appearance frightened the Spanish, who feared the French were once again threatening to settle in Texas. He was arrested and sent to Mexico, but was eventually released and ordered to assist and guide Spanish soldiers to East Texas, where Spain would again build more missions to protect the area. Although his appearance caused Spain to rebuild defenses against French settlement, Saint-Denis must have also been quite likable. The Spanish captain who arrested and sent this French-Canadian back to Texas, also allowed Saint-Denis to marry his step-granddaughter!

MISSIONS & PRESIDIOS

The original European explorers had several goals in mind when they ventured across the Atlantic Ocean to the Americas: new land and potential riches. But there was another mission: a far less selfish reason to settle and colonize an unexplored country. Many wanted to spread Christianity and Catholicism to the Native Americans who had never been exposed to other religions besides their own.

The Franciscans, a group of priests and nuns who were part of the Catholic church, were given the responsibility by Spain to spread Christianity among the Texas Indians. They wanted to do more than just preach. They desired to bring Native Americans into communities where they could be educated and learn Catholic beliefs and practices. By setting up missions in this new territory, an awareness of Christianity and Spanish culture could be spread to local Native Americans. Additionally, a place of safety from tribal enemies and a more constant food supply would be available for those in the community. Trade with local Indians would be improved, and the French would hopefully be discouraged from trespassing and attempting to begin another colony. According to Spain, it was a win-win situation for everyone involved.

Each *mission* settlement was to include a mission, a colony of settlers, and a nearby *presidio* for protection. Once these *settlements* became independent and could provide for themselves, new missions and settlements would be built, resulting in a growing and *prosperous* population, loyal to Spain.

The earliest missions began in the western portion of the territory. After the discovery of La Salle's abandoned colony, when the French became a concern, missions were also established in East Texas. These missions were eventually moved and became the Central Texas San Antonio missions. Each of these missions has an interesting story to tell, and many are open to visitors to this day.

MISSIONS: *How They Worked*

Once a mission spot was selected, the friars, soldiers, and settlers would usually build temporary log houses. Curious Indians who would come upon the scene were offered gifts to assist in the building. Eventually the friars would attempt to convince the local Native Americans to move into the mission in hopes of converting them to Christianity and Catholicism.

While living in the mission, the new inhabitants would be **baptized** and taught the elements of the Catholic faith. Everyone would work to build more housing, **cultivate** gardens, and raise cattle and other livestock; the farm and ranch helped support the mission. The women were trained and encouraged to make baskets, spin, and weave. All were taught the Spanish language, as well as Spanish culture and laws.

Homes consisted of living quarters for the friars, smaller houses or rooms for the Indian families, workshops, gardens, and cooking/storage areas. A fence or wall surrounded the compound to provide protection, as well as to keep the new **converts** from running away.

The Franciscan friars were known as the regular *clergy*, establishing the rules and overseeing the daily activities and teachings. The **secular** clergy were the local **parish** priests and **bishops**. Once the settlement was established, the secular clergy would eventually move in and the Franciscan priests would move on, leaving church life to the local Catholic community and *privatizing* the mission properties by giving them to the local Indians and community.

Although some of the Native Americans who lived within the mission were converted to Christianity and the Spanish way of life, many refused both the religion and life within the mission walls. While thirty-six missions were built in Texas between 1682-1793, they all eventually closed, with very few meeting their true religious goal.

THE PRESIDIOS: *How They Worked*

The presidios were forts built to guard nearby settlements, protect the local missions from Indian attacks, watch for suspicious French activity, patrol the coast, serve as a buffer between raiding Indians and civilian settlements, and control trade.

About ten presidios were built during this period; each presidio would serve a group of missions and settlements. These square or rectangular forts were built using adobe, stone, logs, or other local materials. Walls were often ten feet high, with **bastions** located on diagonal corners where soldiers could fire on potential attackers.

A chapel, storage buildings, and officers' quarters were located inside the complex. Main and rear gates, locked from the inside, kept out unwanted visitors. Usually the soldiers lived in huts within the nearby town. Unfortunately, the soldiers were sometimes known to be cruel to the Native Americans and, rather than help, created additional problems around the settlement.

These strong fortifications were rarely attacked by Indians, and when an attempt was made, it was usually unsuccessful. Horses, however, were kept in a separate area, and were sometimes stolen by Native Americans. Once the horses were taken, it was impossible to chase the raiders on foot!

Today, you can visit a restored presidio in Goliad. Presidio La Bahía is said to be the best preserved presidio in North America. You will learn more about the sad history surrounding this fortification as you read the upcoming unit, *Revolution!*

MAJOR MISSIONS AND PRESIDIOS IN TEXAS

Ysleta and Socorro Missions
(El Paso)

Mission San Sabá
(Menard)

Mission Tejas
(Weches)

Los Adaes

San Antonio Missions:
*The Alamo
(San Antonio de Valero)
*San José
*Concepción
*San Juan
*Espada

Nuestra Señora del Espíritu Santo de Zúñiga Mission
&
Presidio La Bahía
(Goliad)

THE TEXAS MISSIONS

EARLY WEST TEXAS MISSIONS
San Angelo And El Paso

The earliest missions in the New World began in New Mexico, near today's Santa Fe. The first Texas mission was established near San Angelo in 1632 but was only active for about six months, probably because its location was so far away from the New Mexico mission base.

The next missions were established in 1682 near El Paso. During a Pueblo Indian revolt in New Mexico, Spanish settlers, Fransiscans, and Tigua Indian refugees fled to what is now far West Texas near the Rio Grande River. Missions established in this area included Corpus Christi de la Ysleta, Nuestra Señora de la Limpia Concepción del Socorro, and San Antonio de Senecu. Although the majority of the missions were established many miles to the east, several other missions were built over time along the Rio Grande in West Texas.

You can still visit the El Paso mission churches, meet Tigua Indians, and learn about their culture.

THE EAST TEXAS MISSIONS

Think back to your reading about La Salle and the French colony. When the Spanish discovered the French had attempted a settlement on land already claimed by Spain, they became very concerned. The French were already colonizing just to the east, in Louisiana ... would they continue to expand their territory to the west, into Texas? What could Spain do to prevent the French from slowly *encroaching* on their territory?

Most of the land north of Mexico was inhabited only by Native Americans, trees, grass, dirt, and buffalo. Usually not another soul in sight.

Spain decided the best way to protect this land was to settle the territory with individuals and families who would provide not only an increasing population, but also the culture and language of Spain. The Spanish government encouraged and assisted the Franciscans in the founding of missions throughout the eastern and central parts of Texas. The first temporary missions in the province were established in 1690 by the explorer Alonso De León

and Father Damian Massanet (San Fransisco de los Tejas) and in 1691 (Santisimo Nombre de Marfa) near a Hasinai Indian settlement. Unfortunately, both of these missions failed and closed.

Following another threat by the French, three more permanent missions were established in 1716 in East Texas: San Fransisco de los Neches, Nuestra Señora de Guadalupe, and Nuestra Señora de los Dolores. Although some Indians accepted the religious conversion and culture, most were more interested in protection from their enemies and trade. These missions were closed permanently in 1730 and were moved to a better location, with the final two East Texas missions being abandoned in 1773.

CENTRAL TEXAS MISSIONS
San Antonio Missions

Today's most famous Texas missions are located in San Antonio. It was a long way between the missions in East Texas and Mexico, so a halfway settlement was needed to connect the two. A colony in this area would also serve to connect trade between New Mexico and the Gulf of Mexico. The route, once serving as Indian trails and trade routes, became the popular path of missionaries, Indians, and others and was called El Camino Real, "The King's Highway," or the Old San Antonio Road.

In 1718, Mission San Antonio de Valero (the Alamo) and Presidio San Antonio de Béxar (built one mile west of the mission, where the Spanish Governor's Palace stands today) were founded by Franciscan Father Antonio de San Buenaventura y Olivares. He named the mission after Saint Anthony de Padua and Marqués de Valero, the Spanish viceroy of New Spain who agreed to Father Olivares' plan for the mission location. Fifteen families were brought to the area from the Canary Islands in 1731, where they formed the beginnings of the Villa of San Fernando de Béxar (now San Antonio).

These settlers were given supplies in hopes their community would become established and a city would continue to grow. Indeed it did! The city of San Antonio eventually grew around the fort and the nearby mission, and by 1772 San Antonio de Béxar became the capital city of Texas.

The location of the mission changed several times throughout the years, with construction at the current location beginning in the 1720s. Finally, in about 1758, the Alamo chapel, which you can still visit today, opened as an open-air church. It was built with limestone walls three and one-half feet thick, but was not finished—you will notice illustrations of the chapel during the Texas Revolution reveal the roof was incomplete at that time. Original plans included a domed roof and two bell towers, which would have resulted in the look of a more traditional mission chapel.

Some think the Alamo is only the famous building seen in movies and pictures, but that recognizable structure is just the chapel. Originally, the four-acre mission complex had about thirty adobe buildings used for workrooms and living quarters and two two-story wings which served as the convent. Eight-foot walls, 480 feet long by 160 feet wide, surrounded most of the complex to protect the inhabitants from Comanche and Apache attacks.

The Franciscans left the mission in 1793, when it was secularized and the land and supplies were given to the Indians of the mission and the Spanish locals.

Since then, the Alamo has been home to a Spanish *cavalry* outpost, the city's first hospital, a fort, an army *depot*, a store, and a warehouse. Finally, Adina de Zavala and Clara Driscoll worked with the Daughters of the Republic of Texas to save the surviving buildings and turned them into a museum open to the public. Today, the Texas General Land Office controls and oversees operations of the Alamo.

The Alamo is not the only mission located in San Antonio. Mission San José y San Miguel de Aguayo was built in 1720. After the East Texas missions closed in 1730, three missions were moved to the San Antonio area in 1731: Nuestra Señora de la Purísima Concepción, San Fransisco de la Espada, and San Juan Capistrano. If you visit Mission Concepción, you can see the mission just as it was in 1755. Amazingly, it has never had to be rebuilt, as many of the older missions have after crumbling from foundation and other structural issues.

MORE TEXAS MISSIONS
La Bahía (Goliad)
In 1721, a presidio and then the Nuestra Señora del Espíritu Santo de Zúñiga Mission (popularly called *La Bahía*, meaning "the bay") were built at the site of La Salle's failed Fort St. Louis colony. It was moved inland twice, finally settling on the San Antonio River, but called by the same name. This mission and presidio were very important to the mission network since it lay at a major crossroad.

Goliad, named to honor one of the heroes of the Mexican Revolution, is the town which grew around the presidio. "Goliad" is actually an *anagram*—the namesake hero's name was "Hidalgo." If you switch the letters around and take out the "H," you are left with the word *Goliad*!

Like many of the others, the mission was not successful in the conversion of Native Americans.

Santa Cruz de San Sabá
In 1757, the Santa Cruz de San Sabá mission was built to serve and protect the local Apaches from their Comanche enemies on the San Saba River. Sadly, Comanche burned the mission and killed many inside in 1758. Facing multiple Indian attacks, the mission never recovered and the presidio was abandoned in 1768.

Nuestra Señora del Refugio
The last mission built in Texas was Our Lady of Refuge (Nuestra Señora del Refugio) in 1793 near La Bahía. It was often attacked by Comanche and Karankawa Indians, and eventually closed in 1824.

Did You Know?

If you visit the site of the San Miguel de Linares de los Adaes Mission and Nuestra Señora del Pilar Presidio, you'll be surprised when you cross the state line into Louisiana! This mission/presidio was built in 1721 to both Christianize the local Native Americans (Caddo) and to keep the French out of New Spain.

Los Adaes actually became the capital of the province of Tejas from 1729-1770, and was the endpoint of El Camino Real de los Tejas. At that time, most of Louisiana belonged to France, but the land where Los Adaes sits was considered part of Spanish Texas.

When French Louisiana was transferred to Spain, there was no longer a need for this protection from the French. Los Adaes was abandoned and the capital moved to San Antonio. Los Adaes residents then moved to East Texas and became early founders of the Nacogdoches settlement.

MISSIONS OF TEXAS

*Although some have been rebuilt over time or are replicas of the
original mission building, there are still a handful of missions
you can visit today . . .*

Mission San José
Founded 1720

Mission Concepción
Founded 1716

Mission San Antonio de Valero
(The Alamo)
Founded 1718

Mission Espada
Founded 1731

Mission San Juan Capistrano
Founded 1731

The Alamo Mission: Courtesy of photographer Grace Mercado-Marx.

Nuestra Señora del Espíritu Santo de Zúñiga
(Mission La Bahía)
Founded 1722
Goliad, Texas

Mission Ysleta
Founded 1682
El Paso, Texas

San Fransisco de los Tejas
(replica of original mission)
Founded 1690
Grapeland, Texas

Mission Socorro
Founded 1682
Socorro, Texas

Unit Five:
FILIBUSTERS & EMPRESARIOS

From the earliest Spanish explorations and claims of Texas land, through the days of the early missions and settlements, Spain held tightly to its territories through a well-organized system. Commands issued by the king of Spain were passed to the viceroy of Mexico (the highest official position there), then to the provincial capitals, and then to the frontier *outposts*. Although Spain was disappointed great riches were not found as they had hoped, they fiercely protected the territory and attempted to settle the land.

In 1772, San Antonio became the capital of the province. A *province* is different than a state or a country. In Texas's case, it was considered a province because the land was located in territory claimed by the Spanish Empire, but Texas possessed local governments able to make some of their own decisions. A city council, called the *ayuntamiento*, was elected by local land owners; the chief official was called the *alcalde*.

Citizens across the province included those of Spanish heritage, Native Americans, and *mestizos* (a mixture of Indian and Spanish heritage). *Tejano* was the name given to those of Mexican ancestry who made their home in Texas.

San Antonio was very important, as it was one of only three settlements within the Texas *interior*, along with Goliad and Nacogdoches. As hard as Spain tried to attract settlers to the area, it was not very successful. A few settlements were all they had to show after 300 years of Spanish rule. Spain began to *neglect* this territory, and when Spain's ruler was overthrown and their own country turned to chaos, attention turned to matters at home.

As seen throughout history, and as you will still see when we arrive at the Texas Revolution chapter, *strife* and disorganization in a home country will almost always set the stage for some type of revolution or turnover. That's exactly what happened in Texas.

The word *filibuster* means "pirate" in Spanish. This was the name given to people who illegally entered another country with the intent of taking over that country. In this case, the filibusters we will discuss were private adventurers from the United States, who came to Texas with the goal of taking the land from Spain (and later Mexico) and starting their own country.

THE FILIBUSTERS

Philip Nolan Expedition
1800 - 1801

Philip Nolan was an Irishman who came to America and started a successful business illegally capturing wild horses within the Texas border, then selling them to folks in the United States and Spanish military *garrisons* in Louisiana. He confided in friends he secretly hoped Texas would someday be part of the United States. Eventually the Spanish authorities in Louisiana became suspicious and decided not to renew his passport into Spanish territories.

Nolan ignored the Spanish and in 1800, he led twenty-eight armed men into Texas, where he set up camp—along with corrals—near the Brazos River. His men *wrangled* and brought the *confiscated* wild horses to their encampment. They kept the best horses, and slaughtered the rest to make horsehair ropes from the manes and tails.

One day, a large group of Spanish soldiers surprised Nolan's men and a battle commenced. Nolan was killed, and the surviving horse thieves surrendered and were taken to a Mexican prison. As far as Spain was concerned, this illegal entrance and theft of their country's property was *piracy* (and therefore a filibuster attempt).

During their imprisonment, Nolan's men learned the king had *decreed* one of the nine remaining prisoners would be put to death. The fate of the men was determined by tossing a pair of dice. Ephraim Blackburn tossed the dice from a crystal cup onto a drum, threw the lowest number, and was hanged. The rest of the survivors served hard labor time in Mexico.

One man, Peter Ellis Bean, was able to escape and tell the tale of this failed filibuster.

Gutiérrez-Magee Expedition
1812 - 1813

In 1810, a change of power took place in Spain. The country and its colonies, including New Spain, fell into chaos. Realizing it might be a good time for change, some citizens of Mexico began to express their desire for independence from Spain, just like America had recently chosen to declare independence from Great Britain.

One of the men crying for freedom was Father Miguel Hidalgo y Costilla. Another leader of the independence movement was Jose Bernardo Maximiliano Gutiérrez de Lara. Gutiérrez fled to Louisiana and traveled all over the United States, hoping to *garner* support for the establishment of a *republican* government in the Texas portion of New Spain. This original word "republican" meant the people were represented within the government by elected leaders. Of course, Americans were enthusiastic, since that was the type of government they had chosen for their own country.

Gutiérrez was introduced to Augustus Magee, a young U.S. Army officer, who agreed to help Gutiérrez in his cause to invade Texas. Several hundred additional adventurers joined up and these men hoped—after they took Texas from Spanish control—it might become part of the United States. The number of *recruits* grew quickly, and Magee was assigned military leadership of the Republican Army of the North. Gutiérrez was considered commander of the expedition.

These men marched into Texas and captured the city of Nacogdoches in 1812. They then moved towards San Antonio de Béxar, but decided to change course, taking time to replenish their supplies and capture La Bahía first. There Magee died, and was replaced by Samuel Kemper.

In February of 1813, this army, which had increased to 1,400 Americans, Mexicans, and Indians, marched into San Antonio. By the time the expedition reached Béxar, the defenders of the

70

town had heard of the army's success and did not resist the takeover. However, Gutiérrez quickly showed his true colors. When they saw how cruelly he treated the Spanish officials and citizens of San Antonio, he lost the support of his troops and some even abandoned the expedition.

On April 6, 1813, the invaders declared independence from Spain and established a new government. Many of the men became increasingly unhappy with Gutiérrez's leadership, and the new "country" fell into arguments and disorder. Gutiérrez was ousted from his position and returned to the United States . . . but this wouldn't be the last Texas would hear of Gutiérrez.

The tide turned when Spain sent Colonel José Joaquín de Arredondo to fight the Republican Army. Arredondo and his Spanish troops overwhelmed the Republican forces at the Battle of Medina, and Spain once again took control of San Antonio. Captured Republican soldiers were executed, and even civilians were jailed and put to death. Any remaining supporters of the filibuster who were lucky enough to still be alive retreated quickly to the United States.

By Arredondo's side, training at the feet of the ruthless leader, was a young nineteen-year-old officer.

His name? Santa Anna.

Texas Filibusters!

Nolan's Camp
Nacogdoches
San Antonio
La Bahia
Bolivar Point

MAP KEY
Philip Nolan • • • •
Gutiérrez-Magee - - -
James Long ——

James Long Expedition
1819 - 1822

The James Long Expedition was the last major filibuster during this period. You'll remember Gutiérrez was forced out of the Republican Army and **exiled** back to the United States. Gutiérrez never really disappeared, and partnered again with another man—James Long—to organize a second expedition in an attempt to wrestle Texas away from the Spanish.

Long, a former U.S. Army surgeon, and Gutiérrez led 300 men into Nacogdoches, where they created a new independent republic. This time, Long was selected as president of the Supreme Council and general of the army. Long spread his men out, knowing the Spanish would try to break up his army. Some of the men, assigned the job of building trading posts at major river crossings, set out to establish this new system.

The leaders of the filibuster approached the pirate Lafitte and his brother, who lived on Galveston Island, asking for assistance. The filibusters hoped to set up a port of entry and supply line through the gulf: establishing a working relationship with Jean and Pierre Lafitte would help them gain access to the port. The pirates refused. They were having enough problems with the U.S. government and had no desire to add to their headaches.

Once again, the Spanish Army was sent to battle the filibustering invaders. The Spanish were dispatched to East Texas, taking over both the trading posts and Nacogdoches. James Long and his family quickly fled to Louisiana and the rest of the Republican Army was chased across the Sabine River.

Long soon returned to Texas. He joined the remaining troops and journeyed to Bolivar Point, at the tip of the Bolivar Peninsula near Galveston Island. After a trip back to the United States for more supplies and men, Long gathered the Supreme Council and planned another takeover. When Long and his men heard the Lafitte brothers had been ordered to leave Galveston, the Supreme Council decided the door was now open to declare the island their port of entry.

Concerned about Karankawa in the area, the filibusters built Fort Las Casas on Bolivar Point. Meanwhile, in 1821, Mexico declared its independence from Spain. After his unsuccessful attempt to *wrest* land from Spain, it was no surprise when Long decided to support the Mexican independence cause and help capture the fort at La Bahía from the Spanish. His expedition was overpowered by the Spanish Army and Long was taken prisoner. He was killed by a guard while his wife waited at home, unaware of his fate.

Jane Long
Mother of Texas

Jane Long, the wife of filibuster James Long, was one of the earliest Anglo women to live and settle in Texas.

Unaware of James' death in Mexico, Jane (who was expecting a baby) waited for him at Point Bolivar along with her daughter, Ann, and a servant girl, Kian. The women were frequently under threat from the nearby Karankawa Indians and had limited food and supplies.

Jane fired the fort's cannon every now and then and flew a red *petticoat* flag to convince the Indians there were still soldiers at the fort. The women knew they had to fend for themselves and fished in the gulf using an old *hammock*.

Jane soon gave birth to a baby girl, Mary James. As far as we know, this child was one of the earliest Anglo-Americans to be born in Texas. After Jane heard her husband died, she and her children moved and joined the Austin settlement, later running a boarding house and a plantation.

Jane was tough and never gave up; therefore, we call Jane Long, the "Mother of Texas."

Mexico Overthrows the Spanish Empire

In 1808, Napoléon claimed the country of Spain and imprisoned its ruler, King Ferdinand VII. During that period of confusion, people in Mexico began to question who should be running their country. Some wanted to keep things as they were (they were called *royalists*), and some wanted to have the government run by a small council of leaders.

A Mexican priest named Miguel Hidalgo y Costilla spoke for the common people, and in 1810 he cried out for *social change*. This call for independence started a rebellion in Mexico, but the revolutionists were quickly put down and defeated by the royalists.

Even after the Spanish king was returned to the throne, problems continued and many citizens of Mexico were unhappy and ready for freedom. Over time though, change won out and Mexico won its independence from Spain in 1821.

Now, instead of the country "New Spain," the land became known as the "Mexican Empire." In turn, Texas was no longer a province under Spain's rule. Now it was a part of Mexico, and it was joined with Coahuila in 1824 to become the state *Coahuila y Tejas*. It would remain as a combined state with Coahuila until the population increased, at which time Texas would hopefully receive its own state government.

Unfortunately, Texas was located a long way from the state capital; it was 500 miles from San Felipe de Austin (Texas's main settlement) to Saltillo, the capital of Coahuila y Tejas. It was another 550 miles from Saltillo to Mexico City, the national capital. Communication and travel were difficult. Texas was on its own in many ways.

The Mexican Constitution of 1824 was somewhat similar to and designed like the Constitution of the United States; a president and vice-president were elected for four year terms and the president's powers were limited. Mexico was now considered a Representative Federal Republic. As in the U.S., the government was designed with three branches and two houses in the legislature, with two representatives serving from each state. The Constitution also gave many powers and rights to the states, although unlike the United States, the official religion of *Catholicism* was the only form of faith allowed to be practiced within the country.

As we learn more about the settlers who were invited and entered Texas over the coming years, it's important to remember this Mexican Constitution of 1824 was very similar to what the immigrants were accustomed to in the United States. They expected the representation and freedoms which were included in this form of government, and were sorely disappointed when that constitution was taken away from them within a short period of time.

THE EMPRESARIOS

Moses Austin

Moses Austin was at one time a successful American businessman. Unfortunately, during a *depression* which swept the United States in 1819, he lost his job and business. However, Moses had a new idea: what if he approached Spain and offered to help bring settlers to Texas? He knew Spain desperately wanted the land populated, and he also knew many Americans would be happy to move west and purchase land at a very low cost. The inexpensive pricetag wasn't the only attraction, though. The land was fertile, rivers and water were abundant, plenty of trees were available for lumber, and the climate was comfortable and good for farming.

Moses took off for Texas in 1820, before Mexico had won its independence and while Spain was still in control. He arrived in San Antonio and presented his offer, but was immediately turned down. As he was about to leave, Moses ran into an old friend on the street. The friend offered to speak to the governor himself, and convince the Spanish government Moses was an honest man who had no intention of trying to filibuster or take over the land.

Fortunately, Spain agreed to his request. Moses was approved to become the first *empresario* of Texas. The word empresario is Spanish for "businessman." An empresario would be given large plots of land, called *land grants*, by the government (after paying a small fee for the land title), and then would be required to divide it up among the colonists he would bring to Texas. The colonists would pay a small fee for their section of land, and were expected to work the land and follow Spanish (and later Mexican) law. The empresario would then receive payment for his efforts through land for himself and his family.

Depending on the planned use of the land and the size of the family, settlers would receive different sized plots. For instance, a rancher who grazed cattle received a larger *league* of land (4,428

acres), while a farmer only received a *labor* (177 acres) of land.

On his way home from this successful business trip, Moses became ill. Before he died, his last request was that his son Stephen complete his mission and bring the promised 300 families to Texas.

Stephen F. Austin
and the Old Three Hundred

Engraving of Stephen F. Austin
October 18, 1836, Early Texas Documents, Special Collections,
University of Houston Libraries

Moses Austin's son, Stephen, was born in Virginia in 1793. He attended school in Connecticut, and eventually came home to help run his father's lead mining business. When he learned of his father's death, Stephen was studying law in New Orleans.

Honoring his father's wishes, Stephen traveled to Texas and found the land he preferred for his colony: on and between the Brazos and Colorado Rivers. The country was beautiful and fertile, rich with natural resources.

Stephen advertised for colonists in the southern United States, noting that drunkards, gamblers, swearers, and *idlers* need not apply. Although slavery was not legal in Mexico, the law was not enforced in Texas. Mexico realized the acceptance of slavery would *entice* more immigrants and result in greater farming production and land value.

The first settlers arrived in 1821, many leaving homes in Tennessee, Arkansas, Missouri, Kentucky, Mississippi, and Louisiana. They traveled over land by horse and wagon, or by sea through Gulf of Mexico ports.

Serving as the unofficial capital of the colony, San Felipe de Austin was established on the west bank of the Brazos River at the crossing of the Old San Antonio Road. It was here colonists arrived at the land office as their first step to their new life in Texas. Austin surveyed the land and helped the new settlers find their plots. These hardy and courageous immigrants were willing to brave the dangers of travel to purchase land for only twelve and a half cents per acre: about a tenth the cost of public land in the United States. In return, the colonists agreed to become Mexican citizens, practice the Roman Catholic faith, and be of good moral character.

In 1822, Stephen learned Mexico had won its independence from Spain. He traveled to Mexico City, where he spent over a year working with a changing government, trying to regain approval for the new colony. Once the new Mexican government agreed to let Austin proceed with the empresario plan, he returned to Texas.

These brand-new Texans soon found life on the frontier had its dangers. After learning of the Karankawa and other raids by local Native Americans, Austin created a *militia* to protect the settlers.

By 1825, most of the original settlers, known as the "Old Three Hundred," were living and working in Austin's colony. Other empresarios would follow, but Stephen was by far the most successful, ultimately issuing 1,540 land titles.

Other Empresarios

Stephen F. Austin was not the only empresario to bring settlers to Texas. Green DeWitt received a grant in 1825 to settle 400 families southwest of Austin's colony, with its headquarters at Gonzales. Mexican empresario Martin de León settled 200 families from Mexico between the Lavaca and Guadalupe Rivers near the Gulf Coast, founding the settlement of Victoria. Ben Milam and Arthur Wavell planned to settle land in northeastern Texas; even Irish Europeans (James Hewetson and James

Power) acted as empresarios along the Nueces River, with their headquarters located at Refugio.

Other well-known empresarios included David G. Burnet, Lorenzo de Zavala, and Joseph Vehlein. Several of these men would later become active participants in the Texas Revolution.

One *infamous* empresario named Haden Edwards founded a colony near Nacogdoches, but was sent away after leading the Fredonian Rebellion. When older settlers—including Indians and Mexicans who had lived in the area for many years—were required to present proof of their claims to the empresario, they became angry at the possibility of losing their land. Hayden and his brother Benjamin, already involved in several *squabbles* with residents, decided to handle the issue by declaring their colony independent from Mexico. The brothers led a small group of armed men to the Old Stone Fort in Nacogdoches and raised the flag of the Republic of Fredonia.

When both militia from Austin's colony and Mexican troops arrived to put down the rebellion, the participants were either captured or escaped to the United States. This event and threat to Mexico led to the arrival and stationing of Mexican soldiers in Nacogdoches, an early sign of trouble to come.

Most settlers arrived from the southern United States and planned to farm their land. People were excited to move west and begin a new adventure, often leaving a sign with the letters **GTT** (Gone To Texas) on their doors. Families with men, women, and children came to work the land, along with 2,000 slaves and about 150 free African Americans.

Life wasn't easy for these families. Everyone worked side by side to cultivate the land and build their homes. Mexico couldn't afford to provide public schools, so families either educated their children at home, sent them back to the United States, or established private schools in their area.

By 1830, Texas had grown tremendously, with a population of about 20,000 citizens. Older settlements like San Antonio, Goliad, and Nacogdoches continued to grow and towns such as San Felipe and Victoria provided new centers of activity.

Empresario Land Grants

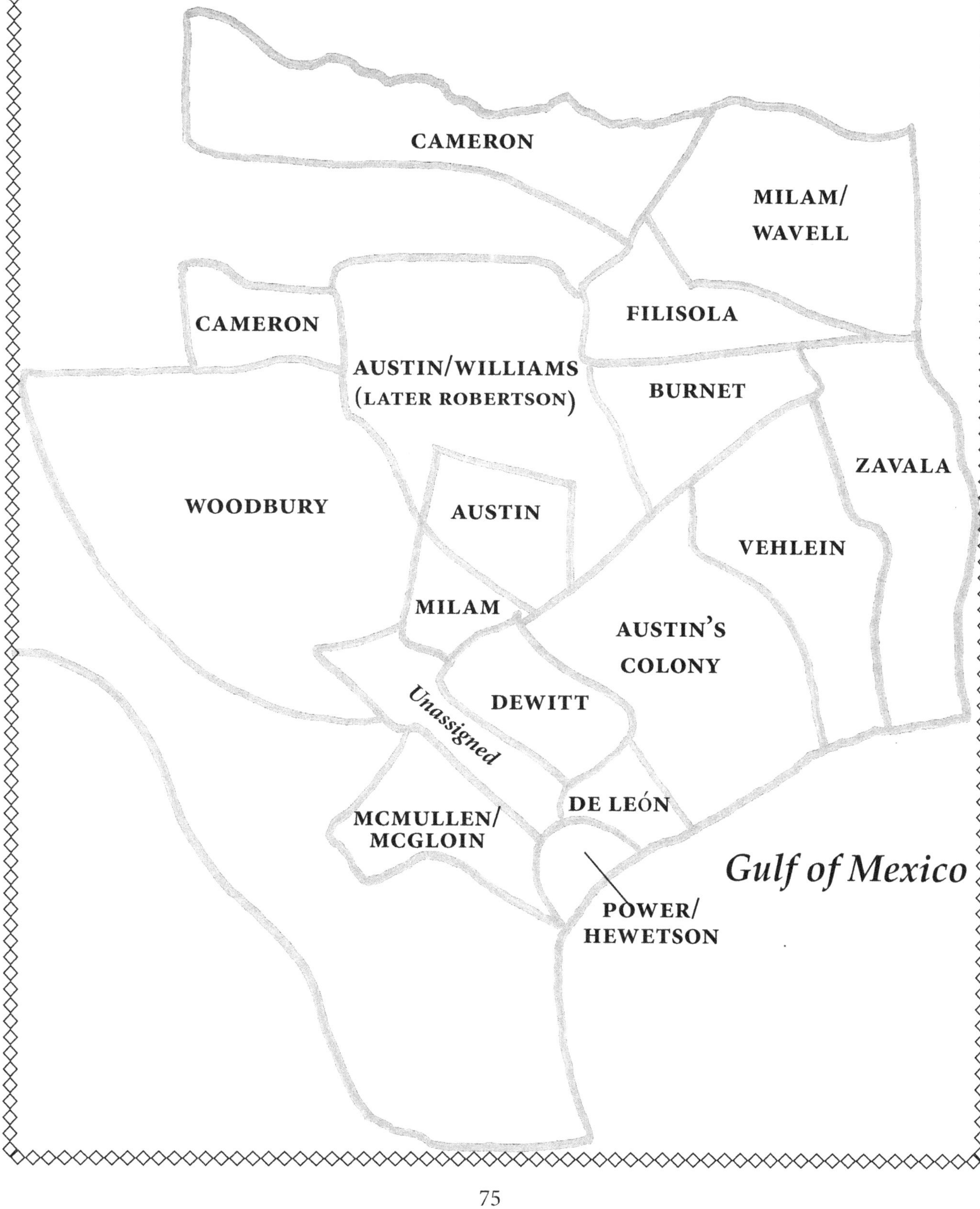

CAMERON

MILAM/
WAVELL

CAMERON

FILISOLA

AUSTIN/WILLIAMS
(LATER ROBERTSON)

BURNET

ZAVALA

WOODBURY

AUSTIN

VEHLEIN

MILAM

AUSTIN'S
COLONY

Unassigned

DEWITT

MCMULLEN/
MCGLOIN

DE LEÓN

POWER/
HEWETSON

Gulf of Mexico

Oxen teams could be used by farmers to plow their fields and prepare for planting.

Tools of the Settlers

Early settlers often brought spinning wheels and looms to make their own clothes.

Unit Six:
REVOLUTION!

Spain ruled Texas for over 300 years. Although they explored, observed, and claimed land for their king, the Spanish did little other than establish the mission system, created to encourage settlement and growth in the province. While the system did not increase population growth as expected, the effect was significant: conversions did occur, and of course it brought the land one step closer to the colonization which eventually began with the empresarios.

Although the empresario system was initiated at the end of their *reign*, the Spanish soon lost control of the land following the Mexican Revolution. Once in power, the Mexican government supported and encouraged immigration from the United States to Texas.

Under Stephen F. Austin and other empresarios, the population exploded by leaps and bounds and the land was cultivated with new farms and crops. Trouble began to brew with the Fredonian Rebellion, and Mexico sent Colonel José de las Piedras and 200 Mexican soldiers to Nacogdoches to keep watch for filibusters and other troublemakers. Mexico began to question its decision to open the doors of Texas to such a large group of settlers.

Terán *and*
The Law of April 6, 1830

Mexico's concern over the rumblings in Texas led them to hire soldier and scientist General Manuel de Mier y Terán to inspect the situation in Texas. After riding many miles and observing the situation among the settlers, Terán found Anglo-American settlers outnumbered Mexican settlers ten to one. He also noted these American settlers were not interested in observing the Mexican culture or practicing the Catholic religion, as the immigrants had promised. He warned the Mexican government Texas would be lost to Mexico forever if they didn't act soon.

By 1830, Mexico had adopted a *centralized* government. This means the majority of the control was held not by the states, but rather by a small group within the federal government. In response to Terán's recommendations, this government decided to issue a new law: the Law of April 6, 1830. This law *halted* all *immigration* of settlers from the United States (although it did allow and encourage settlement from Mexico and Europe). Second, it *suspended* all incomplete empresario contracts.

New forts were built and manned by Mexican soldiers. New taxes, called *custom duties,* were added to goods imported from and exported to other countries. From the settlers' standpoint, these taxes discouraged trade.

The colonists were very upset. Most settlers relied on trade with the United States. Saddened and frustrated when friends and relatives received news they were now banned from joining them in Texas, the colonists realized their success would be limited by this new law. Mexico distrusted the United States and the settlers who came from that country. In turn, the settlers now came to distrust the Mexican government.

Tensions were high.
Trouble lay ahead!

Trouble at Anahuac

One of the Mexican Army garrisons located near the coast was established at Anahuac, a port on Trinity Bay near Galveston. The commander of the fort was a Mexican loyalist, Colonel John Davis Bradburn. Bradburn could be a difficult man and was disliked among the area residents.

The colonel strictly enforced the new Mexican laws. Custom duties were in effect, and these new taxes created a great deal more work and travel for the *merchants* and ship captains. Bradburn was also accused of taking supplies and *harboring* runaway slaves from their masters.

Almost every Texan has heard of William Barret Travis, and this is where the future hero of the Alamo arrived on the scene. Travis and another lawyer, Patrick C. Jack, angered Colonel Bradburn when they tried to retrieve a runaway slave and generally *rile* up local citizens.

Bradburn arrested the two lawyers and declared *martial law*. Once the news got out, the Texas militia came to Travis and Jack's aid. After a small *skirmish* with the Mexican Army, the Texans agreed to release several of Bradburn's men who had been taken prisoner. While the Texans kept their end of the bargain, Bradburn did not.

Travis and Jack remained in prison. The angry Texas colonists came together to issue the Turtle Bayou Resolutions on June 13, 1832. These resolutions stated that while Texans were loyal to Mexico, they supported *federalism* (power shared with the states, instead of centralized among a few) and the Constitution of 1824. Interestingly, they also voiced their support for General Santa Anna, who at that time also publicly supported a federalist government. (While we are fortunate to have the history and *hindsight* to know the Texians should not have trusted Santa Anna, his true intentions were unknown during this pre-revolutionary period. This is common with leaders who eventually become dictators, as we can see throughout history.)

While some Texans stayed to attack the fort at Anahuac, others marched to Brazoria to get a cannon and more men. Luckily for Anahuac, Colonel Piedras (from the Nacogdoches garrison) and some of his men marched to Anahuac to investigate the problem. Piedras relieved Bradburn of his command and released the two prisoners.

William B. Travis by Wyly Martin, 1835, alleged sketch of Travis. Wikimedia Commons/ Public Domain

 Battle of Velasco
June 26, 1832

When the group from Anahuac arrived in Brazoria, they found the cannon they needed and loaded it on a ship. However, the ship would have to pass the fort at Velasco, which was *manned* by Colonel Domingo de Ugartechea and his Mexican Army. Ugartechea refused to let the Texans pass by the fort, and fierce fighting began.

Eventually the Mexican Army ran out of ammunition and surrendered. Lives were lost on both the Texan and Mexican sides, but the Texans finally made it to the Gulf of Mexico and sailed around the coast and bay to Anahuac.

When they arrived, the Texans found the prisoners had been set free, Bradburn was gone, and peace had returned.

 Battle of Nacogdoches
August 2, 1832

After the incidents at Anahuac and Velasco, Colonel Piedras returned to Nacogdoches, concerned about the possibility that something similar might happen under his watch. Piedras issued an order demanding the settlers turn in their *arms*. The Nacogdoches ayuntamiento refused, organized a militia, and sent word out to nearby settlements that help was needed. The settlers' militia captain ordered Piedras to take back his order, but Piedras refused. The Texas militia attacked the Mexican soldiers, who quickly retreated from the Old Stone Fort and other buildings in town to their main fortification, called the *cuartel*.

That night, Piedras and his men decided to

evacuate and quietly left town, marching to San Antonio. James Bowie and a group of settlers chased the Mexican Army, finally overtaking Piedras and his 300 men and initiating a running fight. Piedras lost forty-seven men, and forty soldiers were wounded; four Texans were killed, and four were wounded. The Mexican soldiers surrendered and were eventually *discharged* and sent back to Mexico.

Although the battle was short, the *evacuation* of Piedras and the Mexican soldiers resulted in the freedom of Texans to meet without a military presence.

And meet they did!

Santa Anna

Antonio López de Santa Anna was born in Veracruz, Mexico, in 1794. He was not born of a *high station*; his family was of the *criollo* middle class. Santa Anna began his career as a *cadet* in the *infantry* in a regiment under General Joaquín de Arredondo. You'll remember Arredondo was the *ruthless* leader of the Royalist Spanish Army who defeated the members of the Gutiérrez expedition (filibuster) at the Battle of Medina in 1813.

At that time, Santa Anna was loyal to Spain, and was even *cited* for bravery during the battle. Some say Santa Anna learned his "take-no-prisoners" attitude from Arredondo.

Santa Anna became known as an excellent military officer. Brave in battle and inspiring when he spoke, he was also known for being charming and polite.

General Antonio Lopez de Santa Anna, President of the Republic of Mexico, c1847
Courtesy of Library of Congress.

After supporting Spain for many years, Santa Anna suddenly switched sides and decided to fight with the rebel Mexican Army under General Iturbide as Mexico began its fight for independence from Spain. After they won and Iturbide became emperor, Santa Anna switched sides once *again* and in 1823 joined a group who wanted a more republican (representative) government, overthrowing Iturbide.

Santa Anna served twice as a governor in Mexico. After leading a victorious battle against the Spanish Army, Santa Anna became a national hero. It was no surprise when he was elected President of Mexico in May of 1833. At that time, everyone believed Santa Anna was a supporter of federalism and *democracy*. Unfortunately, it didn't take long for him to show his true colors; the general switched sides once again and became a strong *centralist*, eventually becoming a strict *dictator*. Santa Anna fired governors, dissolved town counsels, and *disbanded* the legislature. Slowly but surely, he disposed of anyone and everyone who might threaten his rise to power or his decisions.

As you can imagine, all of this back and forth flip-flopping was more than any country could bear.

Mexico was confused.

Then there were the Texans: the men who had supported Santa Anna and his promises of freedom and democracy. The settlers had moved to Texas under a constitution and an understanding that the government and their rights as citizens would be similar to those they enjoyed in the United States. The tide had turned.

For the Texans, enough was enough.

The Conventions of 1832 and 1833

The settlers who had been raised in America had a very different view of a proper government and its limitations than those who had grown up in Mexico. Many of the American colonists had fathers and grandfathers who fought in the American Revolution. The idea of fighting for freedom from *tyranny* was still fresh on everyone's mind. They believed strongly a government should have *limited* powers; the American Declaration of Independence and Constitution had been written less than sixty years prior, when America, too, fought a war to break away from Great Britain, who they felt unfairly taxed their citizens, and did not equitably represent them in decision-making.

However, those raised in Mexico, most of that time under the Spanish flag, were used to living under the rule of a king. Decisions were always made without their vote; they didn't have experience with the idea of representation or power shared.

Then Mexico won its freedom from Spain and created a Constitution (of 1824) which was very similar to the American document, and offered a government and freedoms like those in the United States. When these American settlers were invited to live in Texas under the Constitution of 1824, they expected a government somewhat like home.

Unfortunately, change occurred frequently with the new Mexican government. Those in power changed from centralists to federalists and back again. When lawmakers decided to restrict immigration, *levy* duties and taxes, and send soldiers to keep things under control, the Texans rebelled.

After the incidents in Anahuac, Velasco, and Nacogdoches, the settlers decided it was time to meet and make some decisions about how to handle Mexico. Perhaps those in power who had fought for the freedom of Mexico might hear their complaints and help Texas resolve its problems. (Of course, this was during the time prior to Santa Anna's *startling* change of government to a dictatorship.)

The first meeting, the Convention of 1832, was held in San Felipe de Austin on October 1, 1832. Stephen F. Austin served as president of the convention. The men wrote *resolutions* to be presented to Mexico. These included:
1) a request for Texas to become a separate state (from Coahuila), with its own state government,
2) immigration from the United States be permitted again,
3) they would be *exempt* from certain import taxes,
4) and Mexico would provide educational facilities and better protection from Native Americans.

Although two men were appointed to take these requests to Mexico, for several reasons the resolutions were never delivered: the political chief of the province declared the convention illegal, San Antonio did not send delegates to the convention, and Stephen F. Austin felt it was too early to ask permission for statehood.

When six months later the situation had not improved, the Convention of 1833 was held April 1st in San Felipe de Austin (just as Santa Anna was elected president of Mexico). Most of the participants had not attended the first convention.

One very interesting man made an entrance—a man representing Nacogdoches named Sam Houston. This newcomer from the United States had an intriguing history. Houston had lived with the Cherokee Indians for a time, represented Tennessee in the U.S. Congress, and served as Governor of Tennessee. He was also a close friend of his *mentor*, President Andrew Jackson, who encouraged Houston to spend time in Texas and investigate the current situation.

The men attending the Convention of 1833 prepared a set of requests similar to the first convention. However, this time a new constitution was written and proposed for what the men hoped would be the new state of Texas.

Stephen F. Austin agreed to take these proposals to Mexico City as soon as possible.

Austin's Trip to Mexico

Austin left for Mexico in April of 1833. Travel was slow during this time, and he didn't arrive in Mexico City until July. President Santa Anna was away, so Austin was forced to wait until his return. While he sat and waited, Austin wrote a letter home to the *authorities* in San Antonio. The letter discussed his frustrations and encouraged the Texans to go ahead and begin forming their own state government.

In November, the president finally arrived and met with Austin. It initially seemed like discussions were somewhat successful. Santa Anna agreed to grant some of the *reforms*. He said the immigration law would be lifted and settlers would be allowed to come to Texas again. The president also *conceded* Mexico would work to improve the court and postal systems. However, he would not agree to *grant* Texas statehood on its own.

Austin's mission complete, he set off for home on December 10th. When he reached Saltillo, which was the capital of Coahuila y Tejas, Austin was arrested after officials recovered the angry letter he had written back to Texas while waiting for the president's return. He was returned to Mexico City and imprisoned for one year.

Austin was released on bail December 25th, 1834, but was not allowed to leave the city. Finally, he was completely released from custody on July 11th, 1835, and returned to Texas on September 1st.

Austin had been away from Texas for two years and four months. Needless to say, he was more than unhappy.

He was angry.

Trouble Continues . . .

It seemed like, for a little while, things were looking up for the Texas settlers. Immigration from the United States resumed, Texas received better representation in the state legislature, the court system improved, and religion became less of an issue.

By early 1835, problems stirred in Anahuac again. A new Mexican garrison commander and troops were stationed there, and a local merchant was arrested after he and other colonists began complaining about unfair custom duties and refused to pay. William Barret Travis returned to the scene with a group of men, freeing the merchant and forcing the commander and his men out of Anahuac.

While some supported Travis and his actions, other Texans were embarrassed and publicly apologized. Their apologies fell on deaf ears.

Under Santa Anna's orders, General Cos was on his way to Texas to arrest Travis, Lorenzo de Zavala, and other Texans who appeared *disloyal* to Mexico. Cos arrived in Texas, established his headquarters in San Antonio, and made it clear he planned to *quash* any more disturbances.

There were other changes being made as well. Santa Anna began taking more and more power away from the Mexican states. The Constitution of 1824, so much like the United States Constitution and supported by the Texas settlers, was abolished completely and no longer in effect. Now the power in Mexico was placed in the hands of the central government. It had become very clear Santa Anna was no longer a federalist who believed in democracy and states' rights. He had become a centralist, and was not going to put up with Texans who questioned or quarreled with his decisions.

With that realization, the colonists decided to hold a meeting, called the Consultation, to be held in the town of San Felipe in October of 1835 (the meeting was delayed until November). There were different responses to the idea of that meeting. Those who were concerned Mexico would be angry and feared their response were called the Peace Party. Alternately, those who were part of the War Party, including Travis, favored the Consultation. They were ready to declare Texas's independence from Mexico. Everyone realized this approach would likely result in a war.

Meanwhile, as Stephen F. Austin arrived back in Texas, he warned his fellow settlers: Santa Anna had become a dictator. Troops were being sent from Mexico to Texas. The trust was gone.

Austin told Texans to prepare for war.

Replica Cabin
San Felipe, Texas

COME AND TAKE IT!
Battle For Gonzales:
October 2, 1835

Have you ever walked a dog on a leash? And did that dog pull and pull, trying to get away so he could walk on his own? And did you pull and pull back, trying to keep him under control and close to you?

That's exactly what happened in Texas. These Anglo settlers, referred to during this time as *Texians*, wanted independence and the freedom to live under their own control. The more they worked to separate themselves from Mexican rule and power, the harder the Mexican government pulled back, trying to keep those Texians in control.

These Texans who wanted freedom from Mexican tyranny were not just Anglo settlers. Many Mexicans who were born or chose to live in Texas were called "Tejanos." Although their families may have originated in Mexico, they now lived and worked in Texas and realized the importance of *self-government* and the threat of the new Mexican dictator.

Colonel Ugartechea, the Mexican military commander in Texas, sent a small group of soldiers to retrieve a little bronze six-pound cannon which had been given to the Gonzales settlement for protection from Indians in 1831. The citizens refused the order, buried the small cannon in a peach orchard, and sent a call out to the surrounding area for men to hurry to Gonzales, prepared to fight.

When Ugartechea heard the colonists refused to return the cannon, he sent Fransisco de Castañeda and more troops to Gonzales to remove the cannon. When Castañeda arrived at the banks of the Guadalupe River outside the town, he was told by a small group of waiting Texians he would have to wait until Gonzales' alcalde returned.

While the Mexican Army bided their time, Texian *reinforcements* arrived in Gonzales, armed and ready to protect the cannon. They dug up the weapon, mounted it on a cart, took it to the shores of the Guadalupe River, and topped it with a black and white flag *emblazoned* with an *embroidered* cannon image and the words:

"COME AND TAKE IT."

Concerned about the large number of armed Texians camped nearby, Castañeda marched his army upriver to a safer crossing. The Texians moved, too! They crossed to the other side of the river and attacked the Mexican camp on the morning of October 2nd, 1835.

After a brief skirmish, one Mexican soldier lay dead. Realizing he was outnumbered by the Texians, Castañeda and his soldiers retreated to San Antonio.

Guadalupe River near
Gonzales and the battle site.

March to Goliad *and* San Antonio

During the time of the Battle of Gonzales, General Cos marched his soldiers to Goliad, an important town since it lay in a direct *supply line* route. After staying a short time, he left for San Antonio with most of his men, leaving behind a small group to protect Presidio La Bahía.

Hearing this, some of the colonists gathered at Gonzales and other volunteers left for Goliad. Outnumbering the Mexican soldiers, the Texians were able to take the Goliad fort in just a short thirty-minute battle. Although three Mexican soldiers were killed, about twenty escaped and were able to warn not only Cos himself, but also other garrisons taken by Cos and the Mexican Army.

Stephen F. Austin, now having taken on the role of general and commander of the Texian forces, ordered 100 men to stay and protect Goliad. The presidio there housed a large supply of provisions and ammunition. The rest of the soldiers would meet up with other volunteers near San Antonio, where Cos was now in control of the city. Having won short battles at both Gonzales and Goliad, these Texians were feeling confident. They were sure they could take San Antonio back from Cos as well.

Stephen F. Austin led the newly formed Texian Army towards Béxar (now part of San Antonio). He sent a ninety-man scouting party, including Jim Bowie and James Fannin, from Mission San Fransisco de la Espada to locate a safe spot to camp closer to Béxar. Finding an area near Mission Concepción, the men rested and sent a messenger with directions to their location to Austin.

In the meantime, Cos heard Austin's army was divided and sent Ugartechea and 275 soldiers to attack the Texians near Mission Concepción on October 28th. The Texians were able to fend off several attacks by the Mexican Army, who retreated shortly before the rest of the Texian Army arrived. Fourteen Mexican soldiers died, but the Texians only lost one man. The Battle of Concepción is truly considered the first major armed battle (with the Texians' first loss of life) of the Texas Revolution.

Feeling even more confident, the Texians continued on and proceeded to lay *siege*, or set up a military *blockade*, around the city. Austin, along with several other men, was selected to travel to the United States and ask for aid for the Texians. Edward Burleson took Austin's place as commander of the army.

On November 26th, Texian scout Deaf Smith noticed a *caravan* he believed might be carrying a *payroll* of silver for the Mexican Army. Excited, about one hundred Texian soldiers made their way to the expected treasure. After a skirmish leaving several Texians wounded and three Mexican soldiers dead, the caravan was captured—only to discover the sacks did not contain silver, but hay for General Cos's cavalry horses.

This final conflict before the Texians made their way into San Antonio became known as the "Grass Fight."

 ## The Texians Fight Their Way into San Antonio

The Texian Army was restless. Hungry. Cold. Many threatened to give up the siege and either go home or march to Gonzales or Goliad. But something stopped them, and this tip of the dominoes would eventually lead, months later, to the most well-known and *tragic* story in the history of Texas.

A Mexican officer appeared at the Texian camp. Surrendering, he told the soldiers the Mexican troops in San Antonio were *discouraged* and weak. An empresario named Ben Milam knew the Texians must take this opportunity to attack Cos and his army. The time was right. He gathered 300 volunteers, crying out, "Who will go with old Ben Milam into San Antonio?"

On December 5th, 1835, the Texians entered the town and began the assault. Sadly, it is said Ben Milam was killed within the first few days of battle by a sniper as he crawled through a trench between houses. The rest of the troops pressed on, eventually pushing the Mexican forces into the protection of the Alamo mission.

In the end, a mere 400 Texian soldiers defeated a force of 1,000 Mexican troops. About 150 Mexican soldados were either killed, captured, or wounded, whereas only thirty or so Texians were wounded, and two killed.

Realizing his defeat, General Cos surrendered on December 9th. The Texians allowed Cos and his army to return to Mexico after a promise they would never again fight against the Texian colonists.

A promise soon broken!

The Texians were feeling confident. They had taken Goliad and the Alamo from the Mexican forces. It seemed as if peace had finally returned and the colonists could relax. Many chose to return home.

But a storm was brewing on the border.

Ben Milam   *Deaf Smith*

Statue of Ben Milam at the Milam County, Texas:
Photographer: Carol M. Highsmith. Courtesy of Library of Congress.
Erastus "Deaf" Smith, approximately 1836: Wright, Thomas Jefferson. Early Texas Documents, Special Collections, Courtesy of University of Houston Libraries.

Meanwhile, at the Consultation in San Felipe ...

While the Texian soldiers camped and kept watch outside San Antonio, a group of fifty-eight delegates met at San Felipe for the Consultation meeting beginning November 3rd, 1835. The representatives were divided into two groups: the Peace Party believed Texas should oppose Santa Anna and his *aggressive* actions, but should wait to declare independence. This group believed they would more likely receive sympathy and Mexican support if they worked to bring back the Constitution of 1824, now overthrown by Santa Anna, instead of preparing for war.

On the other hand, the War Party was ready to declare independence immediately. They believed the appearance of the Mexican Army was evidence of *imminent* war.

After a vote was called, it became clear the delegates were not yet ready to declare independence. Instead, the members, as loyal citizens of Mexico, declared Texans would continue to support the Mexican Constitution of 1824, but oppose a military dictatorship. They called for all Mexican citizens to support their goal of a democratic government and asked for volunteers to help them in their *quest*. This statement was called "The Declaration of the People."

The Consultation then created a temporary, or *provisional* government. Members selected Henry Smith as governor and James W. Robinson as lieutenant governor, both supporters of the War Party. Stephen F. Austin, William H. Wharton, and Branch T. Archer were selected as *commissioners* sent to the United States to try and obtain the money, supplies, and troops needed as the fight with Santa Anna continued.

Sam Houston was appointed commander of the *regular army*. The "Regulars" were full-time soldiers paid for their service. Unfortunately for Houston, the army members camped in San Antonio were just volunteers. This meant Houston had no real *authority* over the soldiers now involved in the conflict.

This was a rough beginning for a revolution. The citizens and their delegates were torn. Should they give in to Santa Anna and his tyranny? Should they fight for the 1824 Constitution and a democratic government? Or should they begin an all-out battle to win their independence and freedom from Mexico?

Some Texians wanted to invade and capture the Mexican town of Matamoros, but the council and governor would not agree or cooperate. Who would lead the army? The chosen commander could lead a regular army, yet the only army available was a group of volunteers.

Tensions mounted. People argued.

Would the Texans ever come together with a common goal?

Wood Engraving of Alamo, c1844
Courtesy of Library of Congress.

Back in San Antonio ...

Now the Texians held San Antonio and the Alamo. While the Mexican Army had been run out, many Tejano soldiers volunteered to help the Texas effort. In fact, quite a few of the soldiers who remained at the Alamo were Tejano, including Juan N. Seguín. While slavery was practiced by Texans and Americans, Hendrick Arnold (a free African American) helped Ben Milam seize San Antonio. He later served as a scout and fought at the Battle of San Jacinto.

Soldiers who participated were not just from Texas and America; these volunteers were from other countries as well, including England, Ireland, Scotland, and Germany. Those who fought to preserve freedom in the Texas Revolution were diverse in both culture and race.

The Texians settled in at San Antonio, mistakenly assuming Santa Anna would not make another move toward Texas until after the next convention, planned for March 1836, at Washington-on-the-Brazos. Instead, Santa Anna was furious. He would not wait. While he prepared his Mexican Army and began his march toward the rebels, Texans relaxed. The Texian Army became smaller as more and more soldiers returned home and the provisional government continued to quarrel instead of lead.

The number of soldiers in San Antonio was greatly reduced when most of these men volunteered to accompany Colonel Frank W. Johnson and Dr. James Grant in their plan for the invasion of the important port city of Matamoros, Mexico—a mission General Houston did not support. After they departed, Colonel James C. Neill was left commanding the remaining 100 men in San Antonio. Unable to stop the Matamoros Expedition, General Houston decided to take a trip to East Texas and spend time with the Cherokees in that area, hoping to convince them not to side with Mexico when the war broke out.

The remaining Texian troops were limited. Colonel James W. Fannin commanded 450 men at Goliad, and another force was beginning to gather at Gonzales.

With little leadership from the new government and the restrictions placed on General Houston in leading a volunteer army, the Texians were not prepared yet to take on the forces of Santa Anna.

Thousands and thousands of soldiers! Santa Anna's army, perhaps forty to fifty times larger than the number of men left at the Alamo, was moving toward Texas. However, many of his *soldados* were untrained and either prisoners or *enlisted* against their will. They were hungry and poorly dressed for the freezing winter weather which would be encountered along the way, but Santa Anna was angry. He was determined to punish those who rebelled against his authority. He would clean Texas of those disloyal *renegades*.

Santa Anna led his troops toward San Antonio, crossing the Rio Grande at present-day Eagle Pass. He ordered General José de Urrea and his troops to cross the Rio Grande at Matamoros and march toward Goliad along the Gulf Coast.

The armies would sweep Texas clean of the *traitors* and start fresh.

Colonel Neill sent word his army was shrinking. He was in need of both soldiers and guns. In response, General Houston sent Colonel James Bowie and twenty-five men from Goliad to provide support. While Houston believed the Alamo could not be properly defended, he strongly suggested to Bowie the Alamo be destroyed so it could not be used by the Mexican Army. However, he left the final decision to Bowie's judgment. Believing San Antonio's location was too important to *abandon*, Bowie chose to stay and defend the city and mission.

Soon after, Lieutenant Colonel William B. Travis (now a member of the regular army), and about thirty men from San Felipe, joined those gathering in San Antonio. David Crockett and twelve more volunteers arrived on the scene as *reinforcements*. Colonel Bowie stepped up to lead the volunteer soldiers and Lieutenant Colonel Travis commanded the regular army.

Late in February, Bowie became ill and Travis took command of the entire garrison. Crockett, a well-known Tennessee congressman and adventurer, asked to serve only as a *private* with the other volunteers.

Who Was Juan Seguín?

Juan Seguín was from San Antonio, and so fought to protect it from Santa Anna's forces during the Texas Revolution. An original defender at the Alamo, Seguín was sent on a *courier* mission and was away at the time of Santa Anna's final attack. He traveled with Houston and the Texian troops as they retreated and trained, and bravely led a company of Tejano soldiers during the Battle of San Jacinto.

He later served as a Texas senator and mayor of San Antonio. Sadly, as tensions rose again with Mexico, Seguín began to be suspected as a traitor. He fled to and lived in Mexico, telling people he was forced to fight on the side of Mexico in the Mexican-American War. Eventually he braved a return to Texas, where he again became involved in politics. He died peacefully at the age of 83.

Juan Seguín Memorial statue in Seguín, Texas:
Amboo who?/Flickr /CC BY-SA 2.0

THE ALAMO COMPLEX

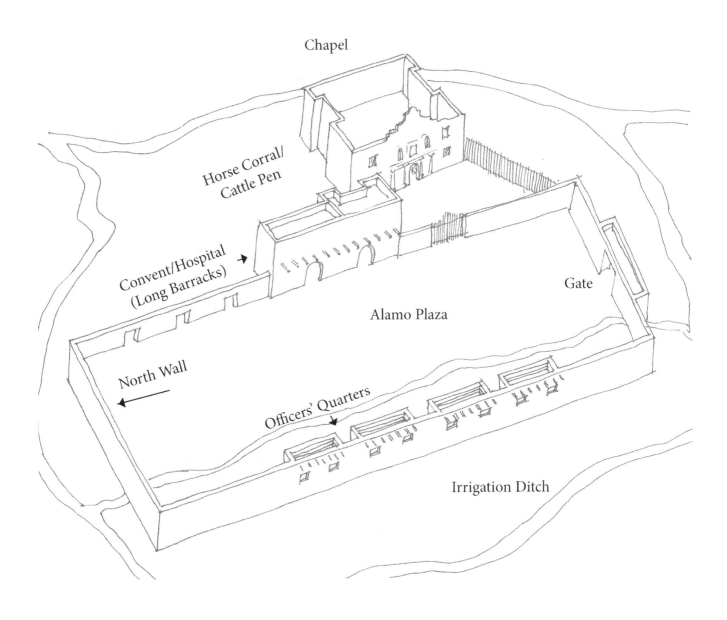

Chapel

Horse Corral/
Cattle Pen

Convent/Hospital
(Long Barracks)

Gate

Alamo Plaza

North Wall

Officers' Quarters

Irrigation Ditch

*Note: An illustration of the incomplete chapel roofline
(as it would have appeared in 1836) can be seen on page 84 of this book.

Illustration by Travis Dougherty.

86

⭐ The Battle of the Alamo ⭐

Aware that Santa Anna would eventually make his appearance, the Texians began to *fortify* the Alamo. *Palisades* were constructed, a new cannon arrived, and eighteen guns were mounted around the *compound*.

On February 23rd, the Mexican general and his huge army were sighted and marched into San Antonio. With only 150 men, the surprised Travis sent a letter to Gonzales requesting assistance. As the army approached, the Texians quickly grabbed supplies and *refugees* from the city and *barricaded* themselves within the Alamo mission *complex*. One of those brought into the compound was Susanna Dickinson, carrying her daughter Angelina, as her husband Almaron hurried his family inside the mission walls.

Santa Anna quickly made his presence known. Beginning the next day, the Mexican Army began the many hours of *bombardment* occurring daily during the siege, drawing closer and closer to the compound. Santa Anna raised the red flag of *"no quarter,"* which meant no prisoners would be taken; no mercy would be shown and all would be executed. Realizing the danger, Travis wrote one of the most famous letters in both Texas and American history, the first of several he sent, pleading for help:

To the People of Texas and All Americans in the World . . .

There was no quiet or rest at night for the Texians. Instead, Santa Anna ensured they received little sleep by playing bugle calls throughout the dark hours. The Texians were exhausted, but it is said Davy Crockett would stand on the walls of the plaza, playing his fiddle to keep the spirits up of his fellow soldiers.

After Travis's request for aide from Gonzales, thirty-two men were able to sneak into the fort, resulting in a total of about 182 Alamo defenders. All survived the constant cannon bombardment which took place day and night. Realizing they were outnumbered and outgunned, Travis brought his soldiers together and told them he would allow any individual to leave, if they could escape the Mexican Army's watch. But his men were committed. They would not give up.

Liberty. Or. Death.

Before the sun rose on March 6th, Santa Anna had his bugler play the *"Deguello,"* a bugle call which reminded the Texians he would take no prisoners. There would be no quarter. The Mexican Army charged the walls of the Alamo, climbing up ladders and each other to scale the walls.

The Texians fought bravely, but the battle was over within ninety minutes. As Santa Anna promised, every single soldier was killed. Only a handful of women, children, and Travis's slave Joe survived. Santa Anna sent Susanna Dickinson, her daughter Angelina, and Travis's slave to Gonzales to warn any Texians who might continue this battle.

𝒟𝒾𝒹 𝒴𝑜𝓊 𝒦𝓃𝑜𝓌?

The bugle call played by order of Santa Anna is known as "Deguello."
The noun deguello comes from the verb degollar . . . which means *to cut the throat* or *slaughter.*

You can find various versions and performances of *Deguello* online.
Close your eyes, listen, and imagine the fear it must have *invoked* for those who knew its meaning.

The Convention of 1836

A Declaration of Independence!

We need to go back in time for a short while to discuss a very important meeting which took place during the siege of the Alamo. The council elected by the Consultation the previous fall decided it was necessary to meet, since it was apparent Santa Anna would soon march into Texas. Delegates assembled March 1st, 1836, at Washington-on-the-Brazos. This small town was still very new, with only one main street and a few buildings. The men met in an unfinished, wooden structure with cloth stretched over the windows to protect them from the cold. And was it COLD! A *blue-norther* had recently blown into town, and temperatures dropped to 33 degrees.

Fifty-nine delegates, led by chairman Peter Ellis, had three major goals. They would write a Declaration of Independence, draft a constitution, and elect a temporary government until freedom was won and a proper election could be held.

The committee responsible for writing the Declaration of Independence completed their task quickly. The document was prepared in just one day, as it was based on the United States' Declaration of Independence, written only sixty years earlier. The Declaration provided a long list of complaints leading to the decision to break away from Mexico. These complaints included the *violation* of the Texans' rights to freedom of religion, trial by jury, the right to bear arms, and the right to *petition*. They were unhappy Mexico had never provided a system of public education, and that the Texans' complaints had been met with force by the Mexican government. They also protested what they saw as unfair import duties and the military stationing of soldiers in important cities and ports. They were angry Santa Anna had *dissolved* the Constitution of 1824, and as they wrote in the Declaration, Mexico had become a "weak, *corrupt*, and tyrannical government."

On March 2nd, the delegates *unanimously* voted to accept the Declaration and each member of the Convention placed their signature on the document. Still today, we celebrate March 2nd as Texas Independence Day.

Independence Hall, Washington-on-the-Brazos

The next point of order was to *draft* a constitution. Again, the resulting document was designed much like the United States' Constitution since the new country's government would be similar to the American style. Three branches of government would provide the basis of this republic: the executive (chief governing officer), the legislative (lawmaking), and the judicial (court) branches.

A Bill of Rights provided many protections seen in the United States, including the right to free speech, freedom of the press and religion, and the right to trial by jury. Parts of the Constitution were based on common Spanish-Mexican legal practices, and even some practices unique to Texas during that time. Although slavery was against the law in Mexico, the new Texas Constitution legalized the practice of slavery. Many Texas citizens had recently moved from the United States where slavery was legal, and were not yet ready to give up this practice.

Finally, it was important officers be selected to act as the *ad interim* (temporary) government until Texas was free and the republic official. David Burnet was elected president, and Lorenzo de Zavala, Vice President. Thomas Rusk was appointed Secretary of War, and of course General Sam Houston continued his position as the army's commander.

On March 6th, the delegates received a final letter written by William Travis, desperately asking for immediate help. Although most of the delegates were ready to jump on their horses and ride to his aid, General Houston argued it was *vital* the Convention continue. Texas must be prepared with a government and leadership in place in order to continue with the revolution.

A decision was made: the delegates would

stay and finish organizing the government, and Houston would leave immediately and gather troops to battle the Mexican Army.

Sadly, the day the letter arrived was the very day the Alamo had fallen, 167 miles away. Little did the **delegates** and Houston know, it was too late to save their fellow Texians in San Antonio.

Disaster in Goliad

While Santa Anna and his army were busy laying siege to the Alamo, General Urrea—along with 1,000 soldiers—began their march through South Texas. Fannin had begun setting up defenses in Presidio La Bahía (renamed Fort Defiance) in Goliad to prepare for their arrival.

One of the letters Travis sent from the Alamo was delivered to Goliad in late February, asking Fannin to send reinforcements. Although he intended to come to Travis' aid and began a trek to San Antonio, Fannin experienced problems with the wagons and had to return to Goliad.

Meanwhile, against Sam Houston's good judgment, a group of Texians decided to invade Matamoros. The men participating in this expedition were attacked by Urrea at San Patricio and Agua Dulce shortly before the final days of the Alamo.

Fearing the arrival of the Mexican Army, the frightened citizens in Refugio sent word to Goliad, asking Fannin for soldiers to protect their community. Fannin sent about thirty men, but all too soon, Urrea arrived in Refugio, surrounding the town. The Texian soldiers and local families took refuge in Mission Señora del Refugio and Fannin sent an additional 100 soldiers for reinforcement. The Texian troops were divided when a group left on a scouting mission; most of the men were killed or captured by Urrea's men.

A few days later, on March 14th, General Houston sent orders to Fannin to retreat to Victoria. Fannin, however, awaiting news from Refugio, did not withdraw from Goliad until March 19th. The army moved slowly, due to their heavy cannon and foggy conditions. Late that day, while resting on a prairie about three miles from Coleto Creek, Fannin and his Texas Army were surrounded by Urrea's troops. Fannin arranged his soldiers into the shape of a square, while Urrea stationed his men in the nearby woods. The Texians were able to drive off the Mexican Army's attacks that day, although over sixty were wounded and seven Texians killed. The second day, with no cover or water for the Texians, began with a cannon attack by Urrea's troops. About three hundred Texians were now surrounded by over one thousand Mexican soldiers. Fannin had no choice and asked to sign an agreement of surrender.

Most of the Texians assumed this meant they would be as taken prisoners of war and treated fairly, hoping for a quick release. The Mexican Army marched them back to Goliad, locking up the prisoners in the old presidio.

Presidio La Bahía

Urrea sent a message to Santa Anna, requesting **mercy** for the Texian prisoners, but the General was insistent they be shown no quarter; all must be executed, just as they were at the Alamo only a few weeks before.

On Palm Sunday, March 27th, the Texians who were able to walk were marched by the Mexican Army into the prairie. Most of the men believed they were either going to be allowed to return home or perhaps were being taken outside for work duty. Instead, the Mexican soldiers took aim and fired their weapons on the unsuspecting men. Those who were still imprisoned in the old presidio were executed within the walls. Fortunately, some of the Texians were able to escape. One group of men fled during the massacre on the prairie. Others were rescued by Señora Francita Alavez, the wife of a Mexican officer, who cared for the men in prison and helped others avoid execution. Her kindness earned Francita the nickname, "Angel of Goliad."

By the end of March, the tide had turned completely. Santa Anna and his army had successfully attacked and destroyed the Texian armies at the Alamo, San Patricio, Refugio, Victoria, and Goliad.

Their march continued. Now the Texians had two very big reasons to prepare to fight.

REMEMBER THE ALAMO!
REMEMBER GOLIAD!

Did You Know?

After the *massacre* at Goliad, the bodies of the executed Texians were burned and left unburied, exposed to the elements and wild animals.

A few months later, Thomas J. Rusk discovered the remains and had what was left of the bodies buried with military honors.

The bodies of the Texians at the Alamo met the same fate ... burned by the soldados and left unburied. Juan Seguín later returned to the site and buried the ashes in an unknown location.

The Runaway Scrape

By now, Santa Anna had conquered and executed the Texian soldiers at the Alamo and throughout South Texas.

Previously, after receiving Travis's cry for help at Washington-on-the-Brazos, Sam Houston instructed the delegates to complete their duties while he gathered soldiers to ride to San Antonio. When he reached Gonzales, where almost 400 volunteers were waiting, he heard the news of the fall of the Alamo. Susanna Dickinson arrived with her daughter Angelina, Travis' slave Joe, and Santa Anna's servant Ben with a message from Santa Anna himself. Susanna told Houston about the *slaughter* at the Alamo, along with Santa Anna's plans to sweep Texas clean of the rebels.

General Houston knew his small Texian Army was not yet ready to fight the much larger and better trained Mexican Army. He knew he would have to retreat east, towards the Sabine River and the safety of the United States. Perhaps this would give him time to better train his men. Maybe more

volunteers would arrive from the United States. And maybe the Texian Army would gather more weapons and ammunition.

He also knew, if Santa Anna and his army followed him, this would stretch their supply lines, and cause the Mexican Army to move further and further away from the provisions they would need. If the situation became desperate, Houston could always *lure* the Mexican Army to the border, where General Gaines and the United States Army might assist the Texians.

Santa Anna, playing right into Houston's hands, headed east to complete his sweep of the rebellious Texans. He sent forces under General Gaona to the north, up and around present day Bastrop, and then to San Felipe. Urrea continued his path along the southern portion of the territory along the Gulf Coast. Santa Anna and General Sesma traveled through the central portion of Texas, following Houston's small army as they retreated. As the soldados swept through the land, the armies were instructed to burn, destroy, and clean Texas of those who would *defy* Santa Anna.

As Houston, his small army, and the frightened families left Gonzales, the general asked the last men out to set fire and destroy the town so Santa Anna would not benefit from the supplies left behind. Houston then headed east to the Colorado River at Burnham's Crossing (present-day La Grange). The river banks had flooded from heavy rains, so the soldiers and families waited at the river for nine days. Houston used this time to *drill* and train his men, while more volunteers arrived from the United States, adding another 1,400 men to the Texian Army. Still, these men were not well-equipped and were unprepared to fight.

Finally, the soldiers and families took up their march and worked their way toward the Brazos River. The roads were muddy and hard to use. Fearing for their lives, these families from Gonzales and other communities left their homes quickly, with little food and few supplies. They were hungry. Many were sick. Contagious illnesses such as whooping cough and cholera spread and made people ill along the way. This frightening retreat by the citizens and soldiers of Texas is known as the *Runaway Scrape*.

General Houston kept up his march toward the Brazos River, with Santa Anna hot on his trail. Both the Texian and Mexican Armies used scouts to spy on the other army's movements. Deaf Smith and his son-in-law Hendrick Arnold proved successful scouts for Houston. In fact, the African American Arnold even posed as a runaway slave to enter and spy within Mexican camps.

When the Texians reached the Brazos River at the town of San Felipe de Austin, Houston left a small section of his army behind to guard the river crossing. He then moved his soldiers upriver to Groce's Plantation (near today's Hempstead). Here they remained for two weeks, as the soldiers continued to drill and prepare for battle. During this time, more volunteers arrived along with two cannon, named the "Twin Sisters": a gift from the state of Ohio. While his men trained, Houston received a letter from the president of the temporary government, David Burnet. Burnet demanded Houston turn and fight the Mexican Army. He *taunted* Houston, telling him people were "laughing him to scorn." Houston's army was anxious to fight as well. They were angry about waiting and constantly begged to begin the battle.

Houston was wise. He was patient. He knew that:
- *every day of training,*
- *every day more volunteers and supplies arrived, and*
- *every day Santa Anna's supply line was stretched* meant a better chance of success.

Santa Anna and his army finally reached San Felipe and the Brazos River. The Texians left at the crossing were able to keep the Mexican Army on the western shore of the river, but Santa Anna just marched his men downriver and crossed there. Hearing the temporary Texas government had moved to Harrisburg (located east of today's downtown Houston), now only about thirty miles away, Santa Anna made a decision which would cost him the war and the land of Texas.

Thinking he could travel faster with a smaller number of men, Santa Anna left most of the Mexican Army at the river and headed with a group of about 900 of his best soldiers to chase down the government officials. Once in Harrisburg, he heard Burnet and his advisors had moved on to the town of New Washington on Galveston Bay. Racing to catch them, the Mexican Army barely missed the officials as they sailed across the bay to Galveston Island.

Hearing the latest news of Santa Anna's actions and knowing Mexico's supply lines were stretched, the timing was perfect for Houston to finally face his enemy. While the families continued on toward the Sabine River and safety, Houston turned his army south to Buffalo Bayou. His men cheered, knowing they would meet Santa Anna when he turned north to Lynch's Ferry on the San Jacinto River. Finally, Houston and his men would meet the Mexican Army in battle.

This time . . . they were ready.

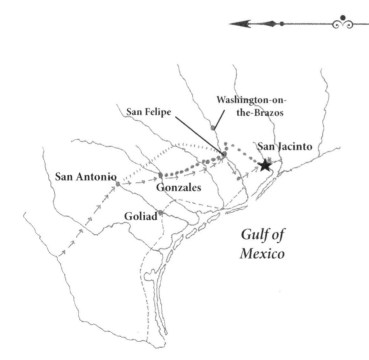

Movement of Troops
Texas Revolution

KEY

→ → → → → Santa Anna's Army (Mexican)

- - - - - - - - Urrea's Army (Mexican)

////////////// Gaona's Army (Mexican)

•••••••••••• Houston's Army (Texian)

The Battle of San Jacinto

While Texians made final preparations to, once and for all, meet the Mexican Army in battle, Santa Anna again separated his army and moved ahead toward Lynchburg, ordering General Cos and his 500 men to meet there as soon as possible. Santa Anna took with him about 700 soldados and a cannon named the *Golden Standard*.

Both armies were well aware of the other's location; scouts continued to keep each side informed. Santa Anna selected a camp site less than a mile away from where the Texians had stationed themselves. The Mexican camp was located in an area with the San Jacinto River and Peggy's Lake to their right and rear, and most of the camp surrounded by marshlands and swamps. The Texians' camp found Buffalo Bayou to their rear and the San Jacinto River to their left.

Testing each other's strength, the two armies held a short skirmish on April 20th. The soldados fired the *Golden Standard*, wounding one Texian. After an unsuccessful attempt to take the Mexican cannon, the Texians retreated to their camp for the night.

For many weeks, General Houston had not slept well. That evening, with a saddle for a pillow, he slept soundly. His patience would finally pay off.

The next morning, the sun rose. Santa Anna was confident, especially after General Cos arrived with 500 reinforcements. However, Cos and his men had marched all night and were tired. Since it appeared the Texians did not plan to battle that day, the soldados decided to rest. Santa Anna went to his tent to take a nap, with only a few soldados left on watch. It was *siesta* time.

Quietly Houston sent Deaf Smith to destroy Vince's Bridge, the only escape for retreat . . . for both armies. Then he gathered his men. He tried to convince Juan Seguín and the Tejano soldiers to wait at the camp since there was a danger they might be mistaken for Mexican Army soldados. They refused. It was their battle, too. They placed cards on their hats to identify themselves as Texians and took their places with the others.

The Texian battle line was ready. Sidney Sherman and his infantry were on the far left, near the river. The *Twin Sister* cannons were in the center, under George Hockley's control. Four infantry units led by Henry Millard were on the right. Finally, Mirabeau Lamar, who had proven himself brave in battle during the skirmish the day before, led the cavalry on the far right.

At 3:30 p.m., the battle line began to move. A popular song of the day, "Will You Come to the Bower," was played on a fife and perhaps a badly battered drum. A soldier carried the San Jacinto Battle Flag, painted on silk with Lady Liberty carrying a *cutlass* and a banner with the words:

Liberty or Death.

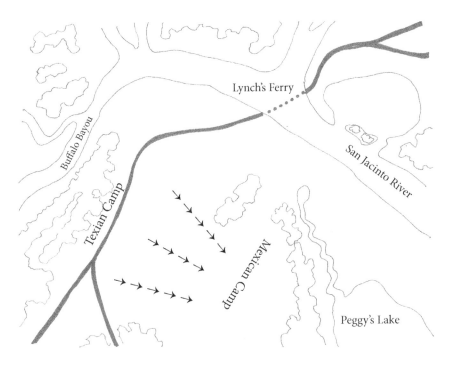

San Jacinto Battleground

Illustration by Travis Dougherty.

92

General Houston jumped on his beautiful gray stallion named Saracen and raised his sword. When they were within firing range, the Texians raced towards the Mexican camp, shouting, "Remember the Alamo! Remember Goliad!"

The Mexican camp was in total confusion. The *Golden Standard* was only able to fire a few times before it was overtaken. The soldados attempted to fight back, but they were unprepared. Houston's horse was shot from beneath him, and he mounted another. Then both Houston and his second horse were shot! Undaunted, he again found another horse and continued to lead his men in battle.

The soldados could not escape. They were surrounded by swamps and most could not swim. Although the battle was over in only eighteen minutes, the Texians *persisted* in their hunt, continuing to capture the soldados until dark.

While less than ten Texians were killed and only thirty injured, over 600 soldados died that day and 730 taken prisoner. *Ironically*, one man could not be found . . . General Santa Anna.

The next day, still searching for fleeing soldados, several men found an escaping soldier not far from the battlefield. Bringing him to camp, it soon became clear this was not just any soldier. It was Santa Anna himself. The Mexican leader was marched to Houston's feet as he lay under a tree recovering from the gunshot wound in his ankle.

The Texians wanted revenge. They hoped to see the leader executed. But General Houston knew Santa Anna was worth far more alive than dead. While the Mexican general made excuses for his actions, Houston calmly stood behind his *convictions* and chose to spare Santa Anna's life.

Santa Anna was soon taken to Velasco, where the new Republic of Texas would establish its first *capital*. He agreed to end the fighting, give back any Texas property taken by Mexico, and send Mexican troops home across the Rio Grande River when he put his signature on the Treaty of Velasco. A different general then led the Mexican Army back home.

Texas was now safe again. Families returned home, many finding their cabins and farms burned and destroyed. Staunchly, they would begin again.

This time, their home was no longer a part of Mexico.

Now it was a new country:

The Republic of Texas.

Battle of San Jacinto Reenactment

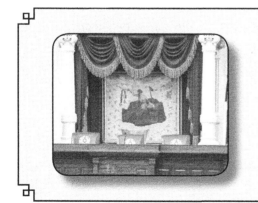

Did You Know?

The San Jacinto battle flag is now carefully preserved and can be found in the state capitol in Austin. You can see the beautiful old banner if you visit the House of Representatives while congress is in session. You'll find it hanging on the wall behind the podium used by the Speaker of the House.

93

Battles of the Texas Revolution

Battle of Velasco: June 25-26, 1832 - Texian victory (John Austin)

Battle of Gonzales: October 2, 1835 - Texian victory (John Henry Moore)

Battle of Goliad: October 10, 1835 - Texian victory (George Collinsworth)

Battle of Lipantitlán: November 4-5,1835 - Texian victory (Ira Westover)

Battle of Concepción: October 28, 1835 - Texian victory (James Bowie & James Fannin)

Grass Fight: November 26, 1835 - Texian victory (James Bowie & William Jack)

Siege of Béxar: October 12 - December 11, 1835: Texian victory
(Austin, Rusk, Milam, Burleson, Johnson)

Battle of San Patricio: February 27, 1836 - Mexican victory (General Urrea)

Battle of the Alamo: February 23-March 6, 1836 - Mexican victory (General Santa Anna)

Battle of Agua Dulce Creek: March 2, 1836 - Mexican victory (General Urrea)

Battle of Refugio: March 14, 1836 - Mexican victory (General Urrea)

Battle of Coleto Creek: March 19-20, 1836 - Mexican victory (General Urrea)

Battle of San Jacinto: April 21, 1836 - Texian victory (General Houston)

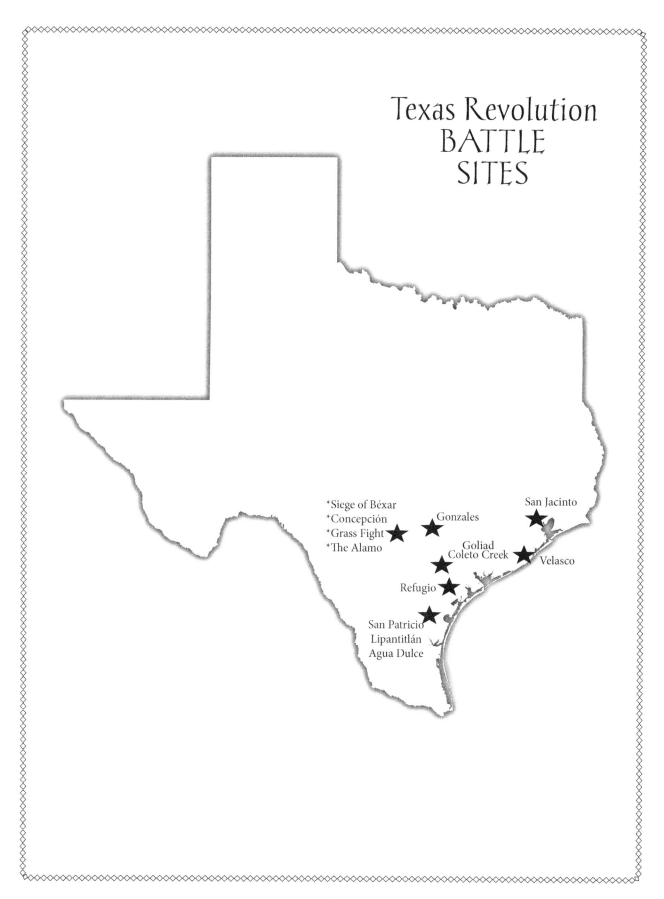

Texas Revolution
BATTLE
SITES

*Siege of Béxar
*Concepción
*Grass Fight
*The Alamo

Gonzales

San Jacinto

Goliad
Coleto Creek

Velasco

Refugio

San Patricio
Lipantitlán
Agua Dulce

Unit Seven:
THE REPUBLIC OF TEXAS

The revolution was won. It was over. Texas was now free.

This unit will help you better understand what it must have been like: beginning a new country from scratch. You'll learn about the three men who served as presidents of the Republic of Texas, and how they pulled together both the people and the government while constantly trying to balance ongoing conflicts with Mexico and Native Americans.

Just as occurs with any new country, there were good decisions made, and there were bad decisions made. Regardless, the country survived and grew, and within ten years Texas would be annexed and become one of the United States of America.

PRESIDENTS OF THE REPUBLIC OF TEXAS

Sam Houston
1836 - 1838
and
1841 - 1844

Mirabeau Lamar
1838-1841

Anson Jones
1844 - 1846

No longer a part of Mexico, Texas was now its own country—the Republic of Texas. That meant Texans would now have to select government *officials* and establish a capital which would be home to the new government as it began to build a new nation. In September of 1836, Texas citizens elected their revolutionary hero, Sam Houston, as the first president of the Republic of Texas, with Mirabeau Lamar as vice president. Houston appointed Stephen F. Austin as Secretary of State and Henry Smith to the office of Secretary of the Treasury.

Sadly, Austin fell ill and died shortly after taking office. At the news of Austin's death, Sam Houston announced, "The Father of Texas is no more." Moses and Stephen F. Austin's great vision and efforts were responsible for a land now blooming with a growing population and new-found freedom.

Until a more permanent capital could be selected, Houston and his *congress* met in the town of Columbia (today the city is known as West Columbia, and is located southwest of Houston, about two miles west of the Brazos River) to organize the new government. Realizing Columbia was too small for their needs, a decision was made to move the capital to the new town of Houston, located on Buffalo Bayou. The Allen brothers, founders of Houston, promised to build a beautiful new city. Eventually a large, two-story *capitol* was built in this town of mosquito swarms and muddy streets, and the government settled down to business.

Did You Know?

The first flag of the Republic of Texas had an *azure* blue background and a gold star in the middle. It was called the National Flag of Texas, or David G. Burnet's Flag. It served as the flag of Texas until the Lone Star Flag was adopted in 1839.

First Things First:
Sam Houston, First President of the Republic of Texas
1836-1838

Many issues faced Texas's first president and government. During the election, it was clear Texans overwhelmingly wished to become part of the United States through a process called *annexation*, but several problems stood in the way.

First, Texas allowed its citizens to own slaves. The United States was split; some states believed in freedom, while other states—especially those states in the South where the economy was based on farming—permitted its citizens to hold slaves. The United States tried to carefully balance the power between the country's slave states and free states, knowing this disagreement might result in a very big conflict from which the nation might never recover. Many within the United States would *reject* the idea of bringing in another slave state.

Second, the United States and its president, Andrew Jackson, did not want to damage the country's relationship with Mexico. Annexing Texas could (and eventually would) cause conflict with their neighbor to the south.

Understanding the road to annexation would be difficult, the Texas government began to work toward gaining *recognition* from the United States, Europe, and Mexico. Texas wanted to be a stable country with the ability to trade and *negotiate* with other nations.

Sometimes Texas's own citizens created problems for the new country. President Houston became uneasy when the new army commander, Felix Huston, along with soldiers still itching to fight, began planning an invasion of Mexico. Houston was concerned about another conflict with Mexico so soon after the revolution. He felt Texas was no longer in need of a large army, and the new country had little money to support its soldiers. Houston quietly *furloughed* most of the troops without the commander's approval. Feeling he had been tricked, Felix Huston was quite unhappy to have his invasion plans blocked by the new president, but for a while, a delicate peace resumed with Mexico.

Since Texas had little money and no *credit* to borrow from other nations, Houston was forced to raise money for the new country in other ways. *Tariffs* were established for *imported* goods, and business and property taxes were *enacted*.

What about the Texas Indians? As new citizens from the United States poured into Texas, conflicts arose over lands which were occupied by Native Americans. Sam Houston, who had spent many years in his youth and adulthood living with the Cherokees, was always very concerned about Texas's relationship with its Native American tribes. He continued his attempts to help the Cherokees in East Texas, who were constantly losing their land to incoming settlers, claiming it as their own. Other tribes in Central Texas also resented the invasion of Anglo settlers, raiding and capturing these newcomers in retaliation.

Comanches and Kiowas led many of these raids. One of the tragic stories of this conflict occurred throughout the life of Cynthia Ann Parker. Kidnapped as a young child and her family massacred by Comanches, Cynthia lived as a captive among the tribe for twenty-four years. After marrying a Comanche chief, Cynthia began a new family and gave birth to three children (including the last free Comanche chief, Quanah Parker). With the best of intentions, Texas Rangers "rescued" Cynthia, taking her away from the tribe she had grown to love. She desperately wanted to return to her Indian family, but was not allowed to do so. She died ten years later, heartbroken.

Sam Houston

Sam Houston was one of the most fascinating heroes in Texas history. He is still the only person in America to have served as governor of two states. He held positions as a U.S. congressman, Tennessee governor, Texas president, Texas congressman, U.S. senator, and Texas governor.

The Republic's Second President:
Mirabeau Lamar
1838-1841

Although Sam Houston proved to be a strong leader for the new nation, the Texas Constitution did not allow *consecutive* terms for its president. He would have to wait to run again. Houston's vice president, Mirabeau Lamar, was elected the second president of the Republic of Texas. Lamar and Houston were very different men, with very different beliefs. While Houston attempted to keep peace with the Native Americans, Lamar did not. Problems arose in East Texas when Lamar became suspicious of the relationship between Mexico and the Cherokees, and declared the Cherokees did not have fair *claim* to the land where they lived. In the summer of 1839, Lamar ordered the removal of the Cherokees from Texas land. After a battle near today's city of Tyler, where approximately 100 Cherokees were killed and their villages and farms burned, the Indian survivors were forced to leave Texas and move across the Red River.

After a series of Comanche raids in 1840, *tribal representatives* were sent to meet and negotiate with officials in San Antonio. Although they were asked to bring any Anglo captives in their possession, the Comanche only brought along one prisoner, who reported there were thirteen more captives still living with the tribes. Upon hearing this news, the Comanche negotiators were then taken hostage by the Texans, and the *Council House Fight* commenced. In the end, seven Texans and thirty-five Comanche were killed, and many of the remaining Anglo captives were killed to *avenge* the deaths of fellow Comanche. Any chance for peace was now gone, and any attempts at treaties in the future were refused.

Problems continued. Other conflicts with Native Americans included the *Battle of Plum Creek*, more Comanche and Kiowa raids, and additional attacks on Comanche villages. Eventually the southern Comanche moved to the area of the Red River, as the Cherokees had done before. President Lamar also decided to restore the Texas Navy. These ships were sent to Mexican waters, where they assisted rebels fighting for freedom from Mexico in the Yucatán province.

Since the city of Houston was considered only a temporary capital, Lamar elected to move the government and its *archives* to a new site on the Colorado River in 1839. Located near the small village of Waterloo, the town would become known as the city of Austin, named after Texas's beloved Stephen F. Austin.

Lamar was a great believer in the importance of public education, ensuring 18,000 acres be set aside in every county to support public schools. He also ensured 288,000 acres in Central Texas were saved as a way to fund two future universities. Because of his great concern that Texas citizens become an educated *populace*, Lamar became known as the "Father of Education" in Texas.

The Indian wars, the *restoration* of the Navy, and the Santa Fe Expedition (discussed in the following section) were expensive, and all added to the republic's growing *debt*. Unable to borrow money from the United States and Europe, the public debt eventually spun out of control. The value of paper money shrunk in value, and one dollar was worth only fifteen cents. Lamar began to look for additional sources of income.

The Santa Fe Expedition:
1841

During this time, Santa Fe (in today's New Mexico, along the upper Rio Grande River) was the most important trade center in the Southwest and the destination for many traders traveling from St. Louis, Missouri. Mirabeau Lamar believed Texas would benefit financially if it had control of Santa Fe and the Santa Fe Trail, and so he organized an *expedition*. Santa Fe would bring more money to Texas and help pay off the country's growing debts. Lamar also hoped New Mexico might be persuaded to join Texas.

Men selected for the expedition included soldiers, merchants, and some men just looking for a good adventure. Unfortunately, the trip turned out to be more difficult than anyone imagined. The expedition suffered from the *intense* summer heat, a shortage of water and food, and the misery of Indian attacks. As the expedition's crew finally neared Santa Fe, they were met and surrounded by soldiers of the Mexican Army, who were very unhappy with these men, clearly trying to take possession of land under Mexico's rule.

The Texans, now prisoners, were marched 1,000 miles to Mexico City. Some died on the long journey, and the rest were held in prison until their release in April of 1842.

The expedition was of course considered a failure, and became just one more issue between Texas and Mexico which would eventually lead to the Mexican-American War.

President Sam Houston's Second Term:
1841 - 1844

Once Lamar's term was over, elections were held and once again Sam Houston was voted in as President of the Republic of Texas. The public debt, a new threat of Mexican invasions, and the attempt to annex Texas to the United States were the central issues of his presidency.

Houston realized he must first reduce the country's expenses, so he cut back the number of government positions and the size of the army. He also tried to repair some of the damage to Indian relations which occurred during Lamar's term by establishing treaties with Native Americans at Bird's Fort and Torrey's Trading House. This led to a greater peace with the earliest residents of Texas.

Mexico had been angered by the Santa Fe Expedition, and in March of 1842, about 500 Mexican soldiers invaded Texas and occupied San Antonio, Goliad, and Refugio for a short time. Concerned for the safety of the government archives, Houston ordered these important documents picked up and moved to Houston. However, the residents of Austin refused to give up the archives, with Angelina Eberly leading the revolt. Angelina aimed a loaded cannon and fired at the men Houston had sent to retrieve the archives. The residents of Austin won what became known as the "Archives War," and the documents remained at home in the capital.

Mexico continued to tweak Texas's nose. In September of 1842, Mexican soldiers led by General Adrián Woll occupied San Antonio. Once again, it was a short *occupation*. The Texas Rangers and militia drove the soldados out and the Mexican Army returned to Mexico.

Even Texas citizens caused headaches for President Houston. In East Texas, a serious *feud* had been brewing for several years between settlers who were arguing over land titles. This ongoing conflict became known as the "Regulator-Moderator War." Citizens were murdered, their properties burned, and lawlessness prevailed. The feud finally came to a resolution after President Houston sent 600 soldiers to bring law and order back to the area.

Angelina Eberly Statue (Austin, Texas)
Sculptor Pat Oliphant

The Mier Expedition
and the Black Bean Episode

After General Woll's short occupation of San Antonio, many Texans were angry with Mexico. Texas had won the revolution, and Mexico had lost. No one appreciated Mexico's annoying threats to Texas freedom.

Houston tried to calm the citizens, sending General Alexander Somervell and 750 militia to *patrol* and protect the land between San Antonio and Laredo, which lay on the border of Mexico. When it appeared the Mexican Army was not present in Laredo, the Texan soldiers were sent back up to Gonzales. Three hundred of the Texans, led by Colonel William S. Fisher, decided to go against orders and marched down the Rio Grande River, instead to attack Mier, Mexico. However, the Texans were outnumbered and surrendered to the Mexican Army. On their march to jail in Mexico City, the Texans escaped but became lost in the mountains. Those who survived were recaptured one week later.

 ←

The Republic of Texas

As you can see, the borders of the Republic of Texas extended farther north and west than our current borders.
In fact, the Republic extended partially through what is now Kansas, Colorado, Wyoming, and New Mexico.
That additional land was sold to the United States in 1850, leaving Texas with the unique shape we know today.

Santa Anna, who had gone into retirement after the Battle of San Jacinto, returned to power in Mexico. Back to his old self, Santa Anna ordered the execution of every tenth Texas prisoner of the Mier Expedition—meaning 17 out of the 176 captives were to die. But how would this decision be made? Each Texan would draw a bean from a jar. If the bean selected was black, that soldier would be executed; if the bean was white, the soldier would be sent to prison in Mexico City. Those who selected white beans either escaped, died in prison, or were released in September of 1844. As promised, those who drew black beans were executed.

Today, this incident is often referred to as the "Black Bean Episode."

Anson Jones,
Last President of Texas
1844 - 1846

Dr. Anson Jones came to Texas in 1833 and set up a medical practice in Brazoria. He also served as a surgeon during the Texas Revolution and was Secretary of State during President Houston's second term. Jones was elected President of the Republic in 1844. He was very concerned with obtaining recognition and peace with Mexico, and became unpopular with the people of Texas when congress and the citizens felt his negotiations with Mexico threatened their plans for annexation with the United States.

Would Texas ever join the United States? The question would be answered during President Jones' term.

Unit Eight:
STATEHOOD
and THE CIVIL WAR

Overview

During the short period between the annexation of Texas and the close of the 19ᵗʰ century, Texas history is filled with stories of war and change. In fact, Texas participated in two wars during this time: the Mexican-American War and the Civil War. With any war comes sacrifice and change. Texas was familiar with both. The Texas Rangers were also busy, protecting Texas citizens from outlaws and Indian raids. This unit will better help you understand the changes Texas went through as it became an official state, as it left the Union to join the Confederate States of America, as it struggled through the Civil War years, and as it worked to meet the standards set to rejoin the Union during the time of Reconstruction.

Texas Joins the United States of America

When Texas won its independence and became the Republic of Texas, the citizens were happy to be free from Mexican rule. By 1844, the Republic of Texas was finally recognized as an independent nation by the United States, France, England, and the Netherlands. This recognition meant Texas could now officially trade with these other countries. However, Mexico refused to recognize the Republic of Texas unless it rejected annexation to the United States.

Many Texas citizens had moved to Texas from the United States, and most hoped the Republic would eventually join the Union and become one of the United States of America. Although the first president of the Republic, Sam Houston, also hoped Texas would be annexed to the U.S., the other Republic of Texas presidents, Mirabeau Lamar and Anson Jones, were not *enthusiastic* about this plan and wished Texas remain an independent country.

The United States was also *wary* about allowing Texas to join the Union. Slavery was legal in Texas, and many Americans were concerned adding a southern slave state would mean a tipping of the balance of power between the free and slave states. Americans were also worried the annexation of Texas might mean a war with Mexico. They were right!

Due to these concerns, the first attempt to annex Texas was *rejected* by the United States Senate in 1844. When James K. Polk won the election for U.S. President in that same year—and it was well-known Polk favored the annexation of Texas—it became clear the *majority* of Americans wanted to see Texas join the U.S. as a state. Americans were also worried England and France might have an interest in *acquiring* Texas and other lands to the west. In fact, Sam Houston cleverly cozied up to these countries in hopes of inspiring a little worry and jealousy in the United States, hoping to speed up the process of annexation.

Many Americans wanted to see the U.S. expand even further west, with its borders reaching from coast to coast. This would mean settlers and merchants could enjoy the many possibilities of plentiful land and ports, which would make both travel and trade with Asia less complicated. The excitement about *expansion* from east to west across the continent during this period is known as *Manifest Destiny.*

The U.S. Congress proposed Texas be annexed by *joint resolution.* A treaty would require a two-thirds majority in the senate to pass, but a joint resolution would only require a *simple majority* of votes in each house. Once the resolution passed, Texas would need to approve the annexation and adopt a new state constitution. It would be allowed to keep *public lands,* but could also sell a portion of those lands to help pay off its many debts. In addition, Texas would agree the state could be divided into up to five states at some future time, with the approval of both the United States and Texas.

Once the resolution was officially submitted to Texas, the Republic's President Anson Jones called a special session of congress. The Texas Congress agreed to annexation and a new state constitution was drafted. On October 13th, 1845, Texans voted and both approved annexation and *ratified* the new constitution. The U.S. *consented* to the constitution, and on December 29th, 1845, President Polk signed the *resolution* and Texas became the 28th state to join the Union.

"The Republic of Texas is No More"

President Anson Jones, Annexation Ceremony, February 19, 1846.
Courtesy of Texas State Library and Archives Commission (1/103-4, Places Collection, Prints and Photographs Collections).

Then on February 19th, 1846, Texas President Anson Jones turned his office over to the newly-elected Texas state governor, James Pinckney Henderson. The Lone Star Flag was lowered and the *Stars and Stripes* raised in its place.

Imagine the mixed emotions of the spectators as Jones announced, "The Republic of Texas is no more."

Texas: A New State and New Citizens

Even before Texas was annexed to the United States, the number of settlers who would make their way to Texas grew quickly. The population of Texas tripled between the victory at San Jacinto in 1836 and annexation in 1845. Most of these settlers left their homes in the eastern United States to make their new homes in Texas. They built houses and farms from Nacogdoches to Austin, and from San Antonio to Laredo. After 1845, new arrivals discovered the least expensive land could be found on the *frontier,* away from the earlier settlements, so many moved into Indian country. A large number of these farmers were originally from the cotton-growing southern states, so they continued cotton raising, along with corn and other agricultural products in the newly available land in Texas, often with the assistance of slave labor.

Immigrants arrived, not only from the United States, but from other countries as well. Europeans from England, France, Germany, and Poland were enticed by the rich land, freedom, and protection offered by the United States. French settlers arrived as well, developing colonies in Castroville and the Dallas area. Although the British did not colonize as other European countries did in this new state, they were actively involved in trading and *investing* in Texas—especially when it came to the cotton needed for their factories.

Many settlers from Germany also made their way across the Atlantic. German princes and *barons* organized transportation and assistance for those who wished to immigrate to Texas. These German colonies were established along the Comal and Pedernales Rivers, just north of San Antonio. In 1845, the first German settlement was founded in New Braunfels; although this land was shared with Comanche, the two cultures were able to live in peace. Other German settlements were established in Fredericksburg, Comfort, and Boerne.

Of course, many Tejanos of Mexican heritage already lived in Texas prior to the revolution. Most of these families made their homes in South Texas along the Rio Grande, between the Nueces and Rio Grande Rivers, in San Antonio, and in Goliad.

With this growing population, more *counties* were created. In 1845, only forty-five counties existed in Texas. By 1860, that number had grown to 122 counties. In addition, the Homestead Act provided settlers free land, as long as they lived on the property for a certain number of years and continued to improve the land.

The first governor of this quickly-growing state was J. Pinckney Henderson. The legislature consisted of two houses: the *House of Representatives* (whose members were allowed to serve two year terms) and the *Senate* (whose members were allowed to serve four year terms). Also established was a state *Supreme Court*, as well as district and county courts.

Since Texas had now joined the Union, representatives could be sent to Washington, D.C., to represent the state. Sam Houston and Thomas Jefferson Rusk were selected to serve as U.S. senators, and two additional men were sent to serve in the U.S. House of Representatives.

The Mexican-American War

Wars begin for many reasons, and in the case of the Mexican-American War, trouble had been brewing between Mexico, Texas, and the United States for many years.

First, Mexico never got over the loss of Texas land after the revolution. When the United States annexed Texas, Mexico became even angrier. The Mexican government had continued to refuse to recognize Texas even as a republic, and now they had been insulted by Texas's new statehood. On top of that, Mexico never did agree to the Rio Grande as the established boundary between Texas and Mexico; they believed the Nueces River was the borderline.

The United States sent a representative to Mexico in hopes of peacefully negotiating the boundary between the two countries, and perhaps purchasing even more Mexican land to the west in return for a large payment to Mexico. Mexico refused to meet with the negotiator, and the discussion *ceased*.

This failed negotiation caused concern in the United States, and in March of 1846—just a few months following annexation—President Polk sent General Zachary Taylor and troops to the area in Texas between the Nueces and Rio Grande Rivers. Shortly thereafter, Mexican and American troops began to *clash* just north of the Rio Grande. The Mexicans considered this area to be Mexico. The Americans considered this land to be Texas, and therefore American soil.

In May of 1846, the U.S. Congress declared war on Mexico. Thousands of men enlisted in the fight against Texas's old enemy. Even Texas Revolution heroes Edward Burleson, Sidney Johnston, and Mirabeau Lamar joined the army. Governor Henderson was given command of all Texas troops, and the Texas Rangers assisted the army as scouts.

The United States was better prepared and equipped for battle than Texas had been during the revolution. Santa Anna, living in *exile* after the revolution, returned once again to Mexico to raise an army but was unable to defeat Texas. General Taylor began his occupation of northern Mexico and moved south, defeating Santa Anna at Buena Vista. Mexico City was captured in September of 1847 by General Winfield Scott, while other troops moved west and occupied California.

Finally, a peace treaty was signed February 2nd, 1848. The Treaty of Guadalupe Hidalgo stated Mexico would abandon its claim to Texas and accept the Rio Grande River as the border between the two countries. Mexico *ceded* all territories from West Texas to the Pacific Ocean. This ceded land, called the Mexican Cession, included California, Nevada, and Utah, as well as parts of Arizona, Colorado, New Mexico, and Wyoming (adding 850,000 square miles of territory to the U.S.).

In return, the United States gave Mexico fifteen million dollars. If a Mexican citizen lived in territory turned over to the U.S., they were allowed to keep their land and were given one year to decide whether or not to become a citizen of the United States.

In 1853, additional territory located on a strip of land along the southern edge of today's Arizona and New Mexico was purchased from Mexico. The U.S. paid Mexico another ten million dollars for what is known as the Gadsen Purchase.

Texas Rangers, Company D, on Rio Grande, 1888-1889
1983/112 R-no number 1-1, Texas Department of Public Safety photographs.
Courtesy Texas State Library and Archives Commission.

The Texas Rangers

Let's travel back in time for a moment, back to the days of empresario Stephen F. Austin and his early settlements in Texas. New settlers were often victims of raiding Comanche, Tonkawa, and Karankawa tribes. Mexican law allowed Austin to form a militia to safeguard the new Texas citizens from unhappy Indians and other dangers to their communities. Austin and his lieutenant did just that: they brought together a group of volunteers to protect the settlers. These men, one hundred of whom would *"range"* the frontier when necessary, were the ancestors of what we today call the Texas Rangers.

In the early days, this group of volunteers was paid only fifteen dollars a month in property. They were known by various names: the national militia, ranging companies, minutemen, scouts, spies, and many other titles until these *law enforcers* were officially and legally named the Texas Rangers in 1874. The early militia was made up of Anglo, Hispanic, and even Native American men who rode on horseback and provided their own steed and most of their needed equipment. The men only furnished temporary assistance; the Rangers would appear when needed and then return to their homes and jobs once the trouble was *alleviated*.

In 1835, just prior to the Texas Revolution, the "Corps of Rangers" was established to protect the citizens from intruders and threats; those threats of course included the Mexican Army. Commanded by R.M. "Three-legged Willie" Williamson, the volunteers were paid only $1.25 per day. Once the revolution began, these rangers helped the Texas Army both in the retreat of citizens during the Runaway Scrape, and in service as scouts and spies to bring *intelligence* from the Mexican Army back to Houston and the Texians.

Probably one of the best-known Rangers was a captain named John Coffee "Jack" Hays. Hays purchased a newly manufactured Colt *revolver*, which became a popular weapon among the Rangers because it could shoot five rounds before the Ranger was forced to pause and reload. Other brave and famous Rangers during this era included Big Foot Wallace and Samuel H. Walker, whose suggested improvements resulted in Colt's even more powerful six shooter.

After Texas achieved statehood and the Mexican-American war began, the Texas Rangers fought bravely alongside the U.S. troops. In fact, the Rangers were sometimes called "Los Diablos Tejanos" (the Texas Devils) by Mexican soldiers because they were known to fight so fiercely.

The Rangers continued protecting Texans during the Civil War. Since many men had to leave the state to fight in the war, the "Regiment of Rangers" helped guard the frontier and families who remained at home.

Following the Civil War, the Rangers continued their protection of Texas citizens, especially from the lawlessness of the Old West. In 1874, congress established two groups within the rangers: the "Frontier Battalion" and the "Special Forces." These Rangers were responsible for capturing train robbers, cattle thieves, *lynch mobs*, and other outlaws. They were viewed as men responsible for taking care of troubles with means beyond local law enforcement. As Texas moved into the 20th century, the Rangers continued to protect citizens from *bandits*, Mexican *raids*, *bootleggers*, and the violence and unruliness associated with new oil boomtowns. Famous criminals like Bonnie and Clyde and Sam Bass had their lawbreaking careers ended by Texas Rangers.

Did You Know?

Legend has it the phrase "One Riot, One Ranger" comes from the story of an illegal heavyweight prize fight set to take place in Dallas. The mayor met Captain "Bill" McDonald, sent to stop the fight, at the train station and asked him where the other Rangers were.

Captain McDonald replied, "Ain't I enough?"

During the 1930s, a new Texas Department of Public Safety law enforcement agency was established. The Texas Rangers continued under their *jurisdiction* and their numbers were reduced, but now the Rangers had access to modern crime labs and better systems of communication. The Rangers still exist today and are responsible for investigating major *felony* crimes and cattle theft. Seven companies share the 134 commissioned Rangers.

Trouble Brewing
Between the North and the South

Just about the time the Mexican-American War ended and the Treaty of Guadalupe Hidalgo was signed, something very exciting was discovered out west in California—gold!

As news spread, people from all over the world flocked to California in hopes of striking it rich. The population of California grew, and soon there were enough inhabitants to apply for admission into the Union. In 1850, Californians asked to be annexed—but as a free state, with no slavery allowed. Of course, cotton planters were unhappy with this arrangement. They wanted to be able to move to this new land and bring along slaves to help them farm.

At just about the same time, the United States purchased sixty-seven million acres of Texas's land. In return, the U.S. took on ten million dollars of Texas debt. This deal was just one part of what is known as the Compromise of 1850. The northwestern boundary of Texas we know today was established after the U.S. purchase of Texas land which lay in today's New Mexico, Oklahoma, Kansas, Colorado, and Wyoming. The Compromise of 1850 also admitted California as a free state (with the same boundaries we see today). Utah and New Mexico Territories were allowed to decide for themselves whether or not to allow slavery, slave trade was banned in the District of Columbia, and the Fugitive Slave Law was enacted: even citizens of free states were required to return escaped slaves to their masters.

Now the question of slavery and states' rights became very important, especially to those Southerners who depended on slaves to help them run their plantations. Some people even wanted to protect their way of life and the ability to own slaves by withdrawing from the United States, forming their own country and government along with other slave states in the South. Those who wanted to break away, or secede, from the Union were known as *secessionists*.

A small group of Texans, including Sam Houston, wanted to protect their state's freedom and yet remain a part the Union, fighting for their rights through the Constitution. Those who didn't want their state to secede from the U.S. were known as *Unionists*.

Sam Houston, having served in the U.S. Senate for thirteen years, was elected Governor of Texas in 1859. He worried Texas would be in grave danger if it joined the secessionists and left the Union. He felt certain a war would be the result, and feared the North, with greater resources, would destroy his beloved state and its southern neighbors.

When Abraham Lincoln was elected president in 1860, some of the states who threatened to secede did just that—including South Carolina, Mississippi, Florida, Alabama, Georgia, and Louisiana. Houston appealed to the Texas legislature and citizens to remain in the Union. He even called a special session of the legislature to discuss the issue, but the excitement of secession had spread and he was unable to change the legislators' minds. Delegates to the Texas Secession Convention adopted the Ordinance of Secession on January 28th, 1861. This *ordinance* (local law) accused the United States of using its power to "strike down the interest and prosperity of the people of Texas."

The delegates also decided to let Texas citizens vote on secession, which they did on February 23rd, 1861. Texans overwhelmingly supported secession, and so Texas left the Union and the United States of America. The seven states which seceded were soon joined by Virginia, Arkansas, Tennessee, and North Carolina, forming the Confederate States of America.

The Texas Secession Convention also ordered state officials to take an oath of allegiance to the Confederacy. Governor Sam Houston, *distraught* and unable to support the *impending* danger associated with Texas joining the Confederacy, refused. Houston was removed from office and was

THE UNION

The United States
of America

PRESIDENT ABRAHAM LINCOLN

GENERAL ULYSSES S. GRANT

The States:
Maine, New Hampshire, Vermont,
Massachusetts, Connecticut, Rhode Island,
New York, Pennsylvania, New Jersey,
Ohio, Indiana, Michigan, Illinois, Iowa,
Wisconsin, Minnesota, Kansas, California,
Nevada, and Oregon.
Some also include Kentucky, Missouri,
Delaware, and Maryland—border states that
did not secede, but also refused to give up
slavery.

Abraham Lincoln: Anthony Berger, photographer, c1864 Feb.9
Courtesy of Library of Congress.
*General Ulysses S. Grant at his headquarters in Cold Harbor,
Virginia*, c1864: Courtesy of Library of Congress.

THE CONFEDERACY

The Confederate States
of America

PRESIDENT JEFFERSON DAVIS

GENERAL ROBERT E. LEE

The States:
South Carolina, Mississippi,
Florida, Alabama,
Georgia, Louisiana,
Texas, Virginia, Arkansas,
North Carolina,
Tennessee

Jefferson Davis: Photograph by Mathew B. Brady, c1858-60
Courtesy of Library of Congress.
Robert E. Lee: A.S. Seer's Litho Print, c1882 June 22
Courtesy of Library of Congress.

replaced by Lieutenant Governor Edward Clark.

The new president, Abraham Lincoln, did not believe in slavery. He also did not believe any state had the right to secede from the United States of America. He told the South he would do whatever he needed and at whatever cost to preserve the Union.

Civil War!

Soon the Confederacy began seizing U.S. garrisons and supplies which lay within its boundaries. The United States troops stationed in one of those forts, Fort Sumter (in Charleston, South Carolina), refused to leave. Confederate troops began firing on the Union soldiers April 12th, 1861.

The Civil War had begun.

Confederate President Jefferson Davis called for volunteers to join the army. It became clear more soldiers would be needed, so the Conscription Act of 1862 was passed requiring young men between the ages of 18 and 35 to *enroll* in military service (later, the age range was extended to men between 17 and 50). Of the 90,000 Texans who joined the Confederate Army, most served along the Texas coast and in the surrounding states, and about one-third served east of the Mississippi River. Many Texans became officers during the war, including Albert Sidney Johnston. Johnston led troops in Tennessee and was the second highest-ranking general in the Confederate Army.

Not every Texan supported the Confederate cause, however. Some Texans remained Unionists and joined the Union Army. Others left Texas or hid within the state, risking arrest or even death if they were caught.

The Confederate Army began to capture U.S. forts and *arsenals* within their territory, even prior to the attack on Fort Sumter. In Texas, the Confederates seized the federal post in San Antonio in February of 1861, and other forts to the west quickly surrendered. Union soldiers were allowed to leave Texas up until the attack on Fort Sumter. Afterwards, Union soldiers who survived battles in Texas were taken prisoner.

Battle For Galveston
October 1862 - January 1863

The location of Texas caused a problem for the Union: it provided an important port for supplies. Thus, the Union Navy attempted to blockade Texas ports to keep supplies from coming in and going out. However, Texas was still able to trade cotton with Europe, *bypassing* the ports and transporting the cotton across Mexico and receiving supplies from Europe in return.

Galveston, Texas's busiest seaport, was one of the ports targeted by the Union Navy. Union soldiers captured Galveston Island in October of 1862. General John B. Magruder was assigned by the Confederate Army to retake Galveston. He loaded two steamers, the *Bayou City* and the *Neptune*, with guns and *cotton bales* for protection. The boats sailed down from Houston by way of Buffalo Bayou and attacked Union ships in Galveston harbor. In addition, Confederate troops marched across the railroad bridge from the mainland to the island to attack Union soldiers stationed there. The Confederates quickly and successfully took back Galveston on January 1st, 1863.

Although Union troops were no longer in control of Galveston, they continued to blockade the port with their ships. Confederate ships (such as the *Denbigh*), known as *blockade runners*, slipped through these blockades and continued to bring important supplies to Texas.

Soldier in Confederate lookout tower at Bolivar Point: c1863-64.
Courtesy of Library of Congress.

The Battle of Sabine Pass
September 8, 1863

When the first Union invasion of Texas failed at Galveston, another attempt was made to attack within the state later that year. Union ships with four *gunboats* and 4,000 soldiers, led by Major General William B. Franklin, sailed up the Sabine River. Franklin's goal was to capture Houston and Beaumont after marching across land from Sabine Pass.

To reach Sabine Pass, the Union troops would have to sail by the Confederate-held Fort Griffin, where forty-seven soldiers were stationed under Dick Dowling. Fort Griffin was located not far from today's Port Arthur, close to where the Sabine River meets the Gulf of Mexico (not to be confused with the cavalry Fort Griffin found in Albany, Texas). As the Union ships traveled near the fort, the Confederates began to shoot and a battle commenced. Dowling and his Davis Guards captured two ships and took 350 Union soldiers prisoner. General Franklin and the rest of the Union troops turned and retreated to New Orleans. The Fort Griffin soldiers were awarded medals for their courage in battle: a clash which kept the Union armies from launching a major *campaign* against Texas.

Battle Near Brownsville
November 3, 1863

With the Gulf Coast under a Union blockade, Texas traders turned to Matamoros, Mexico, using foreign ships to transport cotton to Europe. Brownsville (just across the border from Matamoros and near the mouth of the Rio Grande River) became an important part of an overland supply line as well. Union leaders realized the importance of continuing down the coast and on to the Rio Grande River, taking over any ports along the way. During this campaign, Union forces at one time or another bombarded and/or occupied other coastal towns including Sabine City, Matagorda, Velasco, Port Lavaca, Indianola, St. Joseph's Island, Mustang Island, Corpus Christi, Brazos Santiago, and Point Isabel.

To cut off the supply center, Union troops then invaded and took over Brownsville and Fort Brown, which was then occupied by only 150 Confederate soldiers. Outnumbered, the Confederate troops evacuated Brownsville and abandoned the fort, burning supplies, cotton, and explosives as they retreated. The Union presence caused *disruption* of the cotton trade, forcing the trade route to move up the river to Laredo and Eagle Pass, where *teamsters* would cross the Rio Grande and travel back down the Mexican side of the river to the town of Bagdad, Mexico. Here, the cotton was placed on ships and exported to other parts of the world.

Confederate troops led by Colonel John S. (Rip) Ford eventually pushed the Union Army back, recapturing Brownsville in July of 1864. At that point, however, most of the Union forces were being diverted to the Red River Campaign. Soon, only a small number of Union soldiers remained based along the coast.

Keeping Union Forces at Bay: The Red River Campaign
Spring of 1864

In the spring of 1864, Union troops traveled up the Red River in Louisiana and toward East Texas. Richard Taylor (son of President Zachary Taylor) commanded Confederate troops sent to stop another invasion of Texas. The armies met only twenty-five miles from the Texas border in Mansfield, Louisiana. Although greatly outnumbered, the Confederates won the battle, taking over 2,000 Union Army prisoners and sending the rest of the Union forces into retreat.

Many Texans served east of the Mississippi River during the war as well. Hood's Texas Brigade and Terry's Texas Rangers (the Eighth Texas Cavalry Regiment) were two of these units known for their bravery and extended service during the war.

Life in Civil War Texas
April 1861 - May 1865

Since Texas had joined the Confederate States of America, Confederate leaders took charge of all state and local governments. Texas governors during this time included Edward Clark (who finished out Sam Houston's term), Francis R. Lubbock, and Pendleton Murrah. These governors, of course, spent a large portion of their time dealing with war issues.

Unlike many other Confederate states, Texas did not suffer great destruction since so few battles took place within the state. Farms did suffer though, as the majority of men were fighting or stationed away from home. Women, children, and slaves continued working the land. Since there was a greater need for corn and wheat to support the war effort, less cotton was grown.

MAJOR CIVIL WAR BATTLES IN TEXAS

 Battle of Galveston I:
October 4, 1862
(Union Victory)

 Battle of Galveston II:
January 1, 1863
(Confederate Victory)

 Battle of Sabine Pass:
September 8, 1863
(Confederate Victory)

Battle of Palmito Ranch:
May 12-13, 1865
(Confederate Victory)

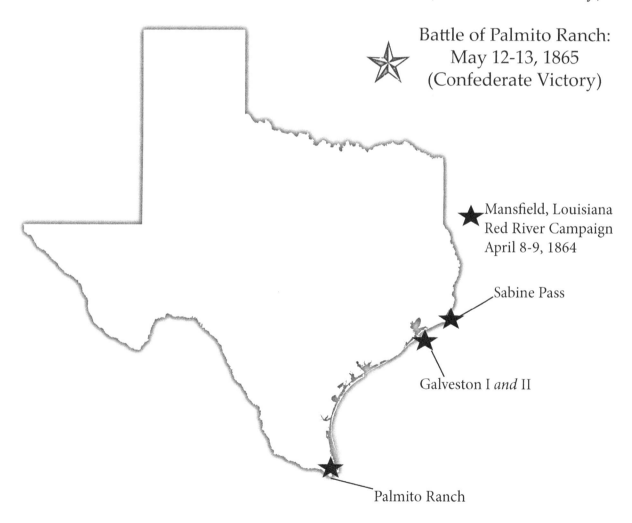

Mansfield, Louisiana
Red River Campaign
April 8-9, 1864

Sabine Pass

Galveston I *and* II

Palmito Ranch

Factories producing cannons, ammunition, and other supplies were built in Texas. Ladies supported the troops by sewing uniforms, while others took over traditional men's jobs, such as shopkeepers and drivers. Southerners were unable to purchase garments normally shipped from the Northern states, so clothing was fashioned from a homemade fabric called *homespun*. Southerners were also unable to purchase coffee and tea, so substitute drinks made of peanuts, sweet potatoes, and corn were consumed instead. Other scarce items during the war included cooking ingredients, paper, medicine, and hospital supplies.

The Civil War is Over
May, 1865

As Sam Houston predicted, the Union Army was at an *advantage* with more resources and manpower provided by the North. After four years of fighting, Confederate General Robert E. Lee surrendered to General Ulysses S. Grant at Appomattox, Virginia, on April 9th, 1865.

News of the surrender took a long time to reach Texas, and one final battle was yet to take place. Union troops, attempting to invade the mainland from Brazos Island, attacked near Brownsville at Palmito Ranch on May 13th, 1865. John S. Ford and his Confederate soldiers battled and captured the invading Union Army, who then informed the Texas troops that Lee had surrendered a month earlier. Ironically, the North won the war, but the final battle of the Civil War was won in Texas by the South.

The governor and other state officials heard of the surrender and quickly escaped to Mexico in June of 1865, leaving Texas without a government for a short time. The new U.S. President Andrew Johnson appointed a provisional (temporary) Texas governor, and the state prepared to make changes to rejoin the Union.

The Civil War was a long and bloody war,

Non-commissioned officers, 19th Iowa Infantry, exchange prisoners from Camp Ford, Texas.
Courtesy of Library of Congress.

devastating families in both the North and the South. A total of over 600,000 soldiers died, with much land and property destroyed. However, the Union had been preserved and slavery ended. Even before the war was over, President Lincoln had issued the Emancipation Proclamation, freeing the slaves of the Confederate states. This freedom would be *enforced*. The nation was soon shocked when Lincoln was assassinated by John Wilkes Booth, only five days after Lee's surrender. Lincoln would not live to see the Thirteenth Amendment (the Constitutional amendment which abolished slavery) ratified.

Reconstruction After the War
1865-1874

The war was over. Slaves were free. Much of the South had been destroyed during the war. How would it rebuild? Where would the newly-freed African Americans work and find housing? What rights would these new citizens have? How could the South recover financially? Many questions were left unanswered.

Since the states who seceded had removed themselves from the Union, there needed to be a way to bring them back once the war was over. The return to the Union would have to be gradual, and these states would need to fulfill many requirements before returning to the United States. This period of time is called *Reconstruction*.

First, Union troops were stationed in all of the Southern states following the war. About 50,000 Union soldiers were sent to Texas, some to the larger towns and some to guard the border of Mexico. The well-known Brigadier General George A. Custer and his troops were assigned to the capital, Austin.

General Gordon Granger and his troops were the first to arrive in Texas at Galveston on June 19th, 1865. Granger issued a *proclamation* announcing slaves were now free, noting "the connection heretofore existing between them becomes that between employer and free laborer. The freedmen are advised to remain at their present homes and work for wages." This was the first the slaves in Texas had heard of their emancipation, and celebrations filled the streets of Galveston. Even

112

today, descendants remember and again celebrate this joyous occasion known as *Juneteenth*.

Although Lincoln did not live to carry out Reconstruction, he had hoped to quickly bring the Southern states back to the Union, "with malice toward none, with charity for all." After Lincoln's *assassination*, Andrew Johnson became president and was faced with this task. He set up provisional governments in each of the Southern states, which would stay in place until the state re-entered the Union. Johnson required these states *outlaw* slavery and cancel their Ordinance of Secession. Men who wished to vote would have to take an oath of allegiance to the United States. Each state would also need to write a new constitution and once again elect representatives.

President Johnson appointed Andrew J. Hamilton as the Texas provisional governor. A federal agency called the Freedman's Bureau was created to manage land seized during the war and to help African Americans in the South adjust to their new freedom. The Bureau worked to help people find jobs, as well as feed and clothe those in need. The agency also defended civil rights in court and opened the first public schools for African American children.

Texas began to meet the requirements for return to the Union. Many men took the oath of allegiance, new officers were elected, and a new constitution was written and ratified which abolished slavery within the state and provided schools and a few other rights to African Americans.

James W. Throckmorton, a former officer of the Confederacy, was elected governor. In fact, most of the representatives elected were former secessionists. Many restrictions were still placed on African Americans throughout the South, although Texas was not as strict as some of the other Southern states. Former slaves were not allowed to vote, serve on juries, testify in court against white defendants, and were restricted in the jobs they could hold. Furthermore, Texas refused to ratify the Thirteenth Amendment (abolishing slavery) and the Fourteenth Amendment (granting citizenship to former slaves) to the U.S. Constitution.

New Rules For Statehood

The Republicans in the United States Congress were unhappy with Johnson's requirements for states re-entering the Union. In 1866, Republican representatives gained control of both the House of Representatives and the Senate in Washington, D.C. Now the Republicans could override the president if he vetoed legislation. President Johnson strongly disagreed with the "Radical Republicans"and battled them over these requirements. In fact, the House of Representatives even voted to *impeach* Johnson for *misconduct* in office when he wouldn't go along with their program, but they were unable to *convict* the president.

> ### Did You Know?
> Only two U.S. presidents have successfully been impeached: Andrew Johnson and Bill Clinton. Impeachment means that formal charges have been brought against a civil officer of the government. The House of Representatives initiates the procedure by impeaching the office holder. The Senate is responsible for trying the impeached person. If the officer is convicted, he/she is removed from office. In both Johnson and Clinton's cases, the presidents were acquitted by the Senate and completed their terms of office.

Johnson could not overcome the strength of Congress, and the rules and requirements for readmission changed. Now the Southern states were divided into five districts, which would be ruled by the military until the new requirements were met. Texas and Louisiana were commanded by Major General Philip Sheridan.

Each state would be required to adopt new constitutions allowing African American men to vote and hold office. States were also required to ratify the Fourteenth and Fifteenth Amendments, and could no longer allow the "Black Codes" restricting the rights of former slaves. If a white man wished to vote, he had to take the Ironclad Oath, which guaranteed he had not served in or assisted the Confederate Army during the war.

In Texas, General Sheridan removed Governor Throckmorton from office and appointed Elisha M. Pease in his place. Other leaders who were not known to be supportive of the Radical Republican plan were replaced as well.

Although the new requirements to vote eliminated many Texans, those who were still considered qualified elected delegates (including some African Americans) to a new convention in 1868. Here, they completed the new Constitution of 1869. This constitution guaranteed the right to vote regardless of race or color, support for public education, protection of public lands, more rights for African Americans, and more power to the governor and legislature. A new governor, Edmund J. Davis, was elected along with a new legislature (also including African American representatives). Texans also ratified the Fourteenth and Fifteenth Amendments to the U.S. Constitution.

Finally, on March 30th, 1870, Reconstruction ended in Texas by a proclamation from the U.S. President, Ulysses S. Grant. The rest of the original Confederate states also met the requirements and were readmitted to the Union by the end of the year.

Texas After Reconstruction

Governor Davis was a strong believer in a powerful government. Taxes had to be raised to meet the extra expense of more law enforcement and public education. The state's debt increased with improved roads, new forts, and new schools, where attendance was now required.

In 1873 another election was held, and Democrat Richard Coke (once a Confederate officer) was elected governor. He was supported by those who wanted to see stronger states' rights and the expansion of railroads and industry in Texas. After some argument about whether the election was constitutional, Davis finally cleared out his office and Coke officially became governor in 1874.

Unit Nine:
COWBOYS AND INDIANS

Every story in history is about change. Changes in ideas, changes in people, changes in countries and laws. After the Civil War, big changes were in store for Texas and the rest of the country. These changes meant more freedom for some, and less freedom for others.

Former slaves could now move freely and own land and businesses. However, increased settlement to the west meant less freedom for the Native Americans who once roamed and hunted across the plains.

The cattle business expanded during this period, leading to the growth of cattle ranches and cattle drives. With the advent of the railroad, these cattle drives were only around for a short period of time. Cowboys and cattle drives are popular themes in Western movies and books, and the real-life cowboys' lives were truly filled with hard work, adventure, and excitement.

Finally, changing technology in the last part of the nineteenth century meant the growth of new businesses and better lives for many. What seems "old fashioned" to us today, was once the wave of the future!

Texas Native Americans
After the Civil War

Native Americans arrived in Texas many thousands of years before Spanish explorers discovered this land. We've already discussed how different tribes led different lifestyles. You'll also remember most of the Native Americans of East Texas were removed to reservations in the Indian Territory during the Republic of Texas period and early statehood.

However, the Indians that lived in the western and Panhandle regions still roamed the plains. Although U.S. soldiers tried to protect settlers in this region after Texas became a state, these military men were needed during the Civil War and were forced to leave the Anglo pioneers open to raids by Comanche, Kiowa, and other Plains Indians.

Some settlers stayed and attempted to defend themselves and their land. Others gave up and abandoned their homes and property.

Plains Indians were unhappy, and their anger was not just due to settlers moving onto their hunting grounds. As you know, many Native Americans depended on buffalo for both food and other supplies. Soon businessmen also discovered the value of the buffalo hide. After the buffalo had all but disappeared to the north in the early 1870s, mass slaughters of the beast began to take place first in Kansas, Nebraska, and Colorado, and then into the High Plains of the Texas Panhandle .

These new *buffalo hunters* would take only the hide, leaving the rest of the buffalo's body to rot. Native Americans began to lose one of the most important resources needed for their existence. While these buffalo slaughters made life more difficult for Indians of this area, the trade did result in new communities and industries related to the business.

Once the Civil War was over and their responsibilities ended, federal soldiers returned to protect this region. These troops were stationed in many towns still present today: Fredericksburg, Brackettville, Eagle Pass, Mason, San Angelo, Albany, Menard, El Paso, Fort Stockton, and Fort Davis. Unfortunately, these forts were short on supplies and located too far apart to be of assistance to each other.

During those times when soldiers and Native Americans battled, Indians at first seemed to have the advantage. *Muzzle-loading pistols* and rifles could take a full minute to reload. The Native Americans, however, could ride quickly and shoot many arrows during the time it took the enemy to reload. With the introduction of the Colt six-shot pistol, the soldiers were finally able to compete without the gap of reloading time. Of course, Native Americans also had *access* to these weapons and soon carried guns as well.

Although a peace treaty called the Medicine Lodge Treaty offered food and supplies for those who moved to reservations in Oklahoma, many Indians in West Texas refused to *comply*. Tribal leaders such as Satanta (Kiowa chief), Lone Wolf (Kiowa chief), Ten Bears (Comanche chief), Victorio (Apache chief), and the famous Quanah Parker (Comanche chief) argued that their people should and would continue to roam the plains as they had long before the settlers arrived.

As Plains Indians continued to raid, General William Tecumseh Sherman was sent by the army to West Texas. After witnessing attacks and raids by Native Americans, Sherman realized negotiations and peace treaties would never be successful. Sherman advised the government to send soldiers to the northwest portion of Texas and rid the area of Native Americans.

Colonel Ranald S. Mackenzie commanded the Fourth Cavalry Regiment and set out to locate Comanche living on the South Plains in 1871. The army was somewhat successful and the number of Comanche raids was reduced in West Texas. Other troops were posted along the Rio Grande in South Texas, where the Apache and Kickapoo were raiding settlements in both Texas and Mexico. These soldiers were able to reduce the number of Indian raids in that area as well.

Quanah Parker:
Courtesy of Library of Congress.

The Plains Indians Attack

You will recall the story of Cynthia Ann Parker. About the time Texas gained its independence from Mexico, Cynthia was kidnapped by the Comanche. After giving birth to three children, she was "recovered" by Texas Rangers and returned to members of her original family. Sadly, she was forced to leave two children behind with the tribe. One of those children was named Quanah. This young man grew up to become a great warrior and chief.

As a Comanche, Quanah Parker was angered by the buffalo hunters and led a group of warriors in the attack of an Anglo buffalo hunter camp in June 1874 at Adobe Walls (near today's Borger and the Canadian River). The hunters defended themselves with their guns, frustrating the Native Americans. Other attacks followed in West Texas settlements, with Indians from Oklahoma reservations joining in the battles. Many Anglo settlers were attacked and killed over the next two months.

As a large group of warriors gathered in the Panhandle canyons and valleys, a larger group of U.S. soldiers approached to attack in August of 1874 and continued through the following spring. This search for Native Americans still living in the area and preparing for war became known as the Red River Campaign (not to be confused with the Red River Campaign during the Civil War). Colonel Mackenzie and his soldiers, along with Major John B. Jones and the Texas Rangers' Frontier Battalion, participated in these battles.

During the Battle of Palo Duro Canyon, Colonel Mackenzie and his Fourth Cavalry set fire to Comanche, Kiowa, and Cheyenne villages located deep in the canyon. Horses, food, and supplies were captured, leaving these tribes without daily necessities.

Eventually, most of the tribes moved towards reservations. The last Comanche bands, along with Quanah Parker, surrendered in June of 1875. Although originally a fierce warrior, Quanah Parker ultimately became a *mediator* and representative for Native Americans in Washington, D.C.

Native Americans on the Rio Grande

The Red River Campaign practically emptied the plains and prairies of Central and West Texas of Native Americans. Raiding by the Kickapoo and Apache, however, continued along the Mexican border and the Rio Grande. Mackenzie and his men moved to South Texas to help protect the region, and along with Mexican units, eventually stopped the Kickapoo attacks.

However, Apache warriors led by Chief Victorio still raided the area. Colonel Benjamin H. Grierson and his African American soldiers were assigned to handle the fierce combatants. These particular troops stationed on the frontier were well-known for their battle skills; in fact, Native Americans named these men *"buffalo soldiers,"* a name of respect in recognition of the soldiers' abilities.

Grierson and his men tracked the Apache into the Big Bend region of far West Texas. They pursued the warriors over the Rio Grande, where Mexican troops cornered and battled the Indians, killing Chief Victorio. After this 1880 battle, the Apache no longer posed a significant problem in Texas.

As the Texas Native Americans surrendered and moved to reservations or other territories, more Anglo settlers moved to Texas from the east. Although no longer needed for protection from Indian raids, settlements were sometimes established around the forts, including Brackettville and San Angelo. Fear of Native Americans no longer stopped settlers from moving west, and towns grew quickly. Wichita Falls, Vernon, Abilene, Sweetwater, and Colorado City developed within a short period of time.

Cattle Business *and* Ranching

Cattle are not native to Texas. The early Spanish explorers and settlers brought them from Europe during the 1500s and 1600s. Although many were *corralled* and raised for food and leather, other cows escaped and became wild cattle on the open range. The cattle brought to Texas from Spain were closely related to what would eventually be bred as *Texas longhorns*. Cattle ranches were developed along rivers where there was plenty of water and grass. The Spanish cattle grazed on *open range* land (public land), and *vaqueros* (cowboys)

were in charge of herding, roping, and *branding* the cows with a hot iron to signify who owned each particular cow. Wild horses called *mustangs* (also descendants of horses brought by the early Spaniards) were *lassoed* and trained as ranch horses.

As time passed and settlers from the United States moved to Texas and built ranches, these new ranchers began to use the Spanish and Mexican ranching and cowboy techniques familiar to us  today. Many of these early ranches were developed in South Texas between the Nueces and Colorado Rivers in the late 1700s and early 1800s. At that time, the cattle hide and tallow (fat) were the most valuable parts because they could be shipped easily. Beef was also valuable, but cattle would need to be driven east to find a market. In the South, cattle were valued at four dollars a head, but folks in the North and East would pay ten times that amount.

Huge ranches developed in South Texas. Some of the largest ranches were owned by Richard King (the famous King Ranch south of the Nueces River), Charles Goodnight and John Adair (the JA Ranch in Palo Duro Canyon), Thomas Bugbee (the Shoe Bar Ranch in the southeastern Panhandle), and H.H. Campbell (the Matador Ranch east of the High Plains).

Sheep ranches appeared in South Texas as well. When the need for wool grew after the Civil War, even more sheep ranchers from the northern U.S. and Europe settled in Texas. Unfortunately, these sheep ranchers did not get along with either the cattle ranchers or farmers; the sheep ate the grass needed by cattle ranchers and sometimes destroyed farmers' crops as they roamed across their land.

These issues led to even more fencing of both ranchers' and farmers' lands. The invention of the *barbed wire fence* was important to both of these professions. The sharp barbs twisted along the wire fencing did not harm the animals, but instead kept them enclosed (and out of farmers' crops). Unfortunately, these fences sometimes caused problems when a fence line was set within a neighboring rancher or farmer's property, leading to wire-cutting wars between the property owners and ranchers who used the open country as *rangeland* for their animals. Eventually, this fence cutting became a felony crime, and by the mid-1800s, most ranches and farmlands were fenced in South and Central Texas. In addition, *windmills* were developed to bring water directly from the ground, so cattle wouldn't have to be driven to other sources of water.

An increasing number of cattle ranches meant a *surplus* of cattle, and the supply eventually became greater than the demand. This, in addition to drought, blizzards, and overgrazing of rangelands, led to the *decline* of the ranching industry. Many ranchers went out of business or divided and sold their ranches.

New breeds of cattle, such as Angus, Brahman, and Shorthorn, were developed to replace the longhorn. Although many ranches closed, some of the larger ranches continued successfully: the King Ranch, 6666, the Matador, and the Waggoner Ranch, to name a few.

The Cow Boy: J.C.H. Grabill, photographer
Courtesy of Library of Congress.

Cowboy Life

Let's return to our discussion of the cowboy. Before the railroad came to Texas, trails were developed to drive cattle from the ranch to railroad towns. Upon reaching their destination, the cows were loaded onto trains and taken to *stockyards* (holding pens) in major cities. About twelve cowboys would move a herd of approximately 2,000 cows north during the spring.

Early *drovers* (cowboys) used the Sedalia or Shawnee Trail to drive cattle from Texas to Sedalia, Missouri. However, this angered farmers, whose fields were often trampled by cattle driven across their land, and they began to put up fences to protect their crops.

Eventually, the railroads moved further west, with towns along the way which could accommodate these cowboys and cattle drives. The new Chisolm Trail was located west of the earlier trail, bypassing Missouri. This popular trail started in South Texas, then ran through Austin, Waco, Fort Worth, across the Red River, finally ending in Abilene, Kansas.

Another popular route was the Great Western Trail. This began at Kerrville (the town where the Matamoros Trail—which originated in Brownsville—met the Old Trail from Castroville), and wound its way up through Fort Griffin, across the Red River, and into Dodge City, Kansas.

If cowboys were moving cattle to New Mexico, Colorado, Wyoming, or Montana, they would travel along the Goodnight-Loving Trail. This trail followed the Concho River west, then north along the Pecos River to Colorado.

Cowhands worked long, hard days. These men were usually young and single, and might have been of Anglo, Mexican (or Tejano), or African American heritage. If working a cattle drive, these tough men would travel ten to twelve miles a day, driving anywhere from a few hundred to several thousand head of cattle. If a cowboy was experienced, he might be granted the lead position in front of the herd. The rest of the drovers rode alongside the cattle or behind the herd. A cook drove alongside in a chuck wagon and provided meals for the cowboys. A *wrangler* (ranch hand) came along to care for the horses. At night, the drovers took turns guarding the herd from Native Americans and *rustlers* (thieves).

Eventually, these cattle drives ended. Once large numbers of cattle reached the north and east, the supply again became greater than the demand, and prices fell. In addition, barbed wire fences caused problems along the trail, not to mention problems related to new laws created to *isolate* cattle that might carry diseases.

Finally, railroads were built across Texas in the late 1800s, so the need to drive cattle cross-country became unnecessary.

The heyday of the cattle drives was over.

Major Cattle Trails

Farming

The development of windmills, the arrival of the railroad, inexpensive land, and new techniques such as *dry farming* led more and more settlers to move to Texas and set up farms after the Civil War.

Cotton was Texas's most important crop, and the new railroads meant easier access for transporting produce to markets. Other important crops grown in Texas during this time included rice, sugarcane, wheat, corn, oats, and even honey.

Not every farmer owned the land on which he farmed. After the Civil War, many of the large *plantations* which depended on slave labor were broken up and sold into smaller farms. Sometimes the landowner would rent out portions of their farm to *tenant farmers*, who would give a portion of their crop to the landowner as payment. If the tenant farmer did not own his own supplies, he would use the landowner's tools. These farmers were known as *sharecroppers*, and were paid about half the value of the crops they produced. Many of these tenant and sharecroppers were former slaves, who had farming skills but were not able to afford to purchase their own land.

Farms required many more workers, resulting in more immigration to Texas. This led to the development of more cities, schools, and businesses.

Even today, farming in Texas continues to dominate over the other states in our nation. Texas has more farms than any other state: 247,500 (that's twice the number of farms located in the second state on the list, Missouri). Even more impressive is the fact that farmland in Texas covers more than 130,400,000 acres!

Change and Progress
Close Out the Nineteenth Century

The Civil War was over. Once slavery became illegal, farmers who once relied on slave labor had to adjust. They either had to pay their workers now as *hired hands*, or size down to smaller farms. The former slaves could hold jobs and even serve as legislators. Barbed wire fences and the railroad changed the way ranchers ran their cattle business and transported the stock to market. Most Native Americans had moved to reservations, and farming techniques and tools had improved. This resulted in more settlers moving and farming out West. A growing population meant more money for the state, but it also meant a greater number of needs and concerns.

As you remember, the Republicans (known as the Radical Republicans at that time) held most of the leadership positions in Texas following the Civil War. Governor Davis believed in a strong and powerful government, and was defeated in 1874 by Richard Coke, a Democrat. Democrats during this time favored states' rights and less government. They were unhappy with the Constitution of 1869, written by the Republicans, and decided to write a new constitution.

Put into effect, the Constitution of 1876 limited the power of the government. It took away some of the governor's powers, set the meeting of the state legislature to just once every two years, set the length of legislators' terms, lowered state employees' salaries, encouraged lower taxes, and reduced the money *allotted* for education. Although there have been many amendments (491 amendments, at the time of this book's publication), as times and needs have changed over the many years since its ratification, this constitution is still in effect today.

It is important to recognize beliefs and *stances* of political parties have changed greatly over the years. We might hold certain assumptions about what someone believes today if they have a sign in their yard promoting Republican or Democrat candidates. However, we can't compare the beliefs of these two parties today with the Republicans and Democrats of the nineteenth century. The parties' beliefs today are not exactly opposite of those they held in the late 1800s; they are just different. Times have changed, issues have changed, and the way we see the world has changed.

Democrats, considered the more *conservative* party during that time period, fought to lower taxes and reduce spending. Although the public schools were *segregated* and African Americans still struggled for equal rights in society, progress inched forward with sixty African Americans serving as legislators and representatives to important conventions from 1868-1898. Women had still not earned the right to vote, but they slowly began entering the work force outside the home. Some women became teachers, and others became store clerks, secretaries, journalists, artists (like Elisabet Ney), and even train engineers.

Texas was in great debt after the costly Civil War. Governor Coke, and his successor Governor Oran M. Roberts, worked hard to cut back on state expenses. Finally, under Governor Roberts, the budget was balanced and Texas was no longer in debt.

In 1881, the state capitol burned. Fortunately, the new constitution already included the goal of building a new capitol. The company hired to build the capitol was paid with three million acres of Texas land, which became the XIT Ranch in the Texas Panhandle. If you visit the capitol in Austin today, you will see the beautiful red granite blocks transported from Marble Falls and built with a similar design to the U.S. Capitol. The new Texas capitol was finally finished and *dedicated* in 1888.

With a growing population, many arriving without jobs and means of support, lawmen had their hands full. The Texas Rangers and other local officers stayed busy dealing with train, stagecoach and bank robbers, feuds, horse thieves, and cattle rustlers.

Although the railroad came to Texas before the Civil War, the track was limited and progress laying track slowed and eventually stopped during the war. After Reconstruction, the railroad companies began building lines again, and soon there were connections made between Texas and other states. Cities were excited to have the railroad pass through their town, since it meant more jobs and more business in their community. In fact, cities where railroads met, such as Houston, Dallas, and Fort Worth, became very important sites for *commerce*. Some lines ran from the Gulf Coast and north, while other tracks ran east-west across the state. By 1900, railroad track covered 10,000 miles across Texas. Now travelers and goods could arrive at their destination in a fraction of the time it took to travel on horse or by foot.

Before *pavement*, roads in Texas were uneven, dusty, and sometimes during rains, very muddy. During this time period, cities began using bricks and other pavers to improve travel on the streets. Before the invention of automobiles, *streetcars* pulled by mules and horses (and later, run by electricity) provided transportation for folks traveling within town.

The first telephone in Texas was installed by A.H. Bellow, publisher of the Galveston News. By 1882,

Train and Cotton: Cotton scene in Houston and Texas Central Railway yards, Houston, Texas.
By John D. Roberts, 1904. Courtesy of Library of Congress.

many other cities had telephone service, with long distance capabilities in place by 1883. Operators running a switchboard connected callers through this old-fashioned equipment.

Before the Civil War and Reconstruction, most people in Texas worked as farmers, ranchers, or in jobs supporting those businesses. *Gristmills* which ground corn and wheat were the biggest actual industries during this time, although lumber, *textile*, brick, and other products were important to the state as well. As ranching grew after the Civil War, *meat packing* and *cottonseed oil* producing plants rose to the top. By the end of the 1800s, the lumber business became the most important Texas industry. With the advent of the railroad and the ability to transport coal, the *mining* business also *surged*.

All of this new industry created progress, but problems sometimes arose. When several businesses worked together to hold a *monopoly*, they were able to control prices and thus limit competition and *free trade*. This angered smaller business owners, who felt it was unfair competition. Farmers were frustrated as well. Many were in debt and had financial problems due to decreasing prices of cotton and other crops, caused by an oversupply of the products; this, of course, led to less demand and lower prices. Some business owners asked the government to help them, and in 1889 the legislature passed an *antitrust* law to keep businesses from creating monopolies and hurting smaller businesses.

About the same time, the U.S. Congress created the Interstate Commerce Commission, establishing rules for railroads connecting states. The Texas Railroad Commission was then established in 1891 to oversee the railroad industry in Texas. Today, the TRC continues to watch over the railroads, but it now also regulates the Texas oil industry.

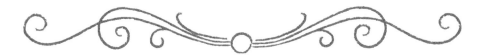

Unit Ten:
TEXAS IN THE 20ᵀᴴ CENTURY

The New Century Opens:
Texas in the 1900s

Agriculture grew, the cattle business grew, industry grew, and technology grew. Railroads expanded throughout the state, and communication improved with the telegraph and eventually telephones.

During this exciting time of change, tragedy struck.

Galveston was devastated by a monstrous hurricane on September 8ᵗʰ, 1900. Over 6,000 Galveston citizens were killed over the twelve-hour course of the horrific storm, still known as the worst natural disaster in the history of the United States. At the time of the storm, Galveston was one of the most important cities in Texas. It was home to the earliest lights and telephone system in the state, and was considered one of the most significant ports in the country for both immigration and trade.

Although thousands lost their homes and businesses, Galveston rebuilt. A *seawall* was created along the shoreline to protect the island from future storms. Residents jacked up many of the homes still standing after the storm and pumped in fill-sand from the harbor entrance, raising the island up to 16 feet in some areas. As their ancestors before them, these tough Texans did not give up.

Unlike its early days, Texas was no longer a distant land. Now interconnected with states all over the country, the Lone Star state became a *thriving* center of trade. Soon Texas would also become a magnet for those seeking their fortune.

Galveston disaster relief party working at
Ave. P and Tremont St., c1900.
Courtesy of Library of Congress.

Man standing on portion of seawall built after
the hurricane and flood of 1900, Galveston, Texas.
Courtesy of Library of Congress.

OIL!

On the heels of the Galveston tragedy came a surprise, and it would bring many new citizens, businesses, and a great deal of money to Texas. It would also change the state's economy for years to come.

Oil itself was not a surprise. People discovered and used oil for countless generations as a medicine and *lubricant*. Others used the sticky *tar* found on the coast to fix leaky boats. *Kerosene* (a product made from *petroleum*) was a valued fuel for lamps. In fact, kerosene was in such great demand, people began drilling for oil in Pennsylvania, Ohio, and West Virginia.

Texas oil was first drilled in 1866 by Lyne T. Barret near Nacogdoches. Another large well was discovered near Corsicana in 1894. A *refinery* was built in the area to process the *crude oil* into different products. Then the real excitement began! Just months after the Galveston hurricane disaster, Anthony Lucas was in charge of drilling a well south of Beaumont on a small hill called Spindletop.

On January 10th, 1901, his workers drilled over 1,000 feet into the ground. First, mud started to come out of the hole. Then . . . a huge tower of mud, gas, and oil spewed up, up, up. It took nine days to cap the well, with over 100,000 barrels flowing out every day! More wells were drilled, and by 1904, oil production in the Spindletop Oil Field had *quadrupled*.

As you can imagine, news spread like wildfire. Many men made their way to this part of Texas to find work and make their fortunes. The city of Beaumont grew rapidly with the multitude of oil businesses and workers who arrived on the scene. Refineries, pipelines, storage facilities, and *ocean tankers* provided jobs and income for citizens and newcomers. New oil fields were found and developed, while *boomtowns* grew almost overnight.

If you travel along the coast in this area today, you will see a large number of refineries, indicating the continued importance of oil to the Texas economy. Located near these oil fields, Houston became the center of oil business activity; the city provided many needed services to assist in the growth of these companies. In fact, the Houston Ship Channel was deepened to allow larger ships access to the city from the coast.

The oil boom created jobs for *support industries* as well. Lumber became a very *lucrative* business, as a great deal of wood was needed to build large *oil derricks*. Construction of additional houses and stores was also required for the many workers who had arrived on the scene.

The new railroad system made transportation of people and goods much more *efficient*. Dallas also benefitted as a major railroad center, although oil was not discovered in the area. Instead, Dallas was known as a major *retail* center, where clothing and other good were *manufactured* and exported to surrounding cities and states. "Big D" grew quickly, and became home to many other services including legal, insurance, and banking.

Oil Gusher: Texas Chief Gusher, c1919.
Courtesy of Library of Congress.

Where Do Oil and Natural Gas Come From?

It's really quite amazing. Your car is almost out of gas, and you pull up to the pump at the gas station. Within a few minutes, you've refilled your tank and now your car can transport you around the city for hours and hours.

Where does this smelly product come from, and how does it make your car or lawn mower engine work?

You might be surprised; the first stage of both oil and natural gas began in ancient times as tiny *microscopic* plants and animals living in the ocean.

You have probably learned that organisms absorb energy from the sun. This energy was stored in the bodies of these sea critters and plants as *carbon molecules*. Over many, many years, the bodies of these dead *microscopic organisms* sank to the bottom of the sea. Layer after layer after layer of these bodies were packed deeper, and deeper, and deeper under the water and sediment. Heat and pressure eventually turned this former life into either oil or natural gas, depending on the original creature or plant and its burial depth. Oil and gas are lighter than water and will always rise to the top. Since the surrounding rock often had tiny little holes, the resulting oil or natural gas would seep through these holes, trying to get to the surface, but would sometimes get trapped under more layers of rock or clay.

Today, when drillers search for oil and natural gas, they use current technology and tools to locate large trapped pockets, and then drill to reach these hidden treasures.

Drilling rigs are set up, and companies drill deep inside the earth and beneath the ocean floor to locate the oil and gas *reservoirs* (some of these ancient seas have dried up, so drilling occurs on dry land as well as under the water). Once the oil and gas wells are drilled, the product is produced out of the ground and carried by pipeline, rail, or ships to a refinery. The refineries (you'll see many of these along the Texas coast) can change the oil or gas into different products (jet fuel, gasoline, and *diesel fuel*) and can also send the fuel to factories and power plants where it is burned to make electricity.

You might be surprised to know plastics are made from natural gas and crude oil. Imagine our lives without plastic. This product has dramatically changed the lives of people throughout the world, from packaging to medical devices. Techniques, such as imaging used in seeking oil wells, have been modified for use in medical imaging. The ability to retrieve oil and gas has allowed our world to

West Texas Oil Pump

progress technologically and made our everyday activities easier and more efficient.

Since oil, natural gas, and coal are products of ancient life, they are called *"fossil fuels."* These fossil fuels are also considered *non-renewable energy* forms, meaning once the fuel is pumped (or mined, in the case of coal) and used, it cannot be replaced. Scientists have been experimenting with other forms of *renewable* energy production, such as *solar* and wind energy, for over one hundred years. These alternatives are used today and may help to sustain us in the future when the fossil fuels are no longer available.

Changes For Women and Minorities

After the Civil War and the establishment of the Fifteenth Amendment, African American men were finally allowed to participate in the election process. However, women still did not have the right to vote. They watched men making decisions all around them, and were ready to have their say in how their city, state, and country were being run. The first convention to support women's voting rights was actually held in 1848 in New York, but it would be many years before change would occur.

Throughout the rest of the 1800s, more organizations were established to support what was called *Women's Suffrage.* By 1910, five states allowed women to vote. In Texas, women made a deal with the governor, William P. Hobby, in 1918. The women promised to support Hobby's re-election if he would sign a bill granting women the right to vote in Texas *primaries* (elections held by a political party to select their candidate who would later run in the *general election*). Hobby signed the bill, the women fulfilled their promise, and they were able to vote (at least in the primary elections) for the very first time.

Eventually, women's suffrage organizations started to come together across the nation to campaign for the right to vote. Finally, in 1920, the 19th Amendment was ratified and all American women were given full voting rights. During World War II, women further proved to the country they were patriotic citizens and deserved the right to participate beyond their traditional roles.

Although African Americans had been granted the right to vote with the Fifteenth Amendment and quite a few black citizens served in government positions and actively participated in politics following Reconstruction, progress slowed around the turn of the century. Southern states began passing laws which discriminated against African Americans. These "Jim Crow" laws required public facilities be *segregated*, and demanded blacks sit in the back of streetcars and theatres, as well as use separate water fountains and restrooms. A *poll tax* was adopted in Texas through a constitutional amendment in 1902, requiring voters to pay $1.50 prior to voting. This charge ensured many minorities would be unable to afford to vote. In fact, the Democratic Party restricted their primary elections to only white voters.

Many African Americans began leaving agricultural life on the farm and moved to cities. There, within segregated communities, blacks began to establish businesses and services for their neighborhoods. Unfortunately, Texas universities only allowed the *enrollment* of white students, so often minorities had to leave the state to obtain training in their chosen fields. As a result, multiple black individuals and families chose to move to cities in the North, where there were more opportunities for training and jobs.

During the Mexican Revolution of 1910-1920, numerous refugees fled over the border of Mexico into Texas to escape the *chaos* of their home country. A military dictator named Victoriano Huerta became the president of Mexico, and revolutionary leaders (such as Emiliano Zapata and Pancho Villa) gathered Mexican fighters to oppose this new dictator. Soon the revolutionaries began fighting each other; Americans were murdered in Mexico, and raids and clashes were rampant along the border. Tensions increased when the United States stepped in to protect its citizens.

The Mexican immigrants who moved to Texas often worked on farms as they began their lives in a new country. There were sometimes conflicts between the newly arrived immigrants and the established Texans; many were based on fears and rumors of Mexican revolutionary leaders, bandits, and on age-old distrust.

Texas Rangers, state militia, and Mexican military patrolled along the Rio Grande to protect citizens in the area. Sadly, many Texans, Mexicans, and Mexican Americans died in conflicts near the border during this time.

The poll tax which kept African Americans from voting in large numbers had the same effect on newly arrived Mexican Americans. These families also faced *discrimination* and lived in separate neighborhoods from their Anglo and African American fellow citizens.

The *pendulum* swings back and forth. Civil rights are sometimes slow to be accepted by all: Texas and the rest of the country suffered the growing pains which come with change. A few steps forward, then one step back. In time, acceptance and progress in rights for all improved . . . and are continuing to improve today.

Help Us to Win the Vote: Suffragist, "Mrs. Suffern" 1914.
Courtesy of Library of Congress.

WORLD WAR ONE

In 1914, World War I (also known as the Great War) began. Relations were tense between European countries for many reasons. Competition existed as each attempted to expand its power and land through *imperialism*. Some countries made secret *alliances* with each other, and a great deal of distrust existed among the European nations. It would take just one incident to be the spark which would turn this fuel into fire.

Archduke Ferdinand (*heir* to the throne of Austria-Hungary) was assassinated in Sarajevo. Austria-Hungary believed Serbia was to blame for the assassination, and when Serbia did not respond to their demands, Austria-Hungary declared war. Russia began to prepare troops to defend Serbia. Soon Germany (an ally of Austria-Hungary) declared war on Russia and France, and then invaded Belgium. In return, Britain declared war on Germany.

With this mix of countries declaring alliances and hostilities, World War I began.

At first, America was *neutral* in this conflict and chose not to side with any particular country. However, German submarines and cruisers attacked ships carrying American citizens, including the *Lusitania*. Then a secret message—known as the Zimmerman Telegram—from a German *diplomat* to the German ambassador to Mexico was intercepted by the British. This letter instructed the ambassador to create an alliance between Germany and Mexico if the U.S. entered the war. The message offered to help Mexico get back land lost to the U.S. (Texas, Arizona, and New Mexico), if Mexico would support Germany. This secret message was decoded and printed for the American public to read.

With Germany's threats and outright attack on Americans, President Woodrow Wilson requested Congress declare war on Germany. It did, joining the British, Russian, French, and Belgium forces (the Allies) against Germany, Austria, Hungary, Italy, Bulgaria, and Turkey (the Central Forces), in a war that had already been raging for almost three years.

American soldiers had to be prepared for war, so training camps and fields were established in cities throughout Texas, including Houston, Waco, Fort Worth, Galveston, Wichita Falls, Benbrook, Everman, Dallas, and San Antonio (home of Kelly Field, a flight training school). These bases served as training grounds for everything from flying and repairing airplanes, to bombing and gunnery skills.

Fort Crockett in Galveston, 1918 (World War I).
Courtesy of Library of Congress.

Over 200,000 Texans served in all branches of the military throughout the war. Participating Texas units included the 36th Division (many from this division died fighting in France) and the 90th Division from Texas and Oklahoma. A large number of African Americans from Texas served as well, although segregation still existed within the military at that time.

Choctaw Native Americans provided an interesting skill to confuse the Germans: *code talking.* They transmitted orders using their own language across wire lines. In addition, many Mexican Americans served bravely in combat and command positions.

11th School Group Consolidated PT-1 trainers, Brooks Field, Texas.
Bwmoll3/Wikimedia Commons/USGOV-PD

War is dangerous and the risks to soldiers are numerous. However, the training and experience provided to all the soldiers, regardless of their race or ethnicity, contributed to further their education. These additional skills meant a brighter future and greater opportunities for themselves and their families following the war effort.

Of course, men weren't the only participants; 450 Texas women contributed their abilities as nurses and ambulance drivers overseas. In addition to military jobs, they worked in factories and farms on the homefront, filling in for the men at war. Texans not serving on the front supported American troops through fundraising with *war bonds* and donations to the Red Cross. Citizens were also careful with food and supplies at home, *rationing* so more could be sent overseas to the soldiers.

Over sixty-five million men fought for four years in what was thought to be the "war to end all wars," with over ten million soldiers killed during the conflict. Most of the fighting occurred with each side shooting and bombing each other across trenches, and with messenger dogs often used to carry information between the trenches.

The fighting finally ended November 11th, 1918 (the eleventh hour of the eleventh day of the eleventh month). Germany admitted they would not win the war through a *general armistice* agreement (now recognized as Armistice Day). Officially, the war ended with the signing of the Treaty of Versailles in 1919.

Texas Following World War One

Although the war was devastating for countless families both in Europe and in the United States, many Texans benefitted as they provided items required for the war effort. Texas oil fields were a source of needed petroleum products. Ranchers and farmers were able to produce necessary meat, grain, leather, cotton, and wool for the troops. The large demand led to higher prices, and in their excitement many ranchers and farmers bought more land and machinery on credit—which meant they were now in debt—taking a risk prices would remain high long enough to *prosper* and pay off that debt.

Unfortunately, by 1921 the price of cotton fell *drastically*. As the price plummeted, the farmers *panicked* and grew more cotton in response. This led to an excess of unneeded cotton, so the price fell even further. This is an excellent example of *supply versus demand*. When the supply is less than the demand, prices go up; when the supply is greater than the demand, prices fall.

Many families decided to abandon their lives as farmers, tenant farmers, and sharecroppers and moved to the city. By this time, most of the homes had electricity, along with refrigerators and other household appliances, making life easier and more efficient.

Women became more active in Texas government as state legislators and lobbyists. Public schools and roads improved, and by the early 1920s, cars became common sights. During this time, radio stations began *broadcasting* throughout the state, bringing music and news into homes, keeping Americans informed and entertained.

Motion pictures (movies) became another fun pastime for citizens, along with a sport which would become a Texas favorite—football!

The Great Depression

Have you ever heard the term *"stock market"*? Larger companies can be owned by more than one or two people. Often, ownership of a company is broken down into many parts, or *shares*. If a business needs money, they might sell shares of stock (or ownership) in their company. Sometimes many different people own a share of a company. When someone buys stock (or partial ownership of a company), they have *"invested"* in that company and are now a *"shareholder,"* or a stockholder. If a company is doing well and making *profits*, then the shareholders enjoy a share in the profits. If a shareholder sells his stock when prices are higher than when he bought the share, he will make money. On the flipside, if the price of the shares goes down and the stock is worth less than when the shareholder purchased the stock, the shareholder will lose money.

The prices of stocks rise and fall many times throughout any given day, for many different reasons. The goal of a stockholder is to purchase shares, hold on to them, and then sell when the price of the share is higher than their purchase price so they can make a profit.

The stock market is the place where company shares are traded (bought and sold). In 1929, when Herbert Hoover was president, stock market prices on Wall Street (where stocks are traded in New York City), fell very quickly. Unfortunately, many investors had borrowed money to purchase their stock. When the stock market plummeted, multitudes of people who borrowed money and banks who loaned the money were financially destroyed.

That wasn't all. Businesses and factories were forced to close, which meant many employees lost their jobs. With no job or income, people could not spend money, meaning even more businesses had to close and more people lost their jobs. This domino effect caused a dark time in America.

New successful oil well drilling by *wildcatters* in the East Texas Oil Fields surprised everyone, especially at a time when many Americans were out of work and desperate for money. *Droves* of people moved to East Texas to work in the oil fields and surrounding towns, and many independents drilled small wells throughout the area. Although this sounds like a happy ending, the law of supply and demand took over. Remember what happens when supply is much greater than demand? These fields produced too much oil; a surplus of oil was left over because the demand had not changed. That, of course, meant the price of oil fell.

Like the farmers after World War One, the drillers panicked and were afraid to stop drilling, causing an even greater gap between supply and demand.

In order to break this cycle, the Texas Railroad Commission sent out an order limiting oil drilling and production. This order was ignored by many, and the Texas National Guard was sent to enforce the law. By 1935, oil production was finally under control and oil prices became more *stable*.

A similar issue with ***overproduction*** occurred in the cotton industry. Since cotton can be stored easily, farmers continued to grow the crop, resulting in large *surpluses*—and again, the price of cotton dropped due to oversupply.

Laws limiting cotton production had very little success, and few voluntarily agreed to stop growing the crop. With oil and cotton prices falling, Texans joined the rest of the country in the struggle for jobs and money during the Great Depression.

The Dust Bowl

During and after World War I, wheat was valuable. Many farmers purchased more land and equipment so they could expand their wheat production. As the price of wheat began to fall, can you guess what the wheat farmers did? Just like we've seen before, they planted even more wheat.

And you know what that means . . . the price of wheat sank!

That wasn't the only problem associated with wheat overproduction. Farmers in the High Plains had to ***plow*** under large fields of grass to plant their crop. This grass had always provided a natural protection for the top layer of soil, safeguarding it from the strong winds which blow across the plains. Tilling of the grass to prepare the soil caused this important defense from ***erosion*** to disappear.

On top of that, a severe drought meant less rain. Precipitation would naturally hold soil down in these high winds, but the lack of grass and rain left fields of loose soil . . . and huge dust storms when

Dust Bowl Farm near Dalhart, Texas. Dorothea Lange, photographer; June 1938. Courtesy of Library of Congress.

the wind blew.

Communities in the Texas Plains suffered from what became known as the Dust Bowl. Blowing dust resulted in lung illnesses, the inability to see more than twenty feet, and failing farms. Adding "insult to injury," this devastating Dust Bowl occurred during the Great Depression.

Child of migrant worker ironing in camp near Harlingen, Texas, 1939. Lee, Russell, photographer. Courtesy of Library of Congress.

People lost their land, their jobs, and sometimes their lives. Those who lost their homes often ***migrated*** across the country, looking for work wherever they could find it.

The New Deal

During this difficult time in American history, a new president was elected with hopes that he could find a way to lift the country out of its economic troubles.

Franklin D. Roosevelt received a large number of votes with his promise of a "new deal." These New Deal programs were developed and put into action through many different new government agencies. The CCC (Civilian Conservation Corps) provided jobs for men who would work on projects to help ***conserve*** the country's natural resources. The PWA (Public Works Administration) offered jobs to those who would build various ***structures*** throughout the state (such as bridges and schools), and the WPA (Works Progress Administration) was responsible for constructing projects from swimming pools to parks.

Laws were passed that ***compensated*** (or paid) farmers NOT to grow as many crops; the goal was to lessen the supply, which would increase the demand, resulting in higher prices. Farmers were also educated in the use of techniques such *alternating crops* and *windbreaks* to reduce the problems of soil erosion, an early contributor to the Dust Bowl.

Even during these difficult times, Texans continued to celebrate their heritage and history. As you travel throughout Texas, you might notice quite a few buildings constructed in 1936, the year of the state's *Centennial* anniversary of independence from Mexico. A huge celebration called the Texas Centennial Exposition was held at Fair Park in Dallas (now home of the State Fair of Texas), and the spectacular San Jacinto Monument was built on the original ground of the final battle for independence.

Miriam Ferguson served for a second term as Governor of Texas, working with President Roosevelt to provide assistance to Texas farmers and the poor in need of food. James Allred followed Ferguson as governor and is known for his reorganization of the Texas Rangers and the development of the Board of Pardons and Paroles. Finishing out the decade, the governor's office was held by a radio show host and sales manager, W. Lee O'Daniel.

Unfortunately, African Americans still experienced some difficulties in their ability to vote in the Democratic Party's election primaries. Eventually this issue would be taken to the Supreme Court, where the justices ruled all-white primaries to be unconstitutional.

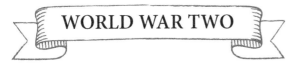

WORLD WAR TWO

As Americans struggled through the Great Depression and the Dust Bowl, other countries throughout the world also experienced *economic* difficulties. During these desperate times, several dictators rose to power to rule their countries: Adolf Hitler in Germany, Benito Mussolini in Italy, and Emperor Hirohito in Japan. Known as the Axis Powers, these three countries decided to expand their territory by taking over other countries, and made an agreement not to attack either of the other Axis countries in the process. The Axis leaders began their quest for more land with Italy's takeover of Ethiopia, Germany's invasion of Poland (with other countries soon to follow), and Japan's attack on China. At first, President Roosevelt and the United States chose to remain neutral, although they were of course concerned about the countries being attacked and provided equipment for their defense. Those nations who battled the Axis Powers became known as the chief Allied Powers: Great Britain, France, China, and the Soviet Union.

On December 7th, 1941, Americans changed their mind! Japan led a surprise attack on American soldiers, sailors, airmen, and Marines at Pearl Harbor in Hawaii. Now, this became America's war as well.

Many Texans hurriedly enlisted in all branches of the military. In fact, over 750,000 Texans served during the war: the largest percentage of any state's population enlisted in World War II. Famous Texan heroes of the war included Dwight Eisenhower (who commanded Allied forces in Europe), Doris Miller (an African American sailor who fired on Japanese pilots during the Pearl Harbor attack), Audie Murphy (who earned more medals than any American), and Oveta Culp Hobby (who directed the Women's Army Auxiliary Corps).

Advance training plane at Naval Air Base, Corpus Christi.
By Howard R. Hollem, August 1942.
Courtesy of Library of Congress.

Over one hundred military bases were located throughout Texas, including numerous Army Air Forces training airfields for pilots and aircrews, Navy air stations along the coast, and Navy pilot training in Dallas.

You might be surprised to know Texas was also home to many *prisoner of war camps*, housing over 45,000 German, Japanese, and Italian prisoners until the war ended. These prisoners were treated well and worked on farming projects during their time in the camps.

Texas was a major oil producer, and oil and petroleum products would be *vital* to win the war. Jobs again became plentiful as factories grew and workers were needed. Shipyards along the coast, airplane factories in the Dallas-Fort Worth area, and steel production near Houston provided major industrial products. A *magnesium* plant in Freeport and *synthetic rubber* plants also contributed to the war effort and aided the Texas economy.

Many Texans moved from the countryside to work in city factories during this period, and women found new roles, taking their place in factories to replace the men who served on the battlefields. Most Texans at home again carefully rationed scarce items and food and planted *"victory gardens."*

After Americans battled for four years in Europe and the Pacific, the war ended in 1945. Once it was over, many of the factories built during the war continued producing materials and other *appliances* now helpful to mainstream society. However, some of these factories and workers were no longer needed and faced closing leading to the loss of jobs. As the servicemen returned home, women who had taken their jobs during the war were now forced to find other employment or return to being full-time mothers and housewives. Many former tenant farmers lost jobs held before the war, as better technology led to farm machinery which could execute many of the tasks humans had always performed.

Veterans, who might never have furthered their education before the war, were given the opportunity to attend college through the GI Bill. America went through great changes as the country and its citizens adapted to new roles and needs.

However, peace was not yet on the horizon. Although the war between the Axis and the Allies had ended, a new threat, *communism*, created tension which would be felt for many years to come. The Soviet Union, our ally during the previous wars, became a communist dictatorship and began taking over other countries. Americans grew concerned about this dangerous spread of a *regime* which could potentially take away the freedoms of both countries and individuals. It wasn't long before this "Cold War" would actually become a real war, as communist North Korea invaded South Korea.

Texas After World War Two

The Korean War would not end with a *decisive* victory, and many Americans—and Texans—participated in battles to stop North Korea's invasion of South Korea. North Korea was supported by the Soviet Union and China, while South Korea was supported by the United States, Great Britain, and the United Nations. Since Korea had been taken over by Japan before World War II, the country was divided following Japan's loss. The Soviet Union took control of the northern half of the country (becoming communist), and the United States took control of the southern half (becoming *capitalist*). Korean leaders were chosen for both halves. These two very different forms of society did not get along, and fighting began along the border. Conflicts continued from 1950 to 1953, finally ending with a treaty. However, the treaty and war didn't resolve the troubles and differences between North and South Korea. Instead, the countries remained independent, and a two-mile *demilitarized* zone was created along the border to discourage fighting.

Dwight D. Eisenhower, 1952
Bachrach, Fabian, 1917-2010, photographer.
Courtesy of Library of Congress.

President LBJ and Lady Bird Johnson
picking wildflowers.
Frank Wolfe, White House Photo Office,
July 5, 1968. Courtesy of LBJ Library.

Lyndon B. Johnson, 1964
Courtesy of Library of Congress.

Shortly thereafter, the Vietnam War began; the communist North Vietnam versus the American-supported non-communist South Vietnam. Many Texans participated and lost their lives in this long (1955-1975), frustrating war fought in the jungles of Vietnam.

Toward the end of the Korean War, a Texan was elected President of the United States. Dwight D. Eisenhower was born in Denison, Texas, and was elected president in 1952. Beforehand, in World War Two, Eisenhower earned his place as a five star general and served as Supreme Commander of the Allied Forces. He helped negotiate a treaty to end the Korean War and, during his presidency, worked hard to ensure civil rights for all in the United States.

John F. Kennedy followed Eisenhower as president, with Texan Lyndon Baines Johnson as his vice president. Sadly, Kennedy was assassinated in 1963 by Lee Harvey Oswald while on a visit to Texas. Johnson, with his wife and Mrs. Kennedy by his side, took the oath of office immediately following Kennedy's death and became the 36th President of the United States.

President Johnson was greatly concerned about racial discrimination and the forced segregation which still existed in much of the South. Many schools and public facilities (libraries, swimming pools, and parks) were still either segregated or denied access to African Americans and other minorities. President Johnson worked with congress to pass the Civil Rights Act of 1964 and the Voting Rights Act.

Almost as famous as President Johnson was his wife, Claudia Alta "Lady Bird" Johnson. Mrs. Johnson wanted to keep America beautiful, and worked for legislation to promote the planting of wildflowers along Texas highways. Now, over 30,000 pounds of wildflower seed are sown each year by the state. Many people think of "Lady Bird" every time they enjoy the bluebonnets which delight Texas drivers each spring.

Cities and Highways

Have you ever driven on the big highway (I-45) connecting Dallas with Houston and Galveston? Or on the big highways (I-30 and I-20) that connect

Highway Sign: by Carol M. Highsmith. Courtesy of Library of Congress.

Dallas and Fort Worth? If you stay on I-20, it will take you all the way to Louisiana or New Mexico. Or how about I-10, which enters Texas at El Paso and passes through San Antonio and Houston, exiting into East Texas and then through Louisiana and beyond? Highway I-35 will take you up to Oklahoma—all the way to Minnesota.

Until Eisenhower became president, long distance car travel was slow. During his term, more and more families and businesses purchased and used cars and trucks, which led to more travel between states. Many roads were only one lane each direction, and some were not even paved.

President Eisenhower experienced slow travel across the country when he served in the military, and believed a system of highways stretching all the way across the country, "*interstate*," would benefit everyone.

In response to these concerns, a new system of highways began in 1956. People could now travel east-west or north-south on one main highway, all the way across the country. Travel became faster and safer, thanks to more lanes and wider shoulders. If people worked downtown, they could live farther away and commute from home to work. This allowed many people to move to smaller towns on the outskirts of large cities. These smaller towns are called *suburbs*, and they would become the centers of new housing developments, schools, shopping areas, and entertainment. More and more people moved to the suburbs, as you can see when you look at maps of the communities surrounding large cities throughout the Texas.

During the 1950s and '60s, as transportation improved and city populations increased, science and technology also progressed. Important medical research and hospitals (such as M.D. Anderson's hospital for cancer research) found a home in Texas, and famous surgeons (including heart surgeons Doctors Michael DeBakey and Denton Cooley) devised new ways to save lives.

Radio and television had become popular

forms of entertainment, and scientists, along with Dallas company Texas Instruments, developed an alternative to the large and fragile *vacuum tubes* used in electronics. These new little *transistors* meant radios could now be *portable* and easily carried and enjoyed outside the home. This same company had an employee named Jack Kilby who invented the *"chip,"* also known as the *integrated silicon circuit.* Computers and calculators began to shrink in size, making them more usable and affordable for regular citizens.

As you remember, Americans had been concerned about the growth of communism throughout the world. The greatest *promoter* of communism, the Soviet Union, launched the first *artificial satellite* and sent the first man into space. America responded by making its own plan for future space exploration and travel, with President Kennedy's urging to have an American man on the moon by 1970.

The National Aeronautics and Space Administration (NASA) led the development of the space program, and Texas was fortunate to become the home of the Johnson Space Center, located near Houston. Americans quickly made their first trips into space and, by 1969, American astronauts landed safely on the moon.

President Kennedy speaks at Rice University about space exploration efforts. Robert Knudsen, White House Photographs. Courtesy of John F. Kennedy Presidential Library and Museum.

In the field of agriculture, improvements in technology meant fewer farmhands were required to run a successful business. Better irrigation, *fertilizers, insecticides,* and *mechanization* resulted in greater production with less manpower. In addition to ranches, the cattle industry discovered how to raise and prepare cattle for meat products through the use of *feedlots*. Since grain grows well in the High Plains, large outdoor areas were established where the cows could be fed until they were ready for slaughter and *meat processing*.

Texas and the Cold War

For many years, Americans worried about the Soviet Union and the potential spread of communism. After the end of World War II, Germany was divided into two different countries, East and West Germany. East Germany was controlled by the communist Soviet Union, while the government of West Germany was based on democratic principles. Many people left East Germany because they believed communism greatly limited their freedom. This led to the 1961 building of the Berlin Wall, which was erected to keep *defectors* from escaping the communist half of the city. Over time, leaders and circumstances changed, and the Soviet Union began to fall apart. Eventually the wall was torn down in 1989, symbolizing the end of the Cold War.

Less fear resulted in new treaties between the U.S. and the Soviet Union, reducing the number of *missiles* owned by each country. This affected Texans when *nuclear weapons plants*, along with some military bases, were no longer needed and therefore closed. The news, however, was good for Texas *geologists* and *petroleum engineers,* who now found jobs working for the former Soviet Union exploring their oil and natural gas reserves.

Trade between the U.S. and Mexico continued, with border factories built combining Mexican labor and American materials. As trade increased, companies moved and brought new businesses to Texas.

Oil remained an important Texas resource. Texas has and will continue to experience economic ups and downs, or "booms and busts," as the price of oil changes due to international and production issues. During good times, when the price of oil is up, companies prosper and more Texans are employed, who then make and spend money. Although the price of gas to fill the tank of a car is higher, these boom times are great for the petroleum industry and employees. When oil prices fall, drilling slows and people lose jobs and move away. These economic ups and downs also affect other industries and workers in Texas, including builders and banks.

Other international issues have affected Texans, although these events have occurred far from home. In 1990, the country of Iraq invaded its neighbor Kuwait, a country rich with oil. Many Texans were called to serve in a military operation called "Desert Storm" or "The Gulf War." Although this war lasted only a short time, a coalition of countries working with the U.S. successfully drove Iraq out of Kuwait.

Following the terrorist attacks of our country on 9/11, more Texans rushed to enlist in protecting the United States and others through military force in Afghanistan and Iraq. Texas continues to be an active home for military training, including four Army bases, seven Air Force bases, and four Navy bases.

Texans served in many important national positions during the last century. George H.W. Bush was the 41st President of the United States (1989-1993), and his son, George W. Bush, was the 43rd President of the United States (2001-2009). Sandra Day O'Connor was a Justice of the Supreme Court, and Vice Presidents who called Texas home included John Nance Garner (1933-1941), Lyndon B. Johnson (1961- 1963), and George H.W. Bush (1981-1989). Oveta Culp Hobby, wife of former Texas Governor William Hobby, became the first Secretary of the Department of Health, Education, and Welfare and the first director of the Women's Army Auxiliary Corps. Congresswoman Barbara Jordan was the first Southern African American woman to serve in the U.S. House of Representatives.

Great leaders have been born and raised in Texas or call it home. Will you be the next one?

Justice
Sandra Day O'Connor

Congresswoman
Barbara Jordan

Presidents
George W. and George H.W. Bush

Colonel
Oveta Culp Hobby

Oveta Culp Hobby: by Al Ravenna, 1942. Courtesy of Library of Congress.
Sandra Day O'Connor: [Between 1981 and 1983] Courtesy of Library of Congress.
Congresswoman Barbara Jordan: by Thomas J. O'Halloran, 1976. Courtesy of Library of Congress.
President George W. Bush and Former President George H. W. Bush in the Oval Office: by Eric Draper, 2001. Courtesy of National Archives.

Unit Eleven:
TEXAS GOVERNMENT TODAY

By now, you should be an expert on Texas, its history, and its heroes. Let's wrap up your Texas experience with interesting facts about the state government and constitution. This information is very important: it reflects how our state government applies to and affects YOUR life.

Some day you will pay property and sales taxes. Some day you might serve on a jury. Someday you may need to contact a *public official* for help with a problem. Our federal, state, and local governments serve their citizens, but it's important to know how the government is organized and who to contact with questions. Plus, learning about our government is a great way to see how our state's history, as well as the men and women of the past, created this wonderful state we call Texas.

Who We Are
and Where We Live

When Texans brag about being the biggest and the best, they aren't kidding! Texas is the second largest state in the nation (land-wise) and only smaller than Alaska. With about twenty-eight million citizens, our state ranks second in the nation in terms of population, with only California claiming more residents.

Of the twenty-eight million Texans, about forty percent are Caucasian, thirty-eight percent are Hispanic, twelve percent are African American, and a little over four percent are Asian (plus a small percentage American Indian or other race). With such cultural and racial diversity, many individuals consider themselves of mixed race. Of course, these numbers change daily, due in part to a quickly growing Hispanic population, brought forth by the sharing of Texas's border with Mexico. Each day in Texas, approximately 1,000 births and 489 deaths take place. With this ratio, it's no surprise the Texas population is growing by leaps and bounds!

These citizens are spread all over the great state of Texas. Texas is home to 1,215 *incorporated* cities and 254 counties. Four of these, Harris, Dallas, Tarrant, and Bexar, are so large over one million people live within each county. In fact, over half of the state's population live within eight counties: those listed above, along with the next largest counties of El Paso, Travis, Hidalgo, and Collin. Many areas in the state are growing quickly, including Dallas/Fort Worth, Austin, San Antonio, Houston, Collin County, and towns along the Texas-Mexico border.

The state's diverse population offers many different languages, cultures, foods, traditions, festivals, and holidays. Some of these cultural celebrations include Cinco de Mayo (Hispanic), Juneteenth (African American), Oktoberfest (German), Westfest (Czech), St. Patrick's Day (Irish), *crawfish* festivals (Cajun), Tet (Vietnamese holiday), and Native American *pow wows*.

You'll find many other delightful *shindigs* and performances held in every corner of the state. Enjoy the Rose Festival in Tyler, Dickens on the Strand and Mardi Gras in Galveston, and the outdoor musical at Palo Duro Canyon. *Stock shows*, rodeos, the Texas State Fair, Renaissance festivals, and even rattlesnake roundups entertain Texans.

History buffs delight in celebrations too, including Texas Independence Day (March 2), San

Photos courtesy of photographers Lauren Tenery, Sharie Dougherty, Laurie Cockerell, and Yvonne Cumberland.

136

Jacinto Day (April 21), Juneteenth Emancipation Day (June 19), American Indian Heritage Day (last weekend in September), and the "Come and Take It" festival in October. Visitors enjoy *reenactments* at several of these events, with booming cannons and actors in period costumes.

Texas Government Today *and* the Texas Constitution

As one of the United States of America, Texas functions under a system called *federalism*. Under this type of system, the powers are divided between the federal (United States) government and the state (Texas) government.

States have the power to *regulate commerce* within their borders, create public school systems, and provide a state militia. Only the United States (federal government) has the power to create money, sign treaties with other countries, and declare war. If you read the U.S. Constitution, it lists all the powers of the federal government. The Tenth Amendment then notes any powers not set aside in the Constitution for the federal government (or prohibited) are reserved for the states.

The constitution Texas operates under today was not the first law of this land. In fact, seven separate state constitutions have been written and ratified over the years. As leaders and circumstances changed, each new version addressed the needs and/or culture of the population at that time (for example, early constitutions allowed slavery). When Texas was considered part of Mexico and the Mexican Constitution of 1824, Texas was combined with Coahuila as a separate state within Mexico. At that time, Coahuila y Tejas established the Constitution of 1827.

When Texas declared its independence from Mexico, representatives created a new Constitution of 1836, which was set up much like the Constitution of the United States. In 1845, when Texas joined the United States, it was required to write a new state constitution.

The Confederate Constitution of 1861 followed after Texas seceded from the Union, although it remained somewhat similar to the previous constitution (and the "Confederate States of America" replaced the words "United States of America"). Two different constitutions followed the Civil War: the Post Civil War Constitution of 1866 and the Reconstruction Constitution of 1869.

Finally, the version we use today, the Constitution of 1876, was approved. Our government works under both the Texas Constitution and the Constitution of the United States. Constitutions are important documents that define the basic law of the land as well as the *functions* and *limits* of its government.

The Texas Constitution:

- outlines the parts and duties of the government
- lists the powers of each governmental body and official
- describes the citizens' rights
- explains the method of *amending* the constitution.

You've probably heard about the Bill of Rights (the first ten amendments) of the U.S. Constitution. The Texas Constitution also has a Bill of Rights. Like the U.S. Constitution, these rights include the right to freedom of speech, religion, and the press. Texas citizens have the right to bear arms (own guns), are guaranteed a speedy trial, and are protected from unreasonable search and seizures.

When changes need to be made to this constitution, it can be updated through the addition of new amendments. An amendment must first be approved by two-thirds of the Texas House and Senate, and then approved through a vote from the citizens of the state.

The Texas Constitution provides for three branches of government. Each of these branches is a separate department with separate powers. This ensures the powers are equally divided, and one branch doesn't have greater authority than another. Each branch keeps a "check" on the powers of the others; we call this the principle of "*checks and balances*."

After the legislature makes a law, the governor can choose to sign the law or he/she can veto the law. If the law is vetoed, the legislature can *override* it and still pass the law with a two-thirds vote. The Texas Supreme Court and the Court of Criminal Appeals have the power to declare state laws *unconstitutional*.

1. **Legislative**: The legislature (consisting of the Senate and the House of Representatives) makes the laws for the state and approves the state *budget*. The Senate is limited to thirty-one members, and the House of Representatives (set up originally with one representative for every 15,000 *inhabitants* in Texas) is currently at its limit of 150 members (each member now represents closer to every 170,000 people). The legislature meets once every two years in odd numbered years, and for only up to 140 days. The governor can call a special session if there is an immediate need which does not fall within the regular session time.

2. **Executive**: The executive department makes sure the laws of the state are carried out properly. This department is made up of the governor (chief executive), the lieutenant governor, secretary of state, comptroller of public accounts, the commissioner of the General Land Office, the commissioner of agriculture, and the attorney general.

3. **Judiciary** (the judicial branch): This branch *interprets* and decides how to apply the laws of the state. This means the courts decide if a person or business is guilty of a crime, and sets the punishment.

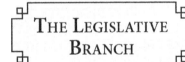 

THE LEGISLATIVE BRANCH

We call both Texas and the U.S. legislatures *bicameral*, since there are two "chambers." The thirty-one Senate members (elected for four-year terms), through committees, watch over issues regarding the state's education system, criminal justice, and health and human services. The lieutenant governor presides over the Senate and is elected by the people of the state.

The 150-member House of Representatives (elected for two-year terms) and its committees deal with many of the same issues as the Senate, along with natural resources, public health, economic development, and other concerns. The Speaker of the House presides over the House, and he/she is selected by members of the House.

Both the House and the Senate work together to write and pass laws, approve the governor's appointments, *appropriate* education and other funds, and make additional decisions regarding taxes and the economy.

Committees do a great deal of research and are responsible for *drafting* bills that may someday become a law. Thousands of proposals for new laws are presented each session, but very few make it through the process successfully.

There are two types of *proposals* which are submitted to the legislature. The first is called a *resolution*: a legislator's opinion regarding topics such as whether an amendment should be proposed or to proclaim certain days to honor individuals or groups.

The second proposal is called a *bill*, which is an idea for a new law. The House or Senate listens to the bill proposal and assigns the bill to a committee. The committee listens to people who either favor or oppose the bill, and then decides whether or not to recommend the legislature continue considering the bill. If it is decided it should *not* continue, the bill "dies in committee."

Alternately, if the committee decides the bill is worthy, either the entire House or the entire Senate *debates* the bill and votes. If a majority of members agree and vote for the bill, it is then passed to the other "chamber" for consideration and vote.

Again, if a majority votes for the bill, then the bill is passed on to the governor. If the governor decides to sign the bill, it will become law, but if he doesn't want to sign the bill and vetoes it, the House and Senate can take a vote and override his veto with a two-thirds vote.

Texas Senate

THE EXECUTIVE BRANCH

Once laws are passed by the legislature, the executive branch is responsible for carrying out those laws. Those who work in the executive branch are either elected or *appointed* by the governor.

Of course, the head of the executive branch is the governor, and the person who holds this position is elected by the citizens of the state. He serves a term of four years, but unlike the U.S. president, the Texas governor can be reelected as many times as the public wants him/her to serve. Anyone who is at least thirty years old, a U.S. citizen, and has lived in Texas for at least five years prior to the election is *eligible* for the position.

As mentioned earlier, the governor is responsible for signing or vetoing bills proposed by the legislature. This means he/she must depend on a staff who researches and helps the governor decide whether or not to sign a bill into law.

The governor also appoints members to boards and commissions, and can, with the approval of the senate, remove *appointees* as well. He also can send messages to the legislature throughout the session and present his recommendations, although the legislature is not required to agree or act on his suggestions.

The governor is the commander in chief of Texas and is in charge of the Texas Guard (includes the Army National Guard, the Texas State Guard, and the Texas Air National Guard). In addition, the governor frequently attends meetings and ceremonies across the state and the nation.

The lieutenant governor is elected by the people, so he/she might or might not be a member of the same political party as the governor. When the governor is out of the state or unable to serve for any reason, the lieutenant governor acts in his/her place with the same powers and duties. Interestingly, the lieutenant governor also serves the legislative branch, since he/she also holds the title of president of the Texas Senate.

Besides the governor and lieutenant governor, other executive positions include the attorney general, the commissioner of the General Land Office, the commissioner of agriculture, and the comptroller of public accounts.

THE JUDICIAL BRANCH

The judicial branch has multiple duties as it works with both *criminal* and *civil* areas of law.

First, it is responsible for trying individuals and businesses accused of crimes and establishing punishments if they are found guilty. It also interprets the meaning of state laws and determines how the laws should be *enforced*. Finally, the judicial branch is responsible for *procedures* which allow settlements of disputes.

These duties are carried out by courts and judges located throughout Texas. Most Texas judges are elected by voters, although some are appointed at a local level.

Some judges and *juries* are responsible for handling *civil law*, or law between private citizens, businesses, and governments. Civil law cases might be related to child custody, money or property, divorce, or insurance claims.

Other courts are responsible for criminal cases, when an individual or business is accused of breaking a law found within the *criminal code.* If the accused is found guilty, punishment must be decided and enforced. Criminal law includes both *felony* and *misdemeanor* offenses. Felonies are very serious crimes, including murder, aggravated assault, kidnapping, and burglary. Punishments might include large fines, prison sentences, loss of the right to vote, or even the death penalty. Misdemeanors are not considered as serious, and might include traffic violations, theft, and simple assault. Punishments more likely given for misdemeanors are fines and shorter jail terms.

Depending on the case, either a judge or a judge and jury may be assigned. Those called to *jury duty* can serve:
- if they are a Texas citizen and at least eighteen years old
- never convicted or under indictment for a felony, *and*
- able to read and write.

If someone is accused of a felony, a *grand jury* is selected to decide if there is enough evidence to issue an *indictment*. If there is enough evidence, a trial will be held at a later date by a *petit jury*. Attorneys who represent both the accused and the state present their case and evidence, and then the jury must decide whether they believe the accused is guilty or innocent. If guilty, either the jury or the judge will decide on the punishment. Sometimes these cases never actually go to court, and a *plea bargain* may be accepted when the accused admits his/her guilt and agrees to a lesser charge.

The judge and juries only hear cases after the accused are captured. Other agencies work to enforce Texas laws and bring criminals to justice. Some of these agencies include the Texas Department of Public Safety, sheriffs and police departments, the Texas Department of Criminal Justice, and the Texas Youth Commission.

The Texas court system has both trial and *appeals* courts. Trial courts are the original court where cases are tried and *verdicts* are *rendered*. If there is a question about whether or not the trial court was unfair and procedures not properly followed, an appeals court may decide to order a new trial.

Trial courts include both criminal and civil cases (most cases are civil). There are three levels of trial courts: municipal/justice of the peace, county courts, and district courts. Smaller towns and rural areas often have justice of the peace courts. Each of Texas's 254 counties have at least one county court. They usually hear civil cases (with less than $5000 at issue) and criminal misdemeanor cases. District courts handle criminal felony and other serious criminal cases, and occasionally civil cases as well.

Appeals can be made in the district court of appeals, or even the highest Court of Criminal Appeals and the Supreme Court of Texas (handles civil and juvenile cases). The high courts have nine justices who are elected to serve staggered terms of six years.

Texas Representatives in Washington, D.C.

As you know, Texas's model of government and its three branches were designed after that of the United States. If we look at the U.S. government, the executive branch is responsible for carrying out laws. It includes the president, the vice-president, and the president's cabinet. The judicial branch is made up of the Supreme Court (with nine justices) and other federal courts. Finally, the legislative branch (Congress) makes the laws and consists of the Senate and the House of Representatives.

The United States is considered a *republic* because the citizens elect people to represent them. As discussed earlier in this unit, some representatives are elected from districts in Texas and serve as that area's representative in Austin. These men and women work together to make laws which affect Texas.

But Texas citizens also elect representatives who serve in the United States *federal* government. There are a total of 435 men or women who are elected across the country to serve in the United States House of Representatives. Each state is allotted a certain number of representatives based on the population of their state. Texas is a big state, so thirty-six congressmen or women are sent to Washington, D.C., by Texans.

The U.S. Senate is composed of two senators from each state, so in total, thirty-eight men/women represent Texas in the U.S. Congress. These delegates are expected to listen to their *constituents* and make the best decisions possible when it comes to creating laws and spending taxpayer money.

The State Capitol and Capital

What is the difference between *capitol* and *capital*? Texas and the United States have both, but the different spellings have different meanings.

A capital is the city or area which is considered the seat of the government of a particular state or country. That's where laws are made and the executives carry out the law. The United States' capital is Washington, D.C. The capital of Texas is the city of Austin.

Just one letter can make a big difference, though! The capitol is the building where a state legislature meets. In Texas, the capitol is that beautiful pink granite building where the state Senate and House of Representatives meet. (Just to confuse things a little more, if you capitalize the letter c, then *Capitol* means the building where Congress meets in Washington, D.C.).

If you have traveled to Austin, you have probably seen the magnificent Texas capitol. The building is very big; in fact, it's the largest of all the state capitols. To give you an idea of the size, the building has over 400 rooms and 900 windows!

Completed in 1888, the building is made from red granite and limestone. The center of the building has a *rotunda*, a circular part of a building covered by a dome. Portraits of all of the presidents of the Republic of Texas and governors of the state of Texas can be found hanging in the rotunda area.

If you look up at the top of the rotunda, you will find the Texas star, surrounded by letters spelling "Texas." You'll find that Texas star again on the floor, right underneath the rotunda dome, surrounded by a *mosaic* depicting the six flags which have flown over Texas.

The large chambers of the Texas Senate and House of Representatives are found in this building, on either side of the rotunda. Each representative and senator, along with the governor, lieutenant governor, and speaker of the house, have offices in the capitol.

TEXAS GOVERNORS

J. Pinckney Henderson February 19, 1846-December 21,1847	Oran M. Roberts January 21, 1879-January 16, 1883	James V Allred January 15, 1935-January 17, 1939
George T. Wood December 21, 1847-December 21, 1849	John Ireland January 16, 1883-January 18, 1887	W. Lee O'Daniel January 17, 1939-August 4, 1941
Peter Hansbrough Bell December 21, 1849-November 23, 1853	Lawrence Sullivan Ross January 18, 1887-January 20, 1891	Coke R. Stevenson August 4, 1941-January 21, 1947
J. W. Henderson November 23, 1853-December 21, 1853	James Stephen Hogg January 20, 1891-January 15, 1895	Beauford H. Jester January 21, 1947-July 11, 1949
Elisha M. Pease December 21, 1853-December 21, 1857	Charles A. Culberson January 15, 1895-January 17, 1899	Allan Shivers July 11, 1949-January 15, 1957
Hardin R. Runnels December 21, 1857-December 21, 1859	Joseph D. Sayers January 17, 1899-January 20, 1903	Price Daniel January 15, 1957-January 15, 1963
Sam Houston December 21, 1859-March 16, 1861	S. W. T. Lanham January 20, 1903-January 15, 1907	John Connally January 15, 1963-January 21, 1969
Edward Clark March 16, 1861-November 7, 1861	Thomas Mitchell Campbell January 15, 1907-January 17, 1911	Preston Smith January 21, 1969-January 16, 1973
Francis R. Lubbock November 7, 1861-November 5, 1863	Oscar Branch Colquitt January 17, 1911-January 19, 1915	Dolph Briscoe January 16, 1973-January 16, 1979
Pendleton Murrah November 5, 1863-June 17, 1865	James E. Ferguson January 19, 1915-August 25, 1917	William P. Clements January 16, 1979-January 18, 1983
Andrew J. Hamilton June 17, 1865--August 9, 1866	William Pettus Hobby August 25, 1917-January 18, 1921	Mark White January 18, 1983-January 20, 1987
James W. Throckmorton August 9, 1866-August 8, 1867	Pat Morris Neff January 18, 1921-January 20, 1925	William P. Clements January 20, 1987-January 15, 1991
Elisha M. Pease August 8, 1867-September 30, 1869	Miriam A. Ferguson January 20, 1925-January 17, 1927	Ann W. Richards January 15, 1991-January 17, 1995
Edmund J. Davis January 8, 1870-January 15, 1874	Dan Moody January 17, 1927-January 20, 1931	George W. Bush January 17, 1995-December 21, 2000
Richard Coke January 15, 1874-December 1, 1876	Ross S. Sterling January 20, 1931-January 17, 1933	James Richard Perry December 21, 2000-January 20, 2015
Richard B. Hubbard December 1, 1876-January 21, 1879	Miriam A. Ferguson January 17, 1933-January 15, 1935	Gregory Wayne Abbott January 20, 2015 to present

Beautiful Artwork
of the Texas Capitol and Grounds

Tejano Monument
Sculptor: Armando Hinojosa

Texas Pioneer Woman Monument
Sculptor: Linda Sioux Henley

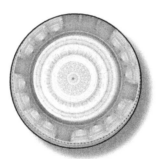

*Rotunda
Dome*

Stephen F. Austin
Sculptor: Elisabet Ney

Vietnam Veterans Memorial
Sculptor: Duke Sundt

Rotunda Floor

Monclova (1682-1720 *and* 1833-35): located in Mexico, it was the first colonial capital. The capital was moved back to Monclova (from Saltillo) in 1833 when it appeared the Texans were beginning to revolt.

Los Adaes (1721-1773): actually located near Robeline, Louisiana, the capital was moved here after concerns about French presence in the area.

San Antonio de Béxar (1771-1824): once France was no longer seen as a threat, the capital was moved here to be closer to Mexico City since a colony had begun to grow near the presidio and mission.

Saltillo (1824-1833): capital moved to Saltillo (in northern Mexico) after Mexico won its independence from Spain. This city was selected because it was located between Mexico City and San Antonio, and would serve as the seat of government for the combined states of Coahuila y Tejas.

San Felipe de Austin (1832-1835): although through the eyes of Mexico, the capital of Texas remained in Mexico, San Felipe became the capital (from the Texans' perspective) when they began to meet and discuss the future of Texas during the Conventions of 1832 and 1833, as well as the Consultation of 1835.

Washington-on-the-Brazos (March 1, 1836): this was the location of the Convention of 1836, where the Texas Declaration of Independence and Constitution were written and signed, and interim officers were selected.

Harrisburg (March 22, 1836): the new interim president, David Burnet, selected this location (now a part of Houston) because it was close to the coast, as well as a supply and communication line.

Galveston (April 1836): the capital was moved to Galveston when it became clear Santa Anna and his army were on their way to Harrisburg to capture the interim officers. It was during this time the Battle of San Jacinto was won by the Texans.

Velasco (May 1836): the capital was moved here (at the mouth of the Brazos River) because it had more to offer than Galveston Island at that time. Santa Anna was sent here to sign the Treaties of Velasco following the Texian victory at San Jacinto.

Columbia (October 1836): Burnet moved the capital once again to Columbia (now West Columbia) because he felt it was a better location for the new Republic's seat of government. The men met in a two-story building and the government was happy to have the use of a printing press.

Houston (1836-1839 *and* 1842): after officers of the new republic were elected, it was time to select a more permanent home for the Republic's capital. Congress and President Houston decided to go with the Allen brothers' offer to create a new city by the name of "Houston." A two-story statehouse was erected and Congress met here until Mirabeau Lamar became the second president of the Republic.

Austin (1840-today): Lamar moved the capital to Austin. Although you will recall Sam Houston had concerns about its location during his second term, proponents of keeping it in place persevered. Austin remains our state capital today.

LOCAL GOVERNMENTS

Your government is active on many different levels. The United States federal government is based out of Washington, D.C., and of course, oversees national issues.

Your state government is based in Austin, the capital city of Texas. There, elected and appointed officials oversee issues directly affecting the state and its citizens.

As we have seen throughout history, the farther away the government and decision-makers are from citizens, the less aware these officials are of local issues and concerns. Sometimes it seems as if our federal and state government don't understand the needs and culture of our community. That's one reason we elect representatives from our district: to represent our concerns on a state and national level.

However, that doesn't mean those representatives can take care of all the needs of the cities and *rural* areas throughout the state. Therefore, we also elect government officials to serve our *local community.* Local government is responsible for taking care of the daily issues. It provides protection by police and fire departments, schools, and water, sewer, and garbage services. The three kinds of local governments in Texas are city, county, and special districts.

City governments can operate under either *general law* or *home rule.* A general-law city usually has populations of less than 50,000 people and is a smaller town. Normally provided are very basic services such as police, fire, water, and sewer.

A city might also be organized as a home-rule city. About one out of four cities in Texas are home-ruled, meaning the city takes care of itself, conducting business and organizing as the citizens choose, as long as they follow state and federal laws.

City governments in Texas can be set up in one of three ways:

• *Mayor-Council*: The mayor is the executive authority. Within this type of government, the city can have either a strong-mayor or a weak-mayor type of government. Strong-mayor cities (such as Houston and El Paso), have mayors who oversee daily operations. In weak-mayor cities, the mayor shares his duties with the city council.

• *Council-Manager*: The mayor only has one vote at council meetings and has less power than mayor-council cities. A professional city manager manages the daily operations of the budget and city (such as Dallas and San Antonio).

• *Commission*: Commissioners are elected to operate the city government and act as a city council (as in Galveston and Sweetwater). The mayor has little power, and the commissioners head various city departments. It is the least common form of local government.

$ How Cities Spend Their Money $

Because cities provide many services to their citizens, they have to create a budget which will cover the costs related to these services. Police and fire protection (including equipment, buildings, and *personnel*), the local jail, street repair, park *maintenance*, garbage and sewer services, water and drainage, libraries, city museums, airports, convention centers and sports arenas, bridges ... you can see how expensive these many projects can be to keep a city safe and appealing.

> ### Did You Know?
> Have you ever wondered how much a big city spends in one year? Here are the annual budgets (2014) for Texas's five largest cities: Fort Worth ($1.4 billion), San Antonio ($2.3 billion), Dallas ($2.8 billion), Austin ($3.3 billion), and finally ... Houston ($4.1 billion)!

HOW CITIES FUND
THEIR GOVERNMENT AND SERVICES

Cities receive money for their operations from several sources:

- *Property Taxes*: Property owners pay taxes each year based on the value of their property. A *tax assessor* inspects and *appraises* (decides on the worth) of each property. Citizens can disagree with the appraisal value and can follow steps to try to have the value—and their taxes—reduced.
- *Sales Taxes:* Cities have the ability to set a sales tax rate on goods sold within the city. That percentage is then added to the set state sales tax when you purchase items. The store where you buy the goods collects and then *remits* the sales tax to the state comptroller.
- *City Service Fees*: Citizens pay fees for the various city services they receive, including trash collection, hospital care, and park usage.
- *Building permit fees*
- *Traffic violation fines*
- *Bonds* can be issued when money is needed for special long-term and expensive projects, such as new parks or recreation areas. These bonds are certificates which guarantee payment, plus interest.
- *State and federal assistance*

There are 254 counties in Texas and each of these counties are operated by locally elected officials. The county government is responsible for helping the state government carry out its duties. You may have visited your *county courthouse.* Inside, county officials maintain *records* pertaining to property ownership, births, deaths, and marriages. The county also helps with the collection of state taxes, issues licenses, and assists with election issues.

Unlike the different forms of city government, each county government must be set up identically. Every county has a *commissioners court* which sets the county's budget, decides how to spend tax money, and sets the property tax rate.

Counties are divided into four *precincts* (districts). One county commissioner is elected (four- year terms) for each precinct. Counties also elect a county judge (four-year term) who takes care of daily operations within the county and heads the commissioners court.

The commissioners court is responsible for directing county business and projects, such as building and repairing roads, jail operations, and the maintenance of airports, county hospitals, museums, libraries, and parks.

HOW COUNTIES FUND
THEIR GOVERNMENT AND SERVICES

- *Property Taxes*: As with cities, the county also collects property taxes on buildings and land. Counties may also collect taxes on cars and airplanes.
- *Bonds*: Bonds can be issued for long-term construction projects.
- *Permit fees*
- *Fuel Taxes*
- *Vehicle Registration Fees*

Special districts are different from cities and counties. These districts are actually units like *school districts*, community college districts, water control, *rapid transit* authorities, and river authorities. They are established to meet very specific needs.

The most common special district is the school district. At the time of printing, 1,247 school districts exist in Texas. The *school board* (an elected board of trustees) directs each school district. This board hires teachers, sets their salaries, chooses the school superintendent, maintains the many schools and related buildings, and arranges transportation. School districts receive their funding from federal, state, and local funds.

YOU CAN MAKE A DIFFERENCE!

Our country and our state were established by men and women who believed in principles such as freedom and the importance of an educated and *moral* society. These principles were put into operation through the creation of governments which ensure the citizens' rights to life and property are protected. There are many different ideas about how to maintain these freedoms and protect society.

How do we ensure these principles are passed down from generation to generation? How do we protect our freedom and preserve safe communities?

You are taking the first step: learn! You have read all about your state's history and how Texas government operates. You understand how men and women have fought and *endeavored* to create this wonderful country and state we enjoy today. You know how important these freedoms are, and why we must all work to protect them. It is said those who do not learn history are *condemned* to repeat it. This means that we must learn from our *forefathers'* mistakes, as well as their successes.

Not everyone can run for political office (although we think it's great if you do!), but once you turn eighteen, and if you are a *native-born* or *naturalized* citizen, a *resident* of the state and county, and registered at least thirty days prior to election day, you can VOTE!

Washington Votes: Harris & Ewing, photographer, 1938 April 30. Courtesy of Library of Congress.

There are four different types of elections:

1. *Primary Election*: This is where you vote for which candidate you want within a political party (Republican, Democrat, Independent, Libertarian, Green Party, etc). The winner of the primary election will serve as the candidate who represents the party in the general election.

2. *General Election:* Candidates representing the different parties run on national and state levels. The general election is held on the first Tuesday after the first Monday in November in even-numbered years; statewide officials are elected in non-presidential election years. Citizens may also vote on special issues and proposed laws at this time.

3. *Special Elections*: These are held when *vacancies* occur in the Texas legislature or the U.S. Congress, to approve local *bond proposals,* taxes, and constitutional amendments. They are also used to fill vacancies in city councils and school boards.

4. *Local Elections:* These are held when it's time to elect city council members, mayors, school board members, and special district boards.

It is important for you to research and study the issues before you cast your first *ballot*. Learn all about the candidates and what they believe. Study the issues and propositions which are up for consideration. Read for yourself, rather than just listen to others and the media. Think about what you have learned from history, and try to apply it to the issues of today.

It's amazing how many times we forget the past and make the same mistakes. Instead, work to break that chain, as you consider those principles which make our country and state so strong.

As you study the issues of the day, look back at our country and state's political history. Today, the Republican and Democratic parties are dominant in Texas. But it's interesting to study the past of each party and how they have changed over the years. Read about what these parties and candidates believe, and see how those beliefs *align* with your own. You might even decide to volunteer to help your political party or candidates by campaigning door to door or at political rallies.

Next Page: *Photo of country road and Fort Worth, Texas.* Courtesy of photographer Lauren Tenery.

Your Neck of the Woods

We've almost reached the end of the trail. You've learned about Texas's place in the world, its beautiful and varied regions, and the fascinating histories of Texas's first citizens, the Native Americans.

You now know about the early explorers, and how the unwanted French presence led to the mission system . . . which led to new settlements and eventually to the empresarios, who brought new immigrants to make their homes in Texas.

The new immigrants displeased the Mexican government, and in the attempt to sweep Texas clean of these rebellious new citizens, Mexico lost the entire state at the Battle of San Jacinto.

Now you know Texas was once its own country, the Republic of Texas. Less than ten years later, Texas was annexed as the 28th state to join the Union of the United States of America. Less than twenty years later, Texas joined ten other southern states and left the Union to form the Confederate States of America. Although Texans were mostly successful in defending their land during the war, eventually the Union won and Texas was forced to undergo Reconstruction before being readmitted to the Union.

Shortly thereafter, Texas saw the advent of the cattle drive and the heyday of the cowboys. Transportation and technology improved, oil changed the face of Texas and brought great wealth to many Texans, and the entire country endured the Great Depression along with two world wars.

The economy improved, although a cold war, a terrible attack on American soil, and more fighting across the seas kept Texans busy providing the military with service people, airplanes, and other supplies. In addition, science and technology improvements placed Texas at the forefront of everything from computers to medical care to space exploration.

You now have a basic understanding of how our government and constitution developed over time. You know how laws are passed and carried out, and you better understand the difference between federal, state, and local governments and representation.

Remember, in *Unit Two* we discussed Texas's place in the world? We imagined zooming out from our window, looking down as we envisioned our homes, our cities, our state, our country, our hemisphere, the world . . .

Let's reverse our direction. Let's zoom back down from space, eventually hovering just over the city or town where you live.

What do you know about the history of your town? When was it established? What type of local government serves your community? For whom or what is your city named? Have you ever wondered about the names of streets, schools, and buildings in your town? Are they named after national, state, or local heroes?

Take time to explore your community. Research its history and find out how and where it falls into the story of Texas.

Keep learning about this great state and its contributions to our country and the world. Take pride in Texas's incredible history and its magnificent heroes.

Finally, take care of Texas's future: the land, the people, and the wildlife. Travel across the state and discover for yourself the historic sites you have learned about.

Remember our forefathers.

Remember the Alamo.

Remember Goliad.

Remember . . .

Because **YOU** are Texas.

BIBLIOGRAPHY

Books:

Anderson, Adrian, et al. ***Texas and Texans.*** New York: Glencoe McGraw-Hill, 2003.

Bailey, Jack. ***A Texas Cowboy's Journal.*** Norman: University of Oklahoma Press, 2006.

Benson, Paul, et al. ***Lone Star Politics.*** Belmont: Thomson/Wadsworth, 2004.

Bevill, James P. ***The Paper Republic.*** Houston: Bright Sky Press, 2009.

Burnett, Carolyn M. ***The First Texans.*** Austin: Eakin Press, 1995.

Chrismer, Melanie. ***Lone Star Legacy: The Texas Rangers Then and Now.*** Gretna: Pelican Publishing Co, 2016.

Connor, Seymore V., et al. ***Capitols of Texas.*** Waco: Texian Press, 1970.

Cooper, Fred. ***Ballads of Texas History.*** Frisco: Sing 'n Learn Publications, 2015.

Cottrell, Steve. ***Civil War in Texas and New Mexico Territory.*** Gretna: Pelican Publishing Co, 2004.

Davis, Lucile. ***The Caddo of Texas.*** New York: Power Kids Press, 2003.

Day, James, et al. ***Six Missions of Texas.*** Waco: Texian Press, 1965.

De Capua, Sarah. ***First Americans: The Comanche.*** New York: Marshall Cavendish, 2007.

Durham, Merle. ***The Lone Star State Divided: Texans and the Civil War***. Dallas: Hendrick-Long Publishing Co., 1994.

Feldman, Ruth Tenzer. ***The Mexican-American War: Chronicle of America's Wars***. Minneapolis: Lerner Publications Co, 2004.

Foster, Nancy Haston. ***Texas Missions: The Alamo and Other Texas Missions to Remember***. Houston: Lone StarBooks, 1995.

Fowler, Mike, et al. ***The Capitol Story: Statehouse in Texas.*** Woodway: Eakin Press, 1988.

Friedman, Mark, et al. ***The Apache.*** New York: Children's Press, 2011.

Gibson, Karen Bush. ***Texas History For Kid***s. Chicago: Chicago Review Press, 2015.

Gilbert, Charles E., Jr., ***Flags of Texas***, Gretna: Pelican Publishing, 1998.

Guerra, Mary Ann. ***The Missions of San Antonio***. San Antonio: The Alamo Press, 1982.

Haley, James L. ***Texas: An Album of History***. Garden City: Doubleday & Company, Inc, 1985.

Holz, Robert K., et al. ***Texas and Its History.*** Austin: Graphic Ideas, Inc, 1972.

Houston History: Volume 4, Number 2, "San Jacinto," Houston: University of Houston Center For Public History, 2007.

Huffines, Alan C. ***The Texas War of Independence 1835-1836***. University Park: Osprey Publishing, 2005.

Jackson, Jack. ***New Texas History Movies***. Austin: TSHA, 2007.

Jerome, Kate. ***Texas: What's So Great About This State***? Mount Pleasant: Arcadia Kids, 2010.

La Vere, David. ***The Texas Indians***. College Station: Texas A & M University Press, 2004.

Levy, Janey. ***The Missions of Texas.*** New York: Rosen Publishing, 2010.

McComb, David G. ***Texas: A Modern History.*** Austin: University of Texas Press, 1989.

My World of Social Studies. Boston: Pearson, 2016.

Moore, Stephen L. ***Eighteen Minutes.*** Lanham: Republic of Texas Press, 2004.

Newcomb, W.W. Jr. ***The Indians of Texas.*** Austin: University of Texas Press, 1990.

Núñez Cabeza de Vaca, Álvar; also Favata, Martin and Fernández.***The Account (Relación)***. Houston: Arte Público Press, 1993 (annotated translation).

Parent, Laurence. ***Official Guide to Texas State Parks and Historic Sites***. Austin: University of Texas Press, 2008.

Patent, Dorothy Hinshaw. ***The Buffalo and the Indians***. New York: Clarion Books, 2006.

Pickman, Richard. *Anglo-American Colonization of Texas.* New York: Power Kids Press, 2010.

Roden, Phil, et al. *Mini-Q's in Texas History*. Evanston: The DBQ Project, 2010.

Sandell, Cindy. *Texas History Supplemental Text*. Plano: VIS Engerprises, 2004.

Schmitz, Joseph W. *Daily Life in the Republic of Texas*. Ingleside: Copano Bay Press, 2007.

Somervill, Barbara A., *Texas*, New York: Scholastic, 20+14.

Sorenson, Richard. *Focus on Texas: History and Geography*. Houston: Hendrick-Long Publishing Co, 1995.

Spearing, Darwin. *Roadside Geology of Texas*. Missoula: Mountain Press Publishing, 1991.

Spradlin, Michael P. *Texas Rangers: Legendary Lawmen*. New York: Walker & Company, 2008.

Stephens, A. Ray. *Texas: A Historical Atlas*. Norman: University of Oklahoma Press, 2010.

"The Texans Are Ready," *The Medallion: World War I Special Edition*, Spring 2017. Austin: Texas Historical Commission

Texas State Historical Association Texas Almanac. Austin: TSHA, 2016.

Wade, Mary Dodson. *Texas History*. Chicago: Heinemann Library, 2004.

Wade, Mary Dodson. *Texas: Native Peoples.* Chicago: Chicago-Heinemann Library, 2004.

Warren, Betsy, et al. *The Story of Texas.* Austin: RanchGate, 1974.

Warren, Betsy. *Explorers in Early Texas.* Dallas: Hendrick-Long Publishing Co., 1992.

Warren, Betsy. *Let's Remember Indians of Texas.* Dallas: Henderson-Long Publishing Company, 1981.

Warren, Betsy. *Let's Remember When Texas Belonged to Spain*. Dallas: Hendrick-Long Publishing, 1981.

Warren, Betsy. *Let's Remember When Texas Was a Republic*. Dallas: Hendrick-Long Pub., 1983.

Warren, Betsy. *Texas History Timeline*. Dallas: Hendrick-Long Publishing Company, 1996.

Weems, John Edward. *The Story of Texas*. Fredericksburg: Shearer Publishing, 1986.

Winegarten, Debra L., *Oveta Culp Hobby*, Austin: University of Texas Press, 2014.

Winfrey, Dorman H. *Six Missions of Texas*. Waco: Texian Press, 1965.

Woodward, Walter M. *Sam Houston: For Texas and the Union*. New York: The Rosen Publishing Group, 2003.

Zappler, George. *Learn About Texas Indíans*. Austin: Texas Parks and Wildlife Press, 1996.

A.P. United States History: *White-Native American Contact in Early American History*, 2008 Curriculum Module.

Websites:

The Portal to Texas History - https://texashistory.unt.edu/

Texas State Historical Association - https://www.tshaonline.org/home/

National Archives - https://www.archives.gov/

The Library of Congress - https://www.loc.gov/

Regions - Texas Parks and Wildlife - https://tpwd.texas.gov/kids/about_texas/regions/

Regions - Texas Parks and Wildlife - http://tpwd.texas.gov/

Regions - Texas Almanac - texasalmanac.com

Tigua Indians - http://www.ysletadelsurpueblo.org/

Texas Indians - www.texasindians.com

Plains Indians - http://www.unl.edu/plains/

Texas Beyond History - https://www.texasbeyondhistory.net/

Texas State Parks - http://tpwd.texas.gov/state-parks/

Texas History - www.lsjunction.com

Archives of Old Documents/Photos - www.tsl.texas.gov

Teaching Texas - www.teachingtexas.org

Texas General Land Office - www.glo.texas.gov

Texas Maps - www.lib.utexas.edu/maps/historical/history_texas.html
Historical Commission - www.thc.state.tx.us/explore-texas
Tour Texas - www.tourtexas.com
Texas Missions - www.texasmissionguide.com
Texas Independence Trail - Texasindependencetrail.com
El Camino Real - www.elcaminorealdelostejas.org
The Alamo - www.thealamo.org
San Jacinto - www.sanjacinto-museum.org
Primary Documents - www.tamu.edu
Texas Republic Constitution - www.tarltonapps.law.utexas.edu/constitutions/texas1836
Civil War - www.civilwartraveler.com/TRANS/TX
Civil War - www.nps.gov//abpp/battles/txmap.html
Texas Rangers - www.texasranger.org/index.htm
Mexican-American War - www.library.uta.edu/usmexicowar/
Buffalo Soldiers - www.buffalosoldier.net
Oil and Gas - www.adventuresinenergy.org; www.oceanstaroec.com
World War One - www.theworldwar.org/education
Texas Government - www.kids.house.state.tx.us/
Texas Capitol - www.tspb.texas.gov/prop/tc/tc/capitol.html
La Salle Expedition - http://www.texascenterforregionalstudies.com/texas-legacy.html
Texas History, Culture, and Historic Sites - http://texastimetravel.com/
Buffalo and Native Americans - http://americanbison.si.edu/american-bison-and-american-indian-nations/
Explorers - http://ageofex.marinersmuseum.org/index.php?page=theexplorers
Tonkawa Indians - http://www.tonkawatribe.com/
Comanche Indians - http://www.texasmonthly.com/articles/the-lost-tribe/

Acknowledgements

Special thanks to the following for their time and expertise: Rachel Galan (Caddo Mounds State Historic Site), Sherri Driscoll and Ernesto Rodriguez (the Alamo), Denton Florian, Kim Rose Bryant, Peggy Purser Freeman, Sharie Dougherty, Taylor Gusler, Wesley Smith, Lauren Tenery (photographs), Grace-Mercado Marx (photograph), Deanna Ford (photograph), Cindy Freeman (photographs), Katheryn Moore (curriculum review), Clark and Becky Richards (oil and gas), Mike Shatynski (military history), Greg Hicks (military history), Kaylyn McCoy (printing assistance), the ever-patient rangers and guides at Texas missions and historic sites, Sam Houston Memorial Museum, Austin, Braeden, Ben, and Kyle (always patient and willing guinea pigs),
and
Travis Dougherty who, always and without complaint, sits down in the middle of his vacation to create illustrations for me.

Photograph and Image Credits
All photos accessed online 03 July, 2017, unless otherwise noted.

Unit One: Texas Symbols
Lone Star Flag: Wikimedia Commons/Public Domain. https://commons.wikimedia.org/w/index.php?curid=28388337
State Seal: courtesy of Texas Secretary of State Registrations Unit.
State Symbol Photographs: photographed by Yvonne Cumberland and Laurie Cockerell.
Bluebonnet: User Ken/Flickr/CC BY 2.0. https://www.flickr.com
Monarch Butterfly, Danaus plexippus: Richiebits/Wikimedia Commons/Public Domain.
https://commons.wikimedia.org/wiki/File:BBGMonarchButterflyWings.jpg
Spanish Flag: Rastrojo/Wikimedia Commons/ CC BY 3.0. https://commons.wikimedia.org/wiki/File:Flag_of_Castile_and_Le%C3%B3n.svg
French Flag: Zippanova/Wikimedia Commons/Public Domain. https://commons.wikimedia.org/wiki/File:Pavillon_royal_de_France.svg
Mexico Flag: Mexico: Alex Covarrubias/Wikimedia Commons/Public Domain. https://commons.wikimedia.org/wiki/File:Flag_of_Mexico.svg
Confederate States of America: Nicola Marschall/Wikimedia Commons/ Public Domain.
https://commons.wikimedia.org/wiki/File:Flag_of_the_Confederate_States_of_America_(March_1861_%E2%80%93_May_1861).svg
United States of America: MSGJ/Wikimedia Commons/Public Domain (implementation of U. S. Code:Title 4, Chapter 1, Section 1 [1] (the United States Federal "Flag Law"). https://en.wikipedia.org/wiki/File:Flag_of_the_United_States

Unit Two: Regions of Texas
Earth as seen from space 36,000 miles above Earth (including Mexico and the Texas gulf) from Apollo 10 mission in 1969: courtesy of NASA.
https://www.nasa.gov/image-feature/may-18-1969-apollo-10-view-of-the-earth
Texas in the United States: courtesy of Public Domain Clipart.
Texas in the Northern Hemisphere: Gringer/Wikimedia Commons/Public Domain.
https://commons.wikimedia.org/wiki/File:Worldmap_northern.svg
Bentsen-Rio Grande Valley State Park, Tx: Vince Smith/Flickr/CC BY 2.0/. https://creativecommons.org/licenses/by/2.0/
The Davis Mountains, Lumber Truck, Galveston Fishing Boat, Cotton Fields: photographed by Yvonne Cumberland.
Ernst Tinaja: courtesy of photographer Deanna Ford.
Lake photos, Enchanted Rock, Galveston Beach, Llana Estacado, Piney Woods, and Horned Toad: photographed by Laurie Cockerell.
Bluebonnets and Fence: courtesy of photographer Lauren Tenery.

Unit Three: Texas Native Americans
An American bison, common in the Elk and Bison Prairie, closes his eyes while resting peacefully: courtesy of National Archives, Identifier 7722894, created by Department of Transportation, Public Domain. https://catalog.archives.gov/id/7722894
Caddo Mound at Caddo Mounds State Historic Site: courtesy of Cindy Freeman.
An American bison at the 1,800-acre Lonesome Pine Ranch, a working cattle ranch that is part of the Texas Ranch Life ranch resort near Chappell Hill in Austin County, Texas: photographed by Carol M. Highsmith (5-10-2014). The Lyda Hill Texas Collection of Photographs in Carol M. Highsmith's America Project, courtesy of Library of Congress, Prints and Photographs Division (LC-DIG-highsm- 28388 (ONLINE) [P&P]).
On the Trail - Buffalo Hunt: courtesy of Library of Congress/Bain Collection, Prints and Photographs Division (LC-B2- 2609-1 [P&P]), ca.1910-15. http://www.loc.gov/pictures/item/ggb2005012290/
Bull Chief-Apsaroke, c1908: Curtis, Edward S., 1868-1952, photographer, courtesy of Library of Congress (LC-USZ62-46963). http://www.loc.gov/pictures/item/2002719697/
Caddo Home Replica and Mound: Courtesy of Caddo Mounds State Historic Site.
Alligator at Brazos Bend State Park: courtesy of photographer Jeanne Diarte.
A running collared peccary or javelina (Pecari tajacu) in Big Bend National Park, Texas, USA: 4 June 2008. Wing-Chi Poon/Wikimedia Commons/ CC BY-SA 3.0. https://commons.wikimedia.org/wiki/File:Running_Javelina.jpg
[Ta-Her-Ye-Qua-Hip or Horse-backs Camp; 4 comanches in front of wigwam, Fort Sill, Indian Territory]: ca. 1873. Photograph. Retrieved from the Library of Congress. https://www.loc.gov/item/2016649448/
Two Apache babies on cradleboards: Department of Defense, Courtesy National Archives, American Indian Select List number 23, ARC Identifier 530904. https://catalog.archives.gov/id/530904
Native American with horse pulling travois: photographed by Richard Throssel, c1910. Museum of Photographic Arts. Flickr Commons, Accession Number: 2003.003.027. https://www.flickr.com/photos/mopa/5711528644/in/photolist-db3d9Y-9GH5tN-nwZ7Gf-nMqUWS-nRg1CV-r7a4Ad-4qje48-oum2RL-owdSKm-nPbqUv-rmqDYd-anHHop-nPtxRgdWKHu2-j827iD-5BCNTR-9GEbWM-5BCNPt-9GEbX2-i8CFVh-9DZb-NB-x5zpud-owb5qa-d925bL-6SUVUr
Mesquite Bean Plant Specimen c1900-1910: photographed by C.C. Pierce, (Charles C.), CHS-2691, California Historical Society Collection, 1860-1960, Public Domain. Release under the CC BY 3.0 Attribution license. Courtesy of University of Southern California. Libraries and California Historical Society. Digitally reproduced by the USC Digital Library; From the California Historical Society Collection at the University of Southern California. http://digitallibrary.usc.edu/cdm/ref/collection/p15799coll65/id/7389
Prickly Pear Cactus in Texas: Sullivan, Jon/ Wikimedia Commons/Public Domain.
https://commons.wikimedia.org/wiki/File:Prickly_pear_cactus_in_Texas.jpg
Ysleta Mission: photographed by Shannon McGee, 07 Jan 2010. Online image. CC BY-SA 2.0/Flickr.
https://www.flickr.com/photos/shan213/9068443819/in/photolist

Unit Four: Explorers and Missionaries
Columbus: engraving by John Sartain from the original portrait presented to William A. Bryan, Esq., of Virginia by H.M. the late Queen Sophia of Holland. Courtesy of Library of Congress (LC-USZ62-1784). http://www.loc.gov/pictures/item/2004671920/
Hernando Cortés: engraving by W. Holl; published by Charles Knight.Courtesy of Library of Congress (Reproduction Number LC-USZ62-33515). https://www.loc.gov/item/2004671921/
Section of Pineda's 1519 map of the Gulf coast: courtesy of Texascounties.net, Public Domain.
http://www.texascounties.net/articles/discovery-of-texas/gulfofmexico.htm
Coronado Sets Out to the North: painted by Frederic Remington. Wikimedia Commons/Public Domain.

https://commons.wikimedia.org/wiki/File:Coronado-Remington.jpg

René-Robert Cavelier, Sieur de La Salle: P.S. Burton/Wikimedia Commons/Public Domain.

https://commons.wikimedia.org/wiki/File:Cavelier_de_la_salle.jpg

La Salle's Expedition to Louisiana in 1684: painted by Theodore Gudin (1844). {{PD-1923}} The ship on the left is La Belle, in the middle is Le Joly, and L'Aimable, which has run aground, is to the far right. The ships are at the entrance to Matagorda Bay. AYER/Wikimedia Commons.

https://commons.wikimedia.org/wiki/File:LaSallesExpeditiontoLouisiana.JPG

Hernando De Soto: J. Maca (engraving): courtesy Library of Congress, LC-USZ62-354. http://www.loc.gov/pictures/item/2004671914

The Alamo Mission: courtesy of photographer Grace Mercado-Marx.

Mission Tejas: photographed by Larry D. Moore, 24 October 2014, Wikimedia Commons/CC-BY-SA-4.0.

https://commons.wikimedia.org/wiki/File:Mission_tejas_2014.jpg

Ysleta Mission: photographed by Shannon McGee, 07 Jan 2010. Flickr/ (CC BY-SA 2.0)/online image.

Mission Socorro Under a Desert Sky: photograph by Jean Fulton, Public Domain. Courtesy of U.S. Department of Transportation Federal Highway Administration.

Missions Espada, San José, Concepción, San Juan, and La Bahía: photographed by Laurie Cockerell.

Unit Five: Filibusters and Empresarios

Engraving of Stephen F. Austin - Front: October 18, 1836, Early Texas Documents, Special Collections, University of Houston Libraries, accessed June 11, 2017. http://digital.lib.uh.edu/collection/earlytex/item/793/show/791

Tools of the Settlers: photographed by Laurie Cockerell and Yvonne Cumberland.

Unit Six: Revolution!

William B. Travis: sketched by Wylie Martin, 1835 (alleged sketch). Wikimedia Commons/Public Domain {{PD-1923}}.

https://commons.wikimedia.org/wiki/File:William_B._Travis_by_Wiley_Martin.JPG

General D. Antonio Lopez De Santa-Anna, president of the Republic of Mexico, c1847: courtesy of Library of Congress (LC-USZ62-21276). http://www.loc.gov/pictures/resource/cph.3a22346/

Replica of Stephen F. Austin's home in San Felipe & Guadalupe River at Gonzales: photographed by Laurie Cockerell.

Statue of Ben Milam at the Milam County, Texas, courthouse in Cameron, Texas, the fourth structure to serve in that capacity. Cameron Milam County Texas United States, 2014: photographed by Carol M. Highsmith and retrieved from the Library of Congress. https://www.loc.gov/item/2014631294/ (Accessed June 14, 2017)

Color portrait of Erastus "Deaf" Smith: painted by Thomas Jefferson Wright (1798-1846),approximately 1836, Early Texas Documents, Special Collections, University of Houston Libraries, accessed July 1, 2017. http://digital.lib.uh.edu/collection/earlytex/item/1120

Texas: Church of Alamo, San Antonio de Bexar. , 1844. Photograph. Retrieved from the Library of Congress, https://www.loc.gov/item/2002725348/. (Accessed September 16, 2017.)

Juan Seguín Memorial statue in Seguín, Tx: Amboo who?/Flickr (CC BY-SA 2.0) - crop/bw. https://www.flickr.com/photos/aboo213/34688464521/in/photolist-URirYv-q58RHB-qYUpTp-7PnEyN-7PiHED-oRzqwo-quBjRX-quBmL8-qKA6ft

Alamo Complex illustration: courtesy of artist Travis Dougherty.

The Alamo: courtesy of photographer Grace Mercado-Marx.

Independence Hall, Washington-on-the-Brazos, Presidio La Bahía & Battle of San Jacinto Reenactment: photographed by Laurie Cockerell.

Battle of San Jacinto Map: courtesy of artist Travis Dougherty.

San Jacinto Battle Flag at Capitol: Pschemp-own work (ssj battle flag 1 November 2015 File:20151101-IMGP1388.jpg)/Wikimedia Commons/CC BY-SA 4.0. https://commons.wikimedia.org/wiki/File:20151101-IMGP1388.jpg

Unit Seven: The Republic of Texas

Engraving of Sam Houston: approximately 1836, Early Texas Documents, Special Collections, University of Houston Libraries, accessed June 11, 2017. http://digital.lib.uh.edu/collection/earlytex/item/1105

Mirabeau B. Lamar: Oldage07(retouch and modifications)Wikimedia Commons, PD-US. https://commons.wikimedia.org/wiki/File:Mirabeaulamar_2.jpg

Anson Jones: Wikimedia Commons/PD-US. https://commons.wikimedia.org/wiki/File:Anson_jones.png

Burnet Flag: Pumbaa80-own work/Public Domain (common property). https://commons.wikimedia.org/w/index

Angellina Eberly Statue: photographed by Laurie Cockerell.

American and Texas Flag: photographed by Yvonne Cumberland.

Unit Eight: Statehood and the Civil War

"The Republic of Texas is no More" - President Anson Jones, Annexastion Ceremony, February 19, 1846: Identifier 0001103_0004, Places Collection, Prints and Photographs Collections. Archives and Information Services, Courtesy of Texas State Library and Archives Commission. https://tsl.access.preservica.com/file/sdb%3AdigitalFile%7C6ac00c1e-e891-4b69-a9d3-51e57a60e739/

American Flag 1846 (28 stars): Jacobolus/Wikimedia Commons/Public Domain. https://commons.wikimedia.org/w/index.php?curid=733555

Texas Rangers, Company D, on Rio Grande, 1888-1889: 1983/112 R-no number 1-1, Texas Department of Public Safety photographs. Archives and Information Services Division, Courtesy of Texas State Library and Archives Commission. https://tsl.access.preservica.com/file/sdb%3AdigitalFile%7C7f7f5405-7ea8-480b-b332-17af8c6ef102/

Abraham Lincoln: Anthony Berger, photographer, c1864 Feb. 9. Courtesy of Library of Congress (LC-DIG-ppmsca-19305). http://www.loc.gov/pictures/item/2009630693/

General Ulysses S. Grant at his headquarters in Cold Harbor, Virginia, c1864: Library of Congress (LC-USZ61-903). http://www.loc.gov/pictures/item/2002736661/

Jefferson Davis: photograph by Mathew B. Brady, c1858-60. Library of Congress (LC-DIG-ppmsca-23852). https://www.loc.gov/item/2004673617/

Robert E. Lee: A.S. Seer's Litho Print, 26 & 28 Union Square, c1882 June 22. Library of Congress (LCUSZ62-11452). http://www.loc.gov/pictures/item/2006677471/

Soldier in Confederate lookout tower at Bolivar Point, c1863-64: Library of Congress (LC-DIG-stereo-1s01419). http://www.loc.gov/pictures/item/2005681147/

Non-commissioned officers, 19th Iowa Infantry, exchanged prisoners from Camp Ford, Texas: photographed at New Orleans on their arrival. United States, None. [Between 1861 and 1869] Photograph. Retrieved from the Library of Congress. https://www.loc.gov/item/cwp2003004635/PP/ (Accessed June 15, 2017)

Unit Nine: Cowboys and Indians

Quanah Parker, Comanche Indian Chief, full-length portrait, standing, facing front, holding feathers, in front of tepee: courtesy of Library of Congress (LC-USZ62-98166). https://www.loc.gov/pictures/item/89714963/
The Cow Boy: photographed by J.C.H. Grabill. Library of Congress (LC-USZ62-13227). http://www.loc.gov/pictures/item/99613920/.
Cotton scene in Houston and Texas Central Railway yards, Houston, Texas: photographed by John D. Roberts, 1904. Library of Congress (LC-USZ62-29471). http://www.loc.gov/pictures/item/2012647874/
Texas Windmill: photographed by Yvonne Cumberland.
Cow & Cotton: photographed by Laurie Cockerell.

Unit Ten: Texas in the Twentieth Century

Galveston Hurricane Aftermath: Galveston disaster, relief party working at Ave. P and Tremont St., c1900: courtesy of Library of Congress (LC-USZ62-71880). http://www.loc.gov/pictures/item/2003663540/
Man standing on portion of seawall built after the hurricane and flood of 1900, Galveston,Texas: courtesy of Library of Congress (LC-USZ62-56461) http://www.loc.gov/pictures/item/2004680402/
Texas Chief gusher, c1919: courtesy of Library of Congress (LC-USZ62-39236). http://www.loc.gov/pictures/item/2016648041/
West Texas Oil Pump: photographed by Laurie Cockerell.
Help Us to Win the Vote - Suffragist, "Mrs. Suffern," 1914: courtesy of Library of Congress (LC-USZ62-23622) George Grantham Bain Collection (Library of Congress) LC-B2-3022-10. http://www.loc.gov/pictures/item/97500240/
Fort Crockett in Galveston 1918 (World War I): courtesy of Library of Congress (PAN US MILITARY - Camps no. 89 (E size) [P&P]) /hdl.loc.gov/loc.pnp/pan.6a30624. http://www.loc.gov/pictures/item/2007664176/
11th School Group Consolidated PT-1 trainers Brooks Field Texas: Bwmoll3/Wikimedia Commons/USGOV-PD. https://commons.wikimedia.org/wiki/File:11th_School_Group_Consolidated_PT-1_trainers_Brooks_Field_TX.jpg
Child of migrant worker ironing in camp near Harlingen, Texas, 1939, Feb.: photographed by Russell Lee, 1903-1986. LC-USF33-011999-M3. Courtesy Library of Congress. https://www.loc.gov/item/fsa1997025214/PP/
Dust Bowl Farm, Coldwater District, north of Dalhart, Texas: photographed by Dorothea Lange, June 1938. Library of Congress (LC-USZ62-130634) https://www.loc.gov/item/fsa2000001757/PP/
Advance training plane at Naval Air Base, Corpus Christi: photographed by Howard R. Hollem, August 1942. Library of Congress,Prints & Photographs Division, FSA-OWI Collection, (LC-DIG-fsac-1a34878). https://www.loc.gov/item/fsa1992000903/PP/
Dwight D. Eisenhower: 1952, photographed by Bachrach, Fabian, 1917-2010, Library of Congress (LC-USZ62-117123). http://www.loc.gov/pictures/resource/cph.3c17123/
Lyndon B. Johnson,1964: courtesy of Library of Congress (LC-USZ62-13036). http://www.loc.gov/pictures/resource/cph.3a53305/
President LBJ and Lady Bird Johnson picking wildflowers: photographed by Frank Wolfe, White House Photo Office, July 5, 1968, Courtesy LBJ Library. https://www.archives.gov/presidential-libraries
Eisenhower Interstate System Sign: photographs in the Carol M. Highsmith Archive, Library of Congress, Prints and Photographs Division. LC-DIG-highsm-15721. http://www.loc.gov/pictures/item/2011633914/
President Kennedy speaks at Rice University about space exploration efforts: 12 September 1962. Robert Knudsen. White House Photographs. Courtesy John F. Kennedy Presidential Library and Museum, Boston Digital Identifier: JFKWHP-KN-23710. https://www.jfklibrary.org/Asset-Viewer/Archives/JFKWHP-KN-23710.aspx
Oveta Culp Hobby, half-length portrait, seated, facing left: World Telegram photo by Al Ravenna, 1942. Photograph. Retrieved from the Library of Congress. https://www.loc.gov/item/99400555/ (Accessed July 02, 2017)
President George W. Bush and Former President George H. W. Bush in the Oval Office: National Archives Identifier: 7431321, photographer Eric Draper, 5/2/2001. https://catalog.archives.gov/id/7431321 National Archives and Records Administration
Barbara Jordan: Photographed by Thomas J. O'Halloran. [Congresswoman Barbara Jordan, head-and-shoulders portrait, possibly seated in a Congressional chamber / TOH]. , 1976. Apr. 7. Photograph. Retrieved from the Library of Congress. https://www.loc.gov/item/2003688128/. (Accessed June 15, 2017)
Sandra Day O'Connor: None. [Between 1981 and 1983] Photograph. Retrieved from the Library of Congress. https://www.loc.gov/item/2002715166/ (Accessed July 02, 2017)

Unit Eleven: Texas Government Today

Texas Capitol and photos on Capitol Art page: photographed by Laurie Cockerell.
Photo collage page 136: Photographs by Lauren Tenery, Sharie Dougherty, Yvonne Cumberland, and Laurie Cockerell.
Texas Governor's Mansion: Larry D. Moore/Wikimedia Commons/CC BY-SA 3.0. https://commons.wikimedia.org/wiki/File:Texas_governors_mansion.jpg
Texas Supreme Court Building: Whisper to Me/Wikimedia Commons/Public Domain. https://commons.wikimedia.org/wiki/File:TexasSupremeCourtBuilding.JPG
Washington Votes: Harris & Ewing, photographer, 1938 April 30, LC-H22-D-3857 [P&P], courtesy Library of Congress. http://www.loc.gov/pictures/item/hec2009011227/
Fort Worth Skyline and Country Road: photographed by Lauren Tenery.
Cover Image/Texas flag and interior ornamental graphics: Shutterstock